Annotated

Checklist of the
Birds of Arizona

Second Edition / Revised and Expanded

Gale Monson
Allan R. Phillips

The University of Arizona Press
Tucson, Arizona

About the Authors

GALE MONSON began studying birds while a boy in his native Red River Valley of North Dakota. He moved to Arizona in 1934 and continued his studies in new surroundings, first on the Papago Indian Reservation, later in the Safford and Bisbee areas and on the Navajo and Hopi Indian Reservations. Joining the U.S. Fish and Wildlife Service in 1940, he spent 17 years along the Colorado River and in southwestern Arizona, where he kept notes on the birds of that region. He left the Fish and Wildlife Service in Washington, D.C., in 1969, and since 1971 has continued his studies of Arizona birds.

ALLAN R. PHILLIPS first studied birds as a youngster in New York and Maine. He attended a boys' school in the Baboquivari Mountains of Arizona in 1931–32, and began serious work on the birds of Arizona in 1934. This occupied him for about 20 years, during which he accomplished a prodigious amount of field work in all parts of the state. In 1958 he moved to Mexico to study the birds of that country, living first in Mexico City and later in Monterrey. He has been engaged in preparing a major publication on the birds of North and Middle America, with emphasis on taxonomy and distribution, since 1975.

Monson and Phillips, besides collaborating on the initial checklist of Arizona birds, joined Joe T. Marshall in writing the first comprehensive work on Arizona birds, *The Birds of Arizona,* which was published by the University of Arizona Press in 1964.

THE UNIVERSITY OF ARIZONA PRESS

This book was set in 11/12 Quadritek 1200 Times Roman.

Copyright © 1981
The Arizona Board of Regents
All Rights Reserved
Manufactured in the U.S.A.

Library of Congress Cataloging in Publication Data

Monson, Gale.
    Annotated checklist of the birds of Arizona.

    Previous ed.: A checklist of the birds of
Arizona, 1964.
    Includes index.
    1. Birds—Arizona.   I. Phillips, Allan R.
II. Title.
QL684.A6M64   1981   598.29791   81–11687
ISBN 0–8165–0753–8 (pbk.)   AACR2

Annotated
Checklist of the
Birds of Arizona

To Sally *and* Juana

Introduction

Our first annotated checklist of the birds of Arizona summarized the known status of the species of recent birds of Arizona up to and including 1960.

The present revision considers the status of Arizona birds up to and including 1980. It follows much the same pattern as the first checklist, but includes subspecies (races) to present a true picture of Arizona bird movements. Historic changes (where such are known) and habitat requirements are given. By using this publication in conjunction with *The Birds of Arizona* and one of the popular field guides to North American birds, the observer in most cases should be able to determine in some detail the identity and status of any bird presently known to occur in Arizona.

PLAN OF THE WORK

We continue to distinguish the proven (dates supported by some sort of tangible evidence) from the unproven by *italicizing* the former. Only those species of birds for which specimen evidence exists were admitted to and numbered in our first Arizona checklist; in the present list we admit three exceptions in which dates are also *italicized.* These are (1) a clearly recognizable photograph preserved in a scientific collection, (2) recorded and published size and weight measurements of a live bird in the hand, when these are diagnostic, and (3) a Yellow Rail in the hand of an experienced collector (M. French Gilman), the specimen not preserved because of Gilman's serious illness at the time. Where the occurrence of a species rests on other than a museum skin, such is stated in the annotation for the species.

Hypothetical species are also listed, in brackets and unnumbered. These are species unconfirmed by a specimen or a distinguishable part thereof, an unmistakable photograph(s), or diagnostic measurements in the hand. Hypothetical species are included on the basis of careful sight records made by competent and experienced ornithologists, preferably more than one, and those supported by good but not entirely diagnostic photographs. We also cite species (and selected auxiliary records) from adjacent parts of surrounding states, including northern Sonora, which we feel will serve to round out and complete a presentation of Arizona ornithology. These and hypothetical species are placed in taxonomic order in the list, not in a separate list.

Classification and nomenclature used herein are concordant, in general, with the Wetmore sequence of orders and families, the latest (5th) edition of the American Ornithologists' Union *Checklist of North American Birds,* and the latter's 1973 and 1976 Supplements. We depart from A.O.U. usage in several cases: (1) combining all cases of massively interbreeding, though distinctive, forms into single polytypic species; i.e., in our list all forms that interbreed more or less freely when in contact are considered to be of the same species, regardless of differences in plumage. An exception for the time being is the *Larus fuscus* group; (2) the order of species within the families Ardeidae (herons and bitterns) and Tyrannidae (tyrant flycatchers) where we follow what is to us a more natural order of species; (3) removing the American vultures from the Falconiformes; (4) placing the family Anatidae (swans, geese, and ducks) after the order Charadrii-formes (shorebirds, gulls, auks, and allies), in which we follow Olson and Feduccia (1980, *Smithsonian Contributions to Zoology* 323); (5) following the arrangement of shorebirds as used by Jehl (1968, *San Diego Society of Natural History Memoir* 3), but retaining generic names for *Calidris, Crocethia, Ereunetes,* and *Erolia* as used in the unsupplemented 1957 A.O.U. Check-list; (6) the insertion of the family Laniidae (shrikes) after the family Corvidae (jays, magpies, crows), following A.M. Rea (personal communication); (7) the removal of the families Ploceidae (weaver finches) and Icteridae (meadow-larks, blackbirds, orioles) to the end of the passerines; (8) the splitting of the family Fringillidae in two, into the families Emberizidae (grosbeaks, buntings, tow-hees, sparrows, longspurs) and Carduelidae (Evening and Pine Grosbeaks, crossbills, finches); and (9) submerging some A.O.U. genera, but maintaining *Dendrocopos*.

We have, as in *The Birds of Arizona*, put the Olive Warbler in the family Sylviidae (Old World warblers, gnatcatchers, kinglets), and we have classified the Dickcissel as belonging in the Icteridae, per Beecher (1951, *Auk* 68: 411–440), Raikow (1978, *Bull. Carnegie Mus. Nat. Hist.* 7), et al. We also depart from A.O.U. usage in employing different names for some genera, following more exactly long-established nomenclatural rules. The reader will forgive us for not explaining in detail the reasons for these departures, as space does not permit us to do this; it is suggested that those interested in the reasons consult the above-cited publications, and patiently await the appearance of Phillips' *Known Birds of North and Middle America* which was in preparation in early 1981.

As a rule, we have not attempted to more than indicate the seasonal status of each species. It should be borne in mind that the fall migration of many birds, especially water birds and hummingbirds, begins early in July, or even late in June, and that many mountain birds begin appearing in the lowlands at the same time. Likewise, "spring" migration may begin in February or even mid- to late January. (For an extreme case of displaced migration seasons, see Phillips, 1975, *Condor* 77:196-205). Where the movements of any species are especially irregular, this is mentioned.

Introduced species are accredited to Arizona if self-introduced (Cattle Egret) or if they arrived here from populations already established in North America from introductions elsewhere (Starling, House Sparrow). Otherwise (i.e., if certainly or probably introduced directly by man) our criterion would be the establishment of self-maintaining wild populations. This has not been met by any other species, not even by the Rock Dove or Domestic Pigeon, which continues to depend entirely on man in Arizona, though remote cliffs abound. One might as well list the Domestic Chicken. The only exceptions are some reintroduced populations of Turkey, and the Chukar.

Even positive identification does not necessarily establish a valid record. Some species, not mentioned in our list, have certainly been seen in southern Arizona, such as Elegant or Douglas Quail, Yellow-headed Parrot, or Magpie Jay; and we have a specimen of an African weaver taken at Tucson.

These must surely have been brought in by man. Only if the specimens show (as with the San Blas Jays) that they were not captives, and if the species are not frequently caged, do we admit such birds to our list.

Whenever a specimen date is given for a record, the observer/collector's name plus location of the specimen or photograph is stated, *except* in the case of records already given in *The Birds of Arizona*. Such earlier published records carry only the locality and date in this publication. Bibliographical citations to records that have been previously published are not usually given, for the sake of brevity.

TERMINOLOGY AND ABBREVIATIONS

In stating the relative abundance of a given bird species it is difficult to find terms that will be uniformly interpreted. In this list, we have employed the following criteria: abundant—in numbers; common—always to be seen, but not in large numbers; fairly common—very small numbers, or not always seen; uncommon—seldom seen, but not a surprise; sparse—always a surprise, but not out of normal range; casual—out of usual range, to be expected every 20 to 50 years; and accidental—far from normal range, and not to be expected again.

Any reference to "A.O.U. Check-List" in the following pages is to the 1957 edition and its 1973 and 1976 Supplements. The "Mormon Lake" referred to is that one about 32 km (20 mi) southeast of Flagstaff, and is not to be confused with another lake of the same name near Show Low. The designations "lower Colorado River" and "lower Colorado Valley" apply to that portion of the stream below Davis Dam in the case of land birds, and to that portion below the head of Lake Mead in the case of water birds.

The following are abbreviations of museums referred to most often in the text as the repositories of specimens and/or photographs:

AMNH American Museum of Natural History, New York

ANSP Academy of Natural Sciences, Philadelphia

ARIZ University of Arizona, Tucson. Includes a number of specimens not yet deposited from the lower Colorado River Valley

ARP Allan Phillips Collection, Monterrey, Nuevo León, Mexico

(collected by Phillips unless indicated otherwise. Most record specimens are now deposited in DEL)

CAN National Museum of Natural Sciences, Ottawa, Canada

CAS California Academy of Sciences, San Francisco

CM Carnegie Museum of Natural History, Pittsburgh

CU Cornell University, Ithaca, New York

DEL Delaware Museum of Natural History, Greenville

DEN Denver Museum of Natural History

GCN Grand Canyon National Park

GM (formerly). Now either ARIZ or US

LSU Louisiana State University, Baton Rouge

MCZ Museum of Comparative Zoology, Harvard University

MNA Museum of Northern Arizona, Flagstaff

NAU Northern Arizona University, Flagstaff

REA A.M. Rea Collection, San Diego

SD Natural History Museum, San Diego

SWRS Southwestern Research Station, Portal, Arizona

US   United States National Museum of Natural
         History, Wasnington (includes Fish and
         Wildlife Service Collection)
UU   University of Utah, Salt Lake City
VPI   Virginia Polytechnic Institute and State Uni-
         versity, Blacksburg
WNMU Western New Mexico University, Silver City
YALE   Peabody Museum, Yale University
ZION   Zion National Park, Utah

ARIZONA LIFE ZONES AND MAJOR HABITATS

A knowledge of the vegetation, topography, and climate of Arizona is necessary to any understanding of the state's birds. A resumé of the principal life zones that are mentioned repeatedly in the text is as follows:

1. *Lower Sonoran Zone.* This is the hot desert zone, whose typical plants are mesquite, palo verdes, large cacti, and creosote bush. It covers much of southern and western Arizona, and follows the Colorado River up to the bottom of the Grand Canyon. Elevation above sea level, 45 to 1000 m (150 to 3500 ft) or more.

2. *Upper Sonoran Zone.* This is also an essentially desert zone, but is not as arid and hot as the Lower Sonoran. Its typical plants are sagebrush and juniper-pinyon ("pygmy conifer") in the north, chaparral (brush) in the central part of the state, and evergreen oaks and junipers of several species in the mountains of the southeast. It also embraces considerable stretches of grassland (almost everywhere seriously modified by a century of overgrazing) both in the north and southeast. Elevation, approximately 1200 to 2000 m (4000 to 6500 ft).

3. *Transition Zone.* This is mainly a ponderosa pine forest, covering most of the Kaibab and Mogollon Plateaus, and large parts of the higher mountains and plateaus elsewhere. Associated trees include Gambel oak and New Mexico locust. Elevation, approximately 2000 to 2600 m (6500 to 8500 ft).

4. *Canadian* or *Hudsonian Zones.* The Canadian Zone occupies only the higher elevations in the state, on the Kaibab Plateau and on the San Francisco, White, Pinaleno, Chiricahua, and Chuska Mountains plus high canyon heads in other mountain ranges. Its typical plants are the Douglas and white firs, limber pine, and quaking aspen. Elevation, approximately 2600 to 3000 m (8500 to 10,000 ft). There are even smaller tracts above 2900 m (9500 ft) that represent the Hudsonian Zone, but this zone is faunally much like the Canadian. Its typical plants are Engelmann spruce, alpine fir, and bristlecone pine. Because of the faunal similarity, both Canadian and Hudsonian Zones are commonly referred to herein as *boreal zones* or *boreal forests.*

On the San Francisco and White Mountains occur timberlines and touches of the treeless *Arctic-Alpine Zone.*

The life zones are often intricately interdigitated or even mixed, especially along canyons and broken mesa lands. Development of extensive tracts of irrigated farmland and the creation of large water impoundments on the major rivers have added variety to a bird habitat already amazingly diverse for a wholly inland, arid region. Everywhere in Arizona streams and marshy areas have disappeared, along with much of the native grassland, as discussed in *The Birds of Arizona* (pages xv–xvii).

RIPARIAN HABITATS

Woodland and shrubland along many of the state's drainageways deserve special attention in any discussion of Arizona habitats. Originally, these were typically cottonwood-willow gallery forests, combined with Arizona sycamore, Arizona walnut, box elder, etc., along mountain canyon bottoms. They are of crucial importance to many bird species, among them some of Arizona's rarest and most interesting birds. These riparian habitats are found now chiefly in high Lower Sonoran and Upper Sonoran Zone areas, and especially where streams leave mountainous terrain to enter more gentle topography. This type of woodland once occupied large stretches along the lower Colorado and the Gila and Salt Rivers, as well as the San Pedro and Santa Cruz Rivers. It has been nearly destroyed along the Colorado, Gila, and Salt Rivers, either through flooding by large dams or by diversion of water from the channels by canals feeding from the same large dams. In lesser drainages the persistence of the gallery forests is threatened by overpumping of ground water or by the livestock that feed on seedlings and saplings, preventing them from reaching the size when they would be immune to grazing and grow to be reproductive trees. The special importance of the gallery forests lies not only in their natural beauty, but in the great contribution they make to the diversity of the flora and fauna of Arizona.

CHECKLISTS AND IDENTIFICATIONS

One function of a checklist should be to guide birders. It should sift the wheat from the chaff and point out what is known, or is highly probable, about local birds' status. In this sifting, unsupported sight identifications pose a problem which has increased by leaps and bounds.

Although the collection of birds for scientific purposes is now largely passé, if not frowned upon, it is still the underlying basis for all serious bird study. For one thing, those who do not actually study collections, or ponder the matter, may well suppose that collections have little or nothing to do with field identification. Actually collections are the basis of local lists. These in turn pass into the American Ornithologists' Union Check-list and ultimately into field guides. When collections have *not* been made and carefully and extensively studied, both the A.O.U. Check-list and field guides fail. See, for example, Phillips, 1975, *American Birds* 29:799-805, on the Semipalmated Sandpiper, supposedly the commonest winter 'peep' in eastern North America but not actually wintering there at all, north of extreme southern Florida.

Given that collecting is the basis of our knowledge, it need *not* always involve the taking of birds. Removal of critical feathers, in a number of cases, or careful preservation of birds (or even parts of birds) found dead, can and will substantiate identifications. In fact, most birds received by museums now are those found dead on the road, killed in collisions with objects such as towers or picture windows, or washed up on beaches. Our knowledge will grow as collections, from whatever source, grow.

Another common idea is that field identification is fully covered by binoculars and field guides, not requiring local checklists. There are three basic flaws to this idea: (1) Field guides are incomplete, omitting juvenal plumages in most cases and often slighting females, immatures, and basic (winter) plumages, partial albinos, etc. They are therefore reliable only for normal breeding adults, even if free of other errors. (2) Likewise the guides do not treat geographic variation, as well as molts (which can turn a Great-tailed Grackle into a stubtailed Starling, for example). (3) Ranges given in field guides are often too general to be definitive, and only a local checklist will tell you whether your supposed observation is predictable or not; obviously an unlikely one will be in need of further investigation.

Some bird-watchers believe that the rejection of their sight reports is a reflection on their competence. They may also think it is a matter of arrogance or prejudice of a "professional" against an "amateur." They forget that all of us reject some of *our own* earlier identifications as we become more knowledgeable and proficient. While we may be willing to agree that a bird was seen that showed certain markings which some book says are found only in a certain species, we may reject the idea that the bird necessarily *was* that species. The question is not one of honesty or accuracy; it may be the book's completeness. *No* book can describe every unusual variation possible in a species (or its hybrids). For example, a female or immature oriole with a brilliant orangeish yellow belly was once seen on an unexpected date (30 Oct. 1955) by the entire Bird Club of the Tucson Natural History Society. According to the standards of many of today's birding groups, this would constitute an accepted record of a Baltimore Oriole (or Scarlet-headed Oriole, or whatever other oriole the group wanted to call it). The bird was collected, however, and calm examination later showed it to be simply an off-color, belated Bullock's Oriole. A potential "state record" of LeConte's Sparrow was lost in the White Mountains on 4 Sept. 1953 when Phillips collected a Savannah Sparrow with much-paled brown tones. Likewise two partly pinkish flycatchers taken in Nayarit, Mexico, proved to be nothing but freak Western Flycatchers. Such specimens prove the existence of birds that cannot be identified correctly, even by the most expert observers, without collecting. To treat the records of less experienced observers as more sacrosanct, simply because they were *not* collected, would hardly be in the interests of science or of those who depend on this checklist for accurate knowledge.

It is obvious that undocumented sight records cannot be ignored. Ideally we must accept the valuable records resulting from careful and scientific field observation, and dismiss those that are inaccurate or doubtful and would only clutter the record and obscure true patterns of occurrence. This ideal requires careful and objective consideration of every record. One criterion to consider is the likelihood of the species' occurrence at the reported place and season. Another important factor is the credibility of the observer, which must be weighed as best it can. In many cases we must also ask by what characteristics the bird was identified: even the most conscientious observer cannot identify birds accurately using unreliable field characters, and unfortunately the popular field guides contain many such misconceptions. All of these factors have been considered in judging each unsupported sight record contained in the species accounts. In exceptional cases what we view as questionable records are included, but with cautionary qualifications stated or implied.

EXPLANATION OF SPECIMEN EVIDENCE

Specimens come in various forms, depending on circumstances, the species involved, whether it has subspecies or close relatives, etc. For research, the ideal specimen is still the traditional museum skin, perhaps modified in special groups to show the under wing or the toes, and accompanied by *full* data—not just sex, locality, date, and collector, but also data on age, sexual condition, molt, amount of fat, colors of soft parts (including the mouth in such groups as flycatchers and corvids), habitat, and behavior (i.e., members of one flock, etc.). In some groups vocalizations are important. Particularly with larger birds, it is well to preserve the trunk skeleton along with the skin.

Emphasis on traditional complete museum skins can be overdone. Important record specimens are often thrown away because the finder cannot prepare skins or the collector or local museum wants nothing that cannot be made into a full, handsome skin. *Something,* however, can always be saved, and often a complete skeleton (with standard wing and tail measurements) is the best way to save a large bird anyway, especially if the species is monotypic, i.e., without known subspecific variation. Here again, other parts may well accompany the main specimen— in this case, wing and tail feathers and other characteristic parts.

We especially urge that unusual birds (or parts thereof) found dead or dying be saved and turned in to museums which will preserve them. Too many such are identified to the *finder's* satisfaction and discarded. Normally the finder has no familiarity with feathers and technical characteristics, and some parts, at least, of a bird are always salvageable. The finder should bear in mind that Phillips, in many years of visiting museums in several countries, cannot recall visiting one that did not have some specimens misidentified—usually at the level of subspecies, but also often at the species level (totaling several hundreds if not thousands of species at this level) and occasionally at even higher levels. If experienced museum curators err so often, it is illogical to expect us to consider the identifications of even the most expert bird-watchers more trustworthy or sacrosanct. Science, after all, is a body of *re-verifiable* data.

With live birds, including those caught for banding, satisfactory specimen evidence (e.g., tail or other distinctive feathers) to identify species (but usually not subspecies) may be secured without harming the bird. More difficult species may require capturing the bird, which should then be photographed, measured, and weighed, if possible; selected feathers should be removed for mounting on a card giving full data and measurements. Careful examination of plumage conditions, feet, and claws (measured) for signs of captivity, etc., should precede release of the bird. Some species (especially large ones) can also be positively identified in museums from shed feathers such as those dropped at favorite preening or roosting spots.

In hummingbirds, for example, one should at least preserve and label unworn tail feathers (e.g., outer and central rectrices) and wing feathers (e.g., a near-outer and an inner primary and an inner secondary). In other groups, feathers from other distinctively colored or patterned areas (e.g., back, breast, rump, crown, and axillars) should be saved. Consult standard works for the critical details involved in the particular group concerned, including Ridgway and Friedmann (1901–1950, *The Birds of North and Middle America*), Brodkorb (1968, "Birds." In *Vertebrates of the United States,* by W.F. Blair, A. P. Blair, Brodkorb, Cagle, and Moore), and Palmer (1962 et seq., *Handbook of North American Birds*). Remember that paleontologists and others routinely identify birds to the species level from scraps of bone, feathers found in aircraft engines, etc. This is perfectly good science, at the species level; but it will not usually tell us the subspecies involved, which commonly require comparison of skins. The specimen card, with feathers and data as above, should be kept in a large envelope prominently labeled with the name of the genus and species (if known), data, and at least a general locality.

Most species of birds are geographically variable, and thus the origin of a stray ordinarily requires preservation of the skin for comparison. Even the most careful comparisons, with skins in the hand at the time, may not lead to permanently conclusive results, as shown by Hubbard and Crossin (1974, *Nemouria,* 14:11). With a preserved skin, one may go back again and again to compare both the old and the new-found characters that may be discovered. Many birds CANNOT be immediately identified to subspecies; because their colors change (by so-called "foxing") they are not comparable to museum series. Even with the best of care, whites become somewhat dulled as decades pass, and dark tones become paler and more reddish ("foxier") in many species. In some, yellowish or red tones fade badly; and the red of fleshy parts may dull enormously at the death of a bird, as with the Black-bellied Whistling-Duck.

The serious student of birds, interested in where the strays are coming from and whether they represent natural occurrences, should collect; if not so author-ized, seek someone who is. Many strays will soon die, in any case, from improper habitat conditions, predation, and/or other factors; even if they should survive to breed somewhere, this may be dysgenic, producing offspring with defective orientation. No conceivable benefit to the species can outweigh the loss to science of being unable to exame the bird's condition, subspecies, and possible abnormalities due to captivity or "pesticide" poisoning (which should certainly be monitored if feasible).

THE WHY OF COLLECTING STRAGGLERS

Field identification is a matter of probability; we ignore birds that have not been documented anywhere near our area. For example, there are other white pelicans in the world than our *Pelecanus erythro-rhynchos,* but we do not worry about them in Arizona because none has been collected in North America. But in most of South America, should a white pelican show up, it would have to be collected for identification as it would be nearly or quite as far from the range of *erythrorhynchos* as from those of Old World species and could not be automatically assumed to be the North American form. Similarly, on migration in Arizona we do not worry excessively about Tennessee Warblers, even though similar birds of other families occur elsewhere, including in Alaska. But in winter Tennessee Warblers are found no closer to Arizona than the coast of Oaxaca in southwestern Mexico. The fact that all museum specimens of similar birds from the main continent of North America (north of the range of Lesser Greenlet, *Hylophilus decurtatus*) are Tennessee Warblers would not necessarily bear on the problem, since none is winter-taken. Obviously, the winter bird would have to be taken to identify it; it could be a Sylviid (e.g., *Phylloscopus*) from Eurasia! Abundant material of a species at one season (summer) may throw no light on the identity of occasional strays at some other season or nearby region; cf. Rea (1970, *Condor* 72:230–233) on the Summer Tanager.

Specimens from adjacent mountains cannot tell us automatically the origin of wanderers to the valleys (cf. Mountain Chickadee, Brown Creeper, Golden-crowned Kinglet, Red Crossbill, etc.). That the many all-red birds with white wing bars taken in the United States are Pine Grosbeaks or White-winged Crossbills does not identify such a bird found at Gila Bend (but unfortunately discarded!) which might conceivably have been the Flame-colored Tanager (*Piranga bidentata*); there simply IS no material of an all-red bird with white wing-bars from the desert anywhere. An apparent Baird's or Pectoral Sandpiper in winter might just as easily be some Asiatic species, since these two winter in southern South America. Water Pipit migrations end in mid-May, and so an odd early June specimen was checked against comparable Asiatic species; the specimen proved to be an accidental Asiatic pipit! Thus, even a two - to three-week gap in records may mean that available material is inapplicable to the meaning of a record, and *dates* need careful consideration as well as places. A Fox Sparrow in May and a Hooded Oriole (from northeastern Sonora) in November, both proved to be of different races than birds found at less exceptional dates. In the northeastern United States, both near-winter specimens of the genus *Empidonax* represent western species (Phillips and Lanyon, 1970, *Bird-Banding* 41:190–197), as do all wintering swift specimens from Louisiana (Lowery, 1939, *Wilson Bulletin* 51:199–201). The frequent and misleading claim that "ample material already exists" in museums is never applicable to strays; in fact, ornithologists who actually *study* museum series and attempt to do research on them usually find themselves handicapped at every critical point by shortage or outright lack of specimens; these researchers make no such irresponsible statements. (Those who do no work naturally need no data.)

The fundamental question is that of a bird's taxonomic status, i.e., its species, subspecies, and origin. This, as we have seen, does not necessarily agree in every case with its supposed "field marks." Thus, an apparently out-of-place stray or off-season straggler presents more possibilities than are implied by books commonly at hand. Hence, the need of critical investigation.

Ornithology can and should continue to be a science—a body of factual data which can be verified and reassessed by anyone willing to study the specimens.

ACKNOWLEDGMENTS

The work in the field of many persons has contributed materially to the greater completeness of this new checklist. Their names are far too many to be set down here in full, but we must especially mention the

work of Bertin W. Anderson, Russell P. Balda, S.W.
Carothers, Douglas Danforth, W.A. Davis, Salome
Demaree, David H. Ellis, Rich Glinski, Sharon
Goldwasser, Grace Gregg, Bill Harrison, Alton
Higgins, John P. Hubbard, the late Lawrence N.
Huber, Betty Jones, R. Roy Johnson, Terry B.
Johnson, Kenn Kaufman, C.S. Lawson, Seymour
H. Levy, G. Scott Mills, Brian Millsap, Arnold
Moorhouse, Robert J. Morse, Phil Norton, Robert
G. Norton, Robert D. Ohmart, Ted Parker, Eleanor
Radke, Amadeo M. Rea, Gary and Kenneth V.
Rosenberg, Stephen M. Russell, E. Linwood Smith,
Steven Speich, Sally and Walter Spofford, Douglas
Stotz, Scott Terrill, Richard L. Todd, Carl S.
Tomoff, P.M. Walters, Bret Whitney, Richard A.
Wilt, and Janet and Robert Witzeman. We are
grateful to Mary C. McKitrick for special assistance.
We wish to thank Anne Pulich of Irving, Texas, for
her contribution of the Black-throated Sparrow draw-
ing on page 1. Finally, we express gratitude to the
University of Arizona Press for effecting publication
of this volume.

Gale Monson
Tucson, Arizona

Allan R. Phillips
*San Nicolás de los Garza,
Nuevo León, México*

Maps

Maps 1 through 3 convey the authors' conception of the various (northern, southeastern, etc.) sections of the state. Please bear in mind that any lines on these maps are, to some degree, necessarily arbitrary. Maps 4, 5, and 6 on the following pages are intended to simplify the reader's attempts to find localities in Arizona and are self-explanatory.

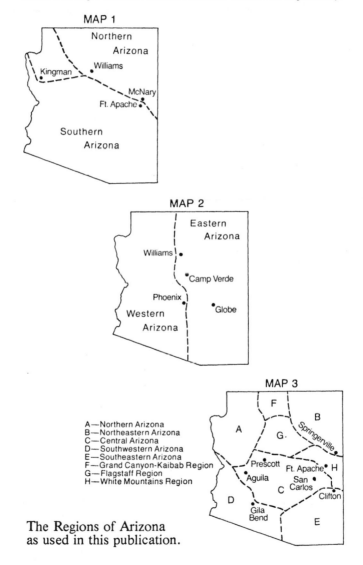

MAP 1

Northern Arizona

Kingman
Williams

McNary
Ft. Apache

Southern Arizona

MAP 2

Eastern Arizona

Williams

Camp Verde

Phoenix

Globe

Western Arizona

MAP 3

A—Northern Arizona
B—Northeastern Arizona
C—Central Arizona
D—Southwestern Arizona
E—Southeastern Arizona
F—Grand Canyon-Kaibab Region
G—Flagstaff Region
H—White Mountains Region

F

B
Springerville

A
G.

Prescott
Ft. Apache   H
San
Aguila   Carlos
C   Clifton

D
Gila
Bend   E

The Regions of Arizona
as used in this publication.

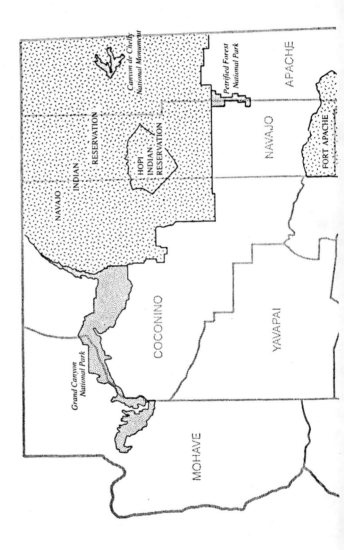

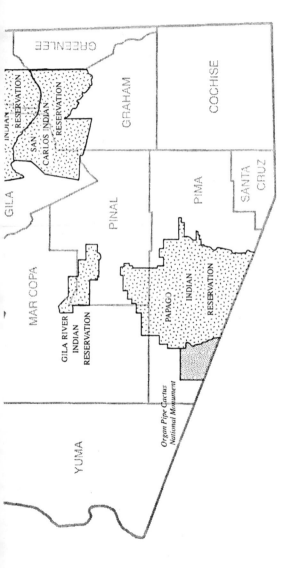

Map 4. Countries, Indian reservations, and some national park areas.

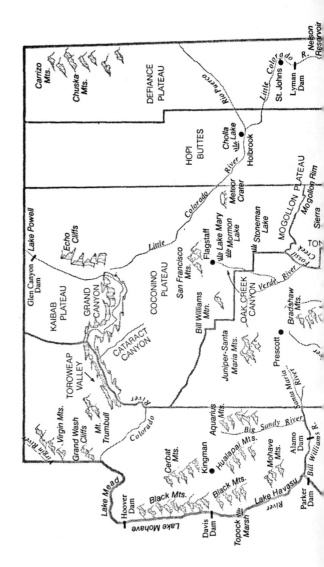

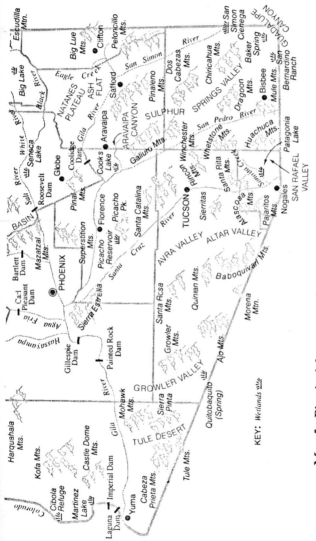

Map 5. Physical features and major dams mentioned in the text.

xxix

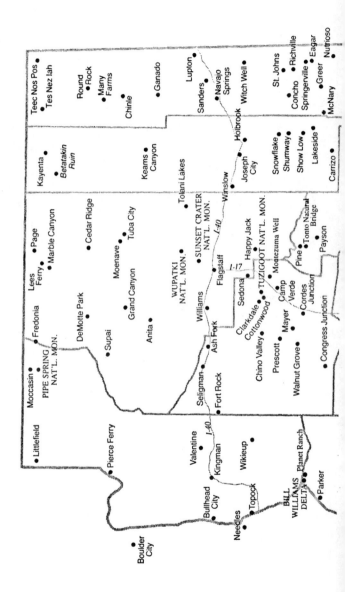

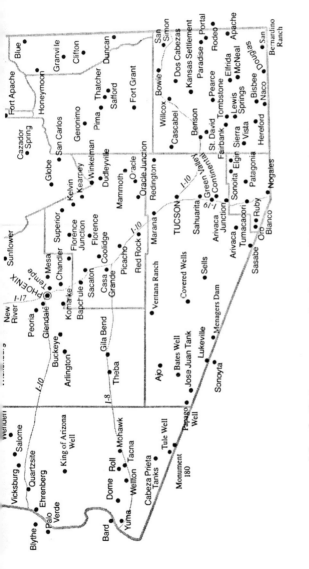

Map 6. Cities, towns, and other localities mentioned in the text.

Checklist

FAMILY GAVIIDAE: LOONS

1. *Gavia immer* (Brünnich). Common Loon. Uncommon transient in fall and sparse winter visitor throughout Arizona, except on Colorado River lakes and the ephemeral Painted Rock Reservoir on the Gila River near Gila Bend, where it is a fairly common transient (sometimes common in Apr.) and uncommon winter visitor and has been found every month of the year including *July* and Aug. At least one seen and heard at Carnero Lake, White Mountains, Apache Co., 22 July 1977 (D.E. Brown).

2. *Gavia arctica* (Linnaeus). Arctic Loon. Uncommon to sparse fall and winter visitant, records mainly from Colorado River lakes; seven specimens, north and east to Camp Verde and Willcox. Up to seven on Lake Havasu in late Oct. to Dec. 1980 (R. Martin et al). The only spring specimen is from Willcox, *4 June 1975* (ARIZ, M. Hansen and B. Jones). Has been seen near Yuma, on Lake Havasu, and at Davis Dam in spring, and on Lake Havasu, 13 Aug. 1954. Also recorded in southeastern Utah.

3. *Gavia stellata* (Pontoppidan). Red-throated Loon. One near Bullhead City, Nov. 1947; one on Lake Havasu, 8 and 15 June 1948; one near Aravaipa, Graham Co., 11 Oct. 1969 (E.L. Smith); one in Bill Williams Arm of Lake Havasu, *29 Mar.* to 2 Apr. *1978* (ARIZ, photo, K.V. Rosenberg); sight record for Painted Rock Reservoir, 26 Nov. 1978 (G. Rosenberg, S. Terrill); and one at upper Lake Havasu, 23 Dec. 1980 and *8 Jan. 1981* (K. Kaufman; ARIZ, photo, J. Witzeman). We have been unable to verify a supposed specimen taken many years ago, and sight records for the Papago Indian Reservation and from near Tuba City, Navajo Indian Reservation, are disregarded.

FAMILY PODICEPIDAE: GREBES

[*Podiceps grisegena* (Boddaert). Red-necked Grebe. One at Boulder Beach, Lake Mead, Nevada side, less than 8 km (5 mi) from Arizona, 5 Dec. 1980 to at least 3 Jan. 1981 (V. Mowbray et al.; photo, ARIZ, *7 Dec. 1980,* C.R. Richards).]

Authors' note: Since completion of our manuscript, a Red-necked Grebe was photographed on lower Lake Havasu by M. Kasprzyk, also seen by C. Romano, *23 Mar. 1981* (ARIZ). This adds another species to the full list of Arizona birds.

4. *Podiceps auritus* (Linnaeus). Horned Grebe. Uncommon fall transient along Colorado River and more sparsely elsewhere in Arizona; only three specimens, lower Lake Havasu, *27 Oct. 1952,* near Tucson, *23 Nov. 1967* (ARIZ, L.N. Huber), and Nogales, *3 Nov. 1975* (ARIZ, G. Gregg and B. Jones). Uncommon to sparse winter resident (but up to 100 at Wahweap Basin, Lake Powell, 25 Feb. 1979, J. Coons and B. Whitney) in southern Arizona and along Colorado River. Sparse spring transient, records from Lake Havasu, Davis Dam, Nogales (3 Apr. 1977, D. Stotz and S. Parker), and Tucson (3 Apr. 1977, E. and C. Wolfe et al.).

5. *Podiceps nigricollis* C.L. Brehm. Eared Grebe. Fairly common to common transient statewide, abundant locally. Winters in smaller numbers along Colorado and Salt Rivers, and on larger bodies of water elsewhere, abundant locally. A few non-breeders may be found in summer throughout the state. Nests on lakes in San Francisco, White, and Chuska Mountains regions, and at Watson Lake near Prescott (1976, C. S. Tomoff).

6. *Podiceps dominicus* (Linnaeus). Least Grebe. Straggler along the south edge of Arizona; recorded from Quitobaquito, Organ Pipe Cactus National Monument, *28 Apr. 1939,* 12 Dec. 1966 (R. Cunningham), and from 13 Oct. 1976 to 30 Nov. 1978 (same individual?; many observers); near Tucson, 28 Dec. 1941 and *26 Sept. 1943;* 16 km (10 mi) north of Sasabe, *14 Jan. 1958;* and Guevavi Ranch north of Nogales, 16 to 20 Dec. 1976 (R. Norden et al.) and 26 to 29 Oct. 1978 (C. Meaker et al.). There is an old sight record for Camp Verde. During the 1960s, seen occasionally at a pond on the west side of the Tumacacori Mountains, Santa Cruz Co.; seven on the pond at the same time in 1964 (S.H. Levy) indicates breeding. Nested at California end of Imperial Dam (West Pond) in *1946,* also possibly at Mittry Lake above Laguna Dam, where 15 reported 5 Jan. 1951 (L. Couch, A.F. Halloran).

    Arizona specimens are of the small subspecies *P.d. bangsi* (van Rossem and Hachisuka).

7. *Aechmophorus occidentalis* (Lawrence). Western Grebe. Resident on Lake Havasu since 1966, about 100 pairs in 1973 and at least 250 pairs in 1977; also nested on Painted Rock Reservoir, lower Gila River, in 1980 (G. Rosenberg et al.). More or less common transient and winter resident elsewhere on Lake Havasu and other lakes of the Colorado River (abundant at times on Lakes Mead and Powell), and on Roosevelt Lake (where sometimes abundant). Sparse to uncommon in summer on Colorado River lakes other than Lake Havasu and Painted Rock Reservoir. Uncommon migrant and sparse winter visitant elsewhere in southern Arizona. Sparse to uncommon transient in the north, including the Mogollon Plateau and the White Mountains.

    The race in Arizona is the large northern nominate one. The matter of dark- and light-phase birds (Ratti, 1979, *Auk* 96:573–586) is not treated here.

8. *Podilymbus podiceps* (Linnaeus). Pied-billed Grebe. Nests in marshy lakes and ponds scatteringly throughout state, sometimes even in late winter in the southeast, but commonly only in lower Colorado Valley, at Picacho Reservoir south of Coolidge, at Seneca Lake (Gila Co.), and in high mountain country. Winters in most ice-free waters, and is an uncommon transient on ponds where it does not nest.

Authors' note: After completion of our manuscript, a Laysan Albatross, *Diomedea immutabilis* Rothschild (FAMILY DIOMEDEIDAE: ALBATROSSES) was picked up alive on a Yuma Street, *14 May 1981* (ARIZ, photo) and brought to Sea World, San Diego, California, cared for, and released after it had recovered. This adds another species to the full list of Arizona birds.

FAMILY PROCELLARIIDAE: SHEARWATERS, FULMARS

9. *Puffinus griseus* (Gmelin). Sooty Shearwater. One found dead along highway near Wellton, Yuma Co., *6 June 1971* (ARIZ, R.J. Quigley).

FAMILY HYDROBATIDAE: STORM-PETRELS

[***Halocyptena microsoma*** Coues. Least Storm-Petrel. Hypothetical. Two on Lake Mohave, 12 Sept. 1976 (W. Prange) and one at Davis Dam, 17 Sept. 1976 (C.S. Lawson). More than 200 were recorded at Salton Sea, California, at the same time (G. McCaskie et al.). The records followed the movement of Tropical Cyclone Kathleen across northern Baja California, Mexico, into the Imperial Valley, California, before dying out, 9 and 10 Sept. 1976.]

FAMILY PHAETHONTIDAE: TROPIC-BIRDS

10. *Phaethon aethereus* Linnaeus. Red-billed Tropic-bird. Accidental straggler; exhausted specimens have been found near Phoenix and in Apache Pass, near Dos Cabezas, Cochise Co., *10 Apr. 1905* and *15 Sept. 1927,* respectively.

The specimens are of the race *P.a. mesonauta* Peters.

11. *Phaethon lepturus* Daudin. White-tailed Tropic-bird. Accidental. An exhausted, emaciated bird came down in a yard at Scottsdale, near Phoenix, *22 Aug. 1980* (US, Paul Rogers; specimen prepared by R.D. Ohmart).

The specimen has been identified by G.E. Watson as the race *P. l. dorotheae* Mathews from the islands of the southwest Pacific Ocean. As such, it is the first record for North America.

FAMILY PELECANIDAE: PELICANS

12. *Pelecanus erythrorhynchos* Gmelin. White Pelican. Regular transient, also wintering and sum-mering, usually in small numbers, along the lower Colorado River. Elsewhere occurs irregularly, subject to great fluctuations over the years but recently chiefly in small flocks or as singles (but about 350 at Painted Rock Reservoir in June and July 1974). No verified breeding record.

13. *Pelecanus occidentalis* Linnaeus. Brown Peli-can. A few enter the state in summer and fall, chiefly in recent years, seldom staying until winter or even spring; most records are for the Colorado and Gila Valleys, but stragglers reach most of the state, exceptionally even the northeast (Tolani Lakes, Navajo Indian Reservation, July 1937). Individuals/ groups reported each year usually do not exceed 25, and all records are of immatures.

The Arizona subspecies is the large *P. o. californicus* Ridgway.

FAMILY SULIDAE: BOOBIES AND GANNETS

14. *Sula nebouxii* Milne-Edwards. Blue-footed Booby. Sparse, irregular late summer and fall straggler to lower Colorado Valley, at least in 1953, 1954, 1971, and 1977, north to Lake Mead (Nevada portion), in 1971 one staying at Martinez Lake above Imperial Dam until mid-Feb. 1972. Also found once at Phoenix, *29 July 1953.*

15. *Sula leucogaster* (Boddaert). Brown Booby. Sparse late summer and fall straggler to lower Colorado Valley, north to Lake Mead (Nevada portion, 1971 only). One present continuously from early Sept. 1958 to Oct. 1960 at Martinez Lake above Imperial Dam.

> The Arizona subspecies is presumably *S. l. brewsteri* Goss.

FAMILY PHALACROCORACIDAE: CORMORANTS

16. *Phalacrocorax auritus* (Lesson). Double-crested Cormorant. Common to abundant transient and winter resident in lower Colorado Valley, where it breeds locally, and is less common on Lakes Mead and Mohave. Fairly common transient and winter resident on larger lakes of the Salt River, and uncommon elsewhere in the south, where chiefly a transient in small numbers. In the north a sparse transient and summer visitant on the Mogollon Plateau. A few nests at San Carlos Reservoir, back of Coolidge Dam, May 1968 (C. and I. Thomas) and at Painted Rock Reservoir in 1979–80 (many observers).

> The Arizona birds are presumably *P. a. albociliatus* Ridgway.

17. *Phalacrocorax olivaceus* (Humboldt). Olivaceous Cormorant. Since *1961* an uncommon straggler to the Santa Cruz Valley downstream to Tucson, usually singles or doubles. In the springs of 1978 and 1979 one was reported at the San Bernardino Ranch, Cochise Co. (D. Danforth). We believe many sight records are actually of the preceding species.

FAMILY ANHINGIDAE: ANHINGAS

18. *Anhinga anhinga* (Linnaeus). Anhinga. Accidental; only one certain record, from Tucson, *12 Sept. 1893.* Old sight records at Yuma, where it probably occurred about 1900, and at California end of Laguna Dam, 9 Feb. 1913, and more recently, but none substantiated.

FAMILY FREGATIDAE: FRIGATE-BIRDS OR MAN-O'-WAR BIRDS

[*Fregata minor* (Gmelin). Great Frigate-bird. Hypothetical. Immatures seen at Tumacacori National Monument, 18 June 1953, and at Picacho Reservoir, 29 Aug. 1962 (the latter sketched) may have been of this species because of their buffy coloration.]

19. *Fregata magnificens* Mathews. Magnificent Frigate-bird. Three documented records: near Yuma, *26 July 1973* (ARIZ, photo, H.R. Guenther), at Davis Dam, *17 Sept. 1976* (ARIZ, photo, C.S. Lawson), and at Painted Rock Reservoir, *22 July 1979* (ARIZ, photo, J. Witzeman), where up to six were seen simultaneously that month (according to Witzeman). Otherwise, about 20 sight records tto end of 1980 from Colorado and lower Gila Valleys north to Lake Havasu. Recorded once at Tucson, 3 Sept. 1971 (D. Prentice). In July and Aug. 1979 at least eight were at Painted Rock Reservoir (R.

Bradley, C. Kangas, et al.). All records are of immatures except for an adult male at Painted Rock Reservoir, 9 Aug. 1979 (according to S. Terrill). All sight records are likely *F. magnificens* but some could be *F. minor.*

FAMILY ARDEIDAE:
HERONS AND BITTERNS

20. *Ixobrychus exilis* (Gmelin). Least Bittern. Fairly common resident in Colorado Valley north to Topock Marsh; also a resident in cattails along Salt River in Phoenix area. Wintered at Picacho Reservoir in 1942–43, where it was common 3 Aug. 1976 (D. Danforth, Monson) and was subsequently seen in the nesting season in 1977 and 1978 (several observers). Elsewhere sparse transient or wanderer except in north, where casual: one at Pipe Spring National Monument, 23 to 24 July 1973 (R. Wilt).

21. *Botaurus lentiginosus* (Rackett). American Bittern. Uncommon winter resident from late Aug. to May in cattail areas in lower Colorado Valley, and locally and sparsely elsewhere in southern and central Arizona. Sparse transient in northern Arizona, where before 1915 it nested at lakes on Mogollon Plateau. Its presence at Martinez Lake above Imperial Dam in June and July 1978 (S. Furness et al.), as well as one in the Bill Williams Delta, 26 May 1980 (R. Martin), may have indicated breeding. One seen near Sunrise Lake, White Mountains, 5 Aug. 1977 (D. Lamm, P. M. Walters); one heard 7 June 1969 at Nelson Reservoir, southeast of Springerville (H.T. Armistead).

22. *Butorides virescens* (Linnaeus). Green Heron. Breeds uncommonly along streams and wooded ponds, particularly in willow areas, south and west of the Mogollon Plateau; found more sparingly in winter in same areas, chiefly since 1940. Sparse summer visitor at bottom of Grand Canyon. One record for northern Arizona: Pipe Spring National Monument, 3 Oct. 1973 (R. Wilt). May occur on stock tanks and other treeless waters during fall, even into Nov.

Only *B. v. anthonyi* (Mearns) has been taken in Arizona.

23. *Ardea herodias* Linnaeus. Great Blue Heron. Found at any season, but in small numbers, throughout the state where there is open water, nesting in scattered small heronries.

Most Arizona specimens are *A. h. treganzai* Court but there is one from Tucson *22 June 1953* of *A. h. sancti-lucae* Thayer and Bangs, and at least one winter specimen that is of the nominate race.

24. *Ardea caerulea* Linneaus. Little Blue Heron. A handful of records, nearly all May and June adults (including one taken near Phoenix, *27 May 1958*) from Nogales, Tucson, and Phoenix vicinities. Exceptions are singles: wounded at Camp Verde, 27 July 1885; near Tucson, 7 to 21 Dec. 1972 (D. Lamm, C. Corchran); Willcox, 29 May 1976 (R. Stallcup); near Hereford, 23 May 1977 (T. Crabtree); Tucson, 25 Sept. 1977 (M. Paulsen); Dome Valley east of Yuma, 9 May 1979 (B. Whitney); and at Arlington west of Phoenix, 15 July 1980 (S. Burge).

25. *Ardea alba* Linnaeus. Great Egret. Common resident, breeding in scattered colonies, along lower Colorado River; fairly common winter resident at Painted Rock and Picacho Reservoirs. Elsewhere found in small transient numbers south of the Mogollon Plateau, a few wintering from Nogales and Safford westward. Sparse summer visitant in southeast. A sparse transient on the Mogollon Plateau, found there only once since the 1930s, Chevelon Creek southeast of Winslow, 27 to 28 June 1977 (R.L. Todd).

26. *Ardea thula* Molina. Snowy Egret. Found year-long in Colorado Valley, especially common as transient and in recent years as a winter resident; has nested in the Topock Marsh and on California side of river at Taylor Lake, 27 km (17 mi) above Imperial Dam. Elsewhere a frequent migrant, in most places in small flocks or singly. Occasional in central and southeastern Arizona all summer, nesting once at Picacho Reservoir (July 1973; Monson). Quite sparse winter visitor east and south of lower Gila Valley and the Phoenix region.

The Arizona race is *A. t. brewsteri* (Thayer and Bangs), a rather unsatisfactory subspecies.

27. *Ardea tricolor* Müller. Louisiana Heron. Very sparse straggler, chiefly in fall, in southern Arizona; has been found north to Camp Verde, *24 Sept. 1884,* and to near Mammoth, 29 July 1979 (D. Abbott, W. Bielstein). One record for the north: Lake Mary, near Flagstaff, *2 Nov. 1975* (ARIZ, photo, C.R. and M.A. Beals). Not more than 20 records in all.

28. *Dichromanassa rufescens* (Gmelin). Reddish Egret. Very sparse; one specimen from near Camp Verde, *27 Aug. 1886.* Also, one seen repeatedly along Colorado River above Imperial Dam, Sept. 1954 to Mar. 1955; one on California side of Lake Havasu, *9 Sept. 1954;* one about 48 river km (30 mi) above Imperial Dam, 2 Sept. 1960; one at Imperial Dam, *11 Feb. 1979* (ARIZ, photo, K.V. Rosenberg, L. Delaney); and. one southeast of Phoenix at Ahwatukee, 14 to 18 *July 1980* (ARIZ, photo, S. Terrill; first found by P. Beall and W.C. Hunter).

The Camp Verde specimen is of the nominate race. The California bird is a juvenile and not identifiable as to race.

29. *Bubulcus ibis* Linnaeus. Cattle Egret. First found in Arizona near Phoenix, *6* or *7 Dec. 1966*

(MNA; emaciated bird with broken humerus brought to Roer Bird Farm). After 1972 uncommon but irregular in southern Arizona, sometimes numerous in the lower Colorado Valley (exceptionally to Lake Mohave) and in the Phoenix area, with as many as 185 found in the Parker vicinity, 18 Dec. 1978 (Christmas Bird Count), and over 500 in the Dome Valley east of Yuma, 7 July 1980 (R. Martin, G. Robinson). Seen much less commonly in summer. Not yet found north of Camp Verde latitude except for one at Ganado, 30 May 1979 (K. Kaufman et al.), and one at Kayenta, 30 Apr. 1980 (C. Sexton); both localities are on the Navajo Indian Reservation.

30. *Nycticorax nycticorax* (Linnaeus). Black-crowned Night Heron. Resident in lower Colorado Valley and near Gila–Salt Rivers confluence, at which places it breeds; seen uncommonly elsewhere as a transient, occasionally in wooded but waterless situations, or as a winter visitant in southern and central Arizona. Nested at least once at Picacho Reservoir, July 1973 (Monson); in tamarisk thickets at head of Lake Mead, June 1974 (R.R. Johnson et al.); and on Gila River near Geronimo, Graham Co., June 1978 (D. Griffith, R. Hanna). Bred formerly on Salt and Verde Rivers; may breed near Springerville and in other localities.

[*Nycticorax violaceus* (Linnaeus). Yellow-crowned Night Heron. Hypothetical. Only two records, one adult at Tucson, 26 May 1968 (C. Coston, G. Gregg), and a subadult at Imperial Dam, 17 Apr. 1973 (R. Webster). A reported specimen from Sullivan Lake, north of Prescott, *14 Oct. 1951* (Institute of Biology, University of Mexico), appears on re-examination to be a hybrid with the preceding.]

FAMILY CICONIIDAE: STORKS

31. *Mycteria americana* (Linnaeus). Wood Stork. Uncommon summer visitant (non-breeding) along lower Colorado and Gila Rivers from mid-June to early Oct.; sparse elsewhere in southern part of state (but 20 at Picacho Reservoir, 20 June 1952, Phillips, L. Sowls) and accidental on and north of Mogollon Plateau. One winter record, from near Tombstone, *24 Dec. 1972* (ARIZ, photo, D. Schmoldt, G. Lasser, R. Willmarch), and no spring record since 1910. More common before about 1960.

FAMILY THRESKIORNITHIDAE:
IBISES AND SPOONBILLS

32. *Plegadis chihi* (Vieillot). White-faced Ibis. Fairly common migrant. A few (seldom up to 50) may be found throughout the summer, but no positive breeding record. Sparse to uncommon in winter in southern Arizona, mainly Colorado Valley south from Ehrenberg (two at Topock, 29 Nov. 1948, Monson), but recorded east to San Pedro Valley.

33. *Eudocimus albus* (Linnaeus). White Ibis. Casual. An adult at Martinez Lake above Imperial Dam, *4* and *5 Apr. 1962* (ARIZ, photo). A flock of ten adults on the Verde River below Horseshoe Dam, *3* to *14 May 1977* (ARIZ, photo, R.L. Todd et al.; first found by B. Campbell.) One reported on California side of Colorado River at Palo Verde, Imperial Co., Mar. 1914; one about 15 km (9 mi) east of Florence, 7 Apr. 1971 (J. Truett); and one adult on Hassayampa River near Wickenburg, 4 June 1977 (S. Terrill, A. Gast), but no substantiations.

[**_Eudocimus ruber_** (Linnaeus). Scarlet Ibis. Hypothetical. While there is no specimen, the identification of a flock of seven or eight near Tucson, 17

Sept. 1890, by so experienced a collector as Herbert Brown can hardly be questioned in the case of so striking a bird.]

34. *Platalea ajaja* Linnaeus. Roseate Spoonbill. Very sparse and irregular in southern Arizona from Yuma region north to Parker and east to Phoenix region, Picacho Reservoir, and Tucson; records extend from late May to Nov. An extraordinary influx occurred in the summer of 1973, when Roseate Spoonbills were found in some numbers along the Colorado River near Yuma and Parker (up to 21 in Yuma) and at Picacho Reservoir (a high of 33), and one or two were seen at other localities (Quitobaquito, Phoenix, and even Nogales). Since 1942, recorded only in 1951, 1959, 1969, 1973, and 1977.

FAMILY CATHARTIDAE: AMERICAN VULTURES

35. *Cathartes aura* (Linnaeus). Turkey Vulture. Formerly common, now fairly common, summer resident, except in extensive forested areas where it is rather uncommon or locally rare. Winters in lower Colorado Valley north to at least Topock, less commonly in Gila Bend, Phoenix, and Nogales areas, the Altar Valley, and the southeastern part of the Papago Indian Reservation; casually north to Tucson. One was seen feeding with Common Ravens on a dead wild burro in the Grand Canyon (Tonto Plateau), 26 Jan. 1965 (J.A. Blaisdell, Robert Todd). In recent years wintering numbers have markedly diminished. Apparently extremely unusual were flocks of eight over Smoke Tree Wash on the east side of the Cabeza Prieta Mountains, Yuma Co., 18 Dec. 1980 (S.H. Levy), and ten at the edge of the Pinacate Lava Flow, extreme southeastern Yuma Co., 31 Dec. 1980 (P.M. Walters, Monson).

Summer resident Turkey Vultures in Arizona (except possibly in the north) are the small southern nominate race. The somewhat larger *C. a. meridionalis* Swann enters Arizona about late Aug. and may be the only wintering race. A reported *C. a. septentrionalis* Wied is probably an exceptional *meridionalis* (A. Wetmore, in litt.).

36. *Coragyps atratus* Bartram. Black Vulture. First found in Arizona in 1920. Resident in generally small numbers of Santa Cruz Valley above Picacho Peak (mainly at Nogales and Sahuarita) and the Papago Indian Reservation west to Organ Pipe Cactus National Monument; also recorded from San Bernardino Ranch, Cochise Co., from Feb. to July. Seen irregularly north to Arlington and near Phoenix, except in the breeding period. Recorded casually from north of Oracle Junction, Pinal Co.; at Papago Well in extreme western Pima Co., *1 May 1972* (ARIZ, photo, J. Creasey); and at Rockfellow Dome, Dragoon Mountains, 18 June 1979 (K. Vernick). Supposed records for Wickenburg, Tonto Basin in Gila Co., Verde Valley, and north are not considered authentic. Only two nests have been found, both on Organ Pipe Cactus National Monument: Twin Peaks, two eggs, 20 Mar. 1967 (W. Hoy, J. Taylor), and Puerto Blanco Mountains, one young, 10 Apr. 1969 (photo, D. Fischer).

37. *Gymnogyps californianus* (Shaw). California Condor. A few sight records, principally in the 1880s, from southeast to northwest (and southwestern Utah). Latest date is apparently 3 Oct. 1924, when one was seen north of Williams (E.C. Jacot). Most of the few bird bones (not petrified) recently recorded from caves in the Grand Canyon are of this species.

FAMILY ACCIPITRIDAE: HAWKS, OLD WORLD VULTURES, AND HARRIERS

38. *Elanus leucurus* (Vieillot). White-tailed Kite. Three substantiated records: Altar Valley about 15 km (9 mi) northeast of Baboquivari Peak, *11 Aug. 1978* (ARIZ, photo, D.H. Ellis); north of Santa Rita Mountains, *22 Aug. 1979* (ARIZ, photo, R. Hudson et al.); and near Hereford, Cochise Co., *27* or *28 Oct. 1979* (ARIZ, photo, P. O'Brien). Other recent reports, all singles, include west side of Dragoon Mountains, 6 Nov. 1972 (D. Danforth); Blue Point cottonwoods east of Phoenix, 25 Feb. 1973 (R.R. Johnson, J. Simpson); Kansas Settlement, Cochise Co., 2 Feb. 1975 (S. Burk); near Sierra Vista, Cochise Co., 15 Dec. 1979 (S. Greenwood); on the Cibola National Wildlife Refuge, Yuma Co., 22 Mar. 1980 (B. Woodbridge); southeast of San Simon, Cochise Co., 19 Apr. 1980 (S. and W. Spofford); and near Poston, Yuma Co., 13 Nov. 1980 (M. Kasprzyk, C. Ramono). A supposed specimen taken years ago cannot be found.

39. *Ictinia mississippiensis* (Wilson). Mississippi Kite. Since its first discovery in the state by S.H. Levy in *1970,* a summer resident locally of the lower San Pedro Valley cottonwoods from Winkelman upstream to the Redington vicinity; also downstream, along Gila River near Kearney. In *1973* the species was found on the Verde River near Camp Verde, *10 June* (MNA, D. Jones), and in 1976 a pair nested successfully on the Verde River in Maricopa Co. just above the Fort McDowell Indian Reservation (R. Glinski). Extralimital records are one southeast of Wickenburg, 12 July 1979 (A. Moorhouse), and near Wikieup, 2 Aug. 1979 (R. Hanna, S. Heckler). Scattered sight records on migration elsewhere in southern Arizona from Phoenix to upper San Pedro Valley.

40. *Accipiter gentilis* (Linnaeus). Goshawk. Sparse to uncommon resident of the mountains of eastern and central Arizona and the Kaibab Plateau. One summer record, an adult seen in the Hualapai

Mountains, 21 June 1978 (K.V. Rosenberg), and a nest found there in 1979 (B. Millsap). In winter it occurs sparsely well away from the pine forests, and irregularly so on the desert, even reaching the Colorado Valley in major flights.

In northern and central Arizona the subspecies is the small, pale *A. g. atricapillus* (Wilson); it is also the race found in atypical habitats in winter. The resident bird of the southeastern mountains is the large, dark *A. g. apache* van Rossem.

41. *Accipiter striatus* Vieillot. Sharp-shinned Hawk. Sparse to uncommon summer resident of the mountains and high mesas of eastern Arizona (even the Mule Mountains, 1979, D. Danforth). Noted in the Hualapai Mountains, July 1977 (A. Higgins, K.V. Rosenberg). Winters commonly in southern and western Arizona, uncommonly on Mogollon Plateau and farther north where it is mainly a transient.

The only subspecies that has been found in Arizona is the northern *A. s. velox* (Wilson), although breeding birds in extreme southeastern Arizona tend toward *A. s. suttoni* van Rossem.

42. *Accipiter cooperii* (Bonaparte). Cooper's Hawk. Nests scatteringly throughout the state, being almost common along Upper Sonoran drainages of the south-central and southeastern parts, but not recently along the lower Colorado River, where nests were found in 1910 (J. Grinnell), near Parker in 1946–48 (Monson), and in the Bill Williams Delta at least in 1953 (Monson). Winters commonly in southern and western Arizona except in higher parts of mountains and in southwestern deserts; uncommonly in the north, chiefly in riparian deciduous situations. Transient in most or all parts of the state.

43. *Buteo jamaicensis* (Gmelin). Red-tailed Hawk. Common resident virtually statewide. Winters to upper part of the Transition Zone and possibly higher. A nest was found on a large sand dune south of the Sierra del Rosario in northwestern Sonora, about 80 km (50 mi) from Yuma, in Mar. 1976 (P. Cowgill, *The Arizona Daily Star,* 28 Mar. 1976).

B. j. calurus (Cassin) winters throughout Arizona and is also the resident form over much of the state. *B. j. fuertesi* Sutton and Van Tyne occupies the southeast, intergrading farther west and northwest with *calurus.* *B. j. kriderii* Hoopes is known only as a rare or casual fall transient on the Mogollon Plateau. *B. j. harlani* (Audubon) is known from two specimens in southeastern Arizona (16 km [10 mi] south of St. David, Cochise Co., *4 Dec. 1959,* and 24 km [15 mi] southeast of Phoenix, *10 Jan. 1962*), where there have been a number of mostly questionable sight records in recent years (but almost none since it was relegated to a subspecies by the A.O.U. Check-list).

44. *Buteo lineatus* (Gmelin). Red-shouldered Hawk. Status unclear; apparently an irregular and sparse visitant to southern Arizona since about 1968, and nesting once near Laguna Dam (*1968,* US, R. Wright and C. Bindner); before that, two indefinite sight records from northern Arizona, plus one on the California side of the Colorado River about 25 km (15 mi) above Imperial Dam. An adult was captured and photographed, then released, in Redington Pass, Pima Co., *15 Jan. 1976* (ARIZ, photo, R. Glinski) after being first seen 20 Dec. 1975 (R. Chapin). One was observed repeatedly in the Bill Williams Delta area, 29 Oct. to 28 Jan. 1978 (K.V. Rosenberg et al.). An adult was seen near Yuma, 11 Mar. 1978 (Rosenberg et al.). Two were found near Needles, California, 21 Jan. 1978, and one was seen there 26 July 1978 (S. Cardiff). A supposed 1853 specimen (US) was finally located by Phillips, and it turned out to be a Red-tailed Hawk. This bird seems prone to such misidentification in the field.

Arizona birds, including the one from Pima Co., are apparently *B. l. elegans* Cassin.

45. *Buteo platypterus* (Vieillot). Broad-winged Hawk. Two specimens: Southwestern Research Station, Chiricahua Mountains, *22 Sept. 1956,* and one found dying at Tucson, *7 Jan. 1965* (ARIZ, M. Whiting). Reported about a dozen times after 1972 from the Huachuca and Chiricahua Mountains, mainly in winter and spring, the Verde River east of Phoenix, 16 and 18 Mar. 1975 (S. Terrill, S. Majlinger), and from Tucson, 6 to 7 Feb. 1979 (K. Kaufman et al.).

46. *Buteo swainsoni* Bonaparte. Swainson's Hawk. Common summer resident of grassy plains and agricultural valleys of eastern Arizona west to Baboquivari Mountains and Florence; also, but sparingly, to central and central-southern Arizona, and possibly to eastern Mohave Co. A migrant state-wide except in forests, but irregular in western Arizona where flocks seen rarely. No records of healthy birds in winter. An old breeding record near Yuma is not considered authentic, nor do we believe it is a "common migrant," starting in Feb., in adjacent parts of Nevada.

47. *Buteo albonotatus* Kaup. Zone-tailed Hawk. Fairly common to uncommon summer resident of mountains and tall deciduous riparian woods in northwestern, central, and southeastern Arizona, but only formerly in the Santa Cruz Valley, the Rillito Valley at Tucson, on the Gila River, and near mouth of Bill Williams River (1946 to 1947). May nest irregularly west to Organ Pipe Cactus National Monument, where individuals seen 9 and 13 May 1939, and north to the Kaibab Plateau, where seen 4 and 12 July 1973 (R. and M. Wilson). A nest with two young found in a palo verde about 72 km (45 mi) southwest of Sasabe, Sonora, 18 July 1975 (D. Lamm, Monson). Occurs rarely in migration west to Colorado River, where seen recently in the Bill

Williams Delta, 1977–78 (D. Wells, K.V. Rosenberg et al.). A very few winter records for the Tucson region, including mountains, and some old ones from Yuma.

48. *Buteo albicaudatus* Vieillot. White-tailed Hawk. Probably casual; one or two specimens from Phoenix, *1899*; nest recorded (*Auk* 14:403, 1897) between Florence and Red Rock, Pinal Co., 1897; one seen repeatedly near Marinette, northwest of Phoenix, winter of 1954–55; and one seen several times in Avra Valley, Pima Co., Dec. 1964–Jan. 1965 (D. Prentice). Three reported west of Gila Bend in the 1954–55 winter. One identified as this species was observed repeatedly in the San Rafael Valley, Santa Cruz Co., 5 Jan. to 8 Feb. 1971 (E. Noble et al.). The White-tailed Hawk (especially immatures) can be confused with *B. jamaicensis harlani* or *B. regalis.*

49. *Buteo lagopus* (Pontoppidan). Rough-legged Hawk. Uncommon in winter, mostly in irrigated or grassy sections, probably of state-wide occurence, including the irrigated southwest. Specimens south to near Douglas (Whitewater Draw) at Sonora border. Fall records prior to Oct. require substantiation. A bird identified as this hawk was seen about 24 km (15 mi) south of Chinle, Navajo Indian Reservation, 10 June 1977 (S. Alden). One recorded at Puerto Peñasco, Sonora, 19 Mar. 1965 (W. Bulmer, J. Haugh).

50. *Buteo regalis* (Gray). Ferruginous Hawk. Uncommon to sparse and widely distributed resident of grassy plains of northern Arizona, more common in winter, and formerly locally and irregularly near Prescott and in southeastern Arizona. Fairly common in winter in open country throughout the south, mainly in irrigated and grassy areas, sparse in other situations.

51. *Buteo nitidus* (Latham). Gray Hawk. A fairly common resident along wooded streams in the southeast: the San Pedro River, Portrero Creek and Santa Cruz River near Nogales, Sopori Wash, Sonoita Creek, and Arivaca Creek. Reported to have nested in 1974 near New River, Maricopa Co. (C. Stensrude), but no substantiation. Before deforestation, common along streams in the Tucson vicinity; and until 1960s nested along Tanque Verde Creek near Tucson. One adult seen along Verde River east of Phoenix, 13–19 Apr. 1975 (S. Burge, S. Terrill, K. Kaufman); one immature found at Paradise, Cochise Co., 22 July 1979 (R. Stallcup et al.). Winter records include one near Nogales to 21 Dec. 1976 (B. Harrison et al.), an immature in Tonto Canyon, western Santa Cruz Co., 2 Jan. 1978 (K. Kaufman, D. Stotz), and a pair of adults at "Dudleyville," Pinal Co., 10 Dec. 1978 (R. Glinski). Old records east and west of above locations are not considered authentic.

52. *Parabuteo unicinctus* (Temminck). Harris' Hawk. Locally resident in palo verde-saguaro desert in a triangular area from north of Phoenix southeast to Tucson (including Florence Jct. and Florence to Winkelman areas) and southwest to Organ Pipe Cactus National Monument. Until recently a common resident along the lower Colorado River north to Topock, but almost absent since some time in the 1960s. One at Cooks Lake, lower San Pedro Valley, 21 Aug. 1979 (B. Harrison, Monson) to at least 5 Nov. 1980 (Monson, P.M. Walters). Rarely seen in migratory raptor flocks, usually with Swainson's Hawks, in Tucson region and westward. Apparently some local dispersion occurs in winters. Old records from upper San Pedro Valley, *1890;* upper Verde Valley, *1886;* San Bernardino Ranch, Cochise Co., *1892;* and Fort Buchanan (later Camp Crittenden, near Sonoita) in the *1850*s or *1860*s. An odd record is of five (four adults and one juvenile) found south of the San Simon Cienega, N.M., 25 Oct. 1980 (R. Fisher); they were seen by others; one of the five was seen flying over the Arizona side, 26 Nov. (W.S. Spofford et al.). They were not seen later in this locality.

Native Arizona race is *P. u. superior* van Rossem, but it is now being mongrelized by falconer-introduced stock of unknown origin. The San Simon Cienega birds could likely be *P. u. harrisi* (Audubon).

53. *Buteogallus anthracinus* (Deppe). Black Hawk. Fairly common summer resident along permanent streams, chiefly those in canyons, in southeastern and central Arizona and in the adjacent Arroyo Cajón Bonito of Sonora, also to the northwest to the Big Sandy drainage and even the Virgin River drainage of the extreme northwest. In migration, one was seen northeast of the Santa Rosa Mountains, Papago Indian Reservation, in late Mar. 1964 (T.D. Burleigh, S.H. Levy). Sight records from Cataract Canyon adjacent to Grand Canyon; near Parker; Bill Williams Delta, Mar. to May 1979 (T. Brush et al.); at Ehrenberg, Yuma Co., 11 Apr. 1978 (M. Lange); and north of Ehrenberg, 5 May 1979 (B. Whitney). The last may have been *B. urubitinga* (Gmelin). Presently the only breeding birds in Arizona south of the Gila River are in Aravaipa Canyon and Redfield Canyon in the Galiuro Mountains, although a pair nested at Patagonia as recently as 1976. No authentic winter records.

The Arizona birds were named *B. a. micronyx* van Rossem and Hachisuka, but they apparently are not separable from the nominate race.

54. *Aquila chrysaetos* (Linnaeus). Golden Eagle. Distributed fairly commonly throughout state in all mountain areas; somewhat more common in the lower mountains in winter, when it also occurs along the Colorado River. Virtually absent in summer, after breeding, in some desert regions (viz., lower Little Colorado Valley), from early May to Aug. or mid-Sept.

55. *Haliaeetus leucocephalus* (Linnaeus). Bald Eagle. Ten to twelve pairs resident on Salt River (mostly above Roosevelt Dam) and in lower reaches of the Verde River; also one nesting attempt near Topock in 1975 and 1976. Formerly nested at Stoneman Lake, Coconino Co.; reported nesting at Foxboro Lake in the same county in 1975 (R.P. Balda). Said to leave after nesting, at least on Salt River; the birds may join gatherings elsewhere. Transient in northern mountains, Kaibab Plateau, and in the Grand Canyon. Winters fairly commonly about lakes and streams on and along the Mogollon Plateau, in the Roosevelt Lake region, about Prescott, along the lower Colorado River, and in the San Rafael Valley, Santa Cruz Co. There are scattered winter records from the southeast, aside from the San Rafael Valley, mostly in mountainous areas.

The subspecies in Arizona are in need of clarification.

56. *Circus cyaneus* (Linnaeus). Marsh Hawk. Common winter resident of better-vegetated open areas below Transition Zone. Before 1890 nested in parts of eastern Arizona; a pair was found on Chevelon Creek southeast of Winslow, 27 and 28 June 1977 (R.L. Todd et al.). An almost unbelievable report of a nest found and photographed in desert grassland near Vicksburg, Yuma Co., 23 Apr. 1980 (B. Millsap); the nest with three eggs was later destroyed by a bulldozer. Summer reports along North Rim of Grand Canyon probably do not indicate breeding. Occasional birds spend the summer in the south, including such records as one at Topock, 12 June and 25 July, 1950; one in Avra Valley, Pima Co., 15 June 1971 (E. Yensen); one near Coolidge, 28 May 1978 (S. Demaree); and one at Willcox Playa, 12 July 1979 (Monson). Fall-returning birds may appear as early as mid-July.

FAMILY PANDIONIDAE: OSPREYS

57. *Pandion haliaetus* (Linnaeus). Osprey. Nests locally along streams below Mogollon Rim; nested until 1951 at Granite Reef Dam, Maricopa Co. (R.R. Johnson et al.); nested successfully near Lakeside, Navajo Co., in 1978 (C. and E. Wolfe); also at Lake Mohave area, where seen carrying food to a nest below Eldorado Canyon, 27 Apr. 1950 (R. Grater). Found sparsely in summer on Mogollon Plateau, along Colorado River and upper Salt and Verde Rivers, and even at other waters statewide. May occur almost anywhere on migration. Occasionally winters in lower Colorado and Gila Valleys, and formerly did so at Roosevelt Lake.

FAMILY FALCONIDAE: CARACARAS AND FALCONS

58. *Caracara cheriway* (Jacquin). Caracara. Resident in small numbers on the eastern part of the main Papago Indian Reservation. Outside of breeding range is seen east to Santa Cruz Valley at and south of Tucson and south to Nogales. About 16 records otherwise since 1950 (almost all of them of single birds), extending from breeding range east to near Pearce, Cochise Co., 1 May 1954, north to east of Flagstaff, 6 Oct. 1973 (W. Fleming et al.), and west to east of Wellton, Yuma Co., 5 Dec. 1978 (V. Hink, D. Laush), and to Mittry Lake above Laguna Dam, Jan. 1964 (C. Lovelace). As many as six observed near Red Rock, Pinal Co., 27 Nov. 1965 (D. Prentice). Old records extend to Salt River Valley (including Phoenix), Florence, Oracle, Gillespie Dam (16 Sept. 1925, V. Housholder), and Yuma. Considerably more common before 1920.

59. *Falco peregrinus* Tunstall. Peregrine Falcon. Nests at cliffs throughout state in small numbers (about 30 pairs in all), even at some distance from water. Found sparsely statewide in migration. Winters occasionally along lower Colorado River, in very small numbers in central and even in the lower parts of southeastern Arizona; no definite records in the north.

Arizona birds belong to the race *F. p. anatum* Bonaparte, as far as known. *F. p. tundrius* White should occur.

60. *Falco mexicanus* Schlegel. Prairie Falcon. Fairly common to uncommon resident statewide in rocky, mountainous situations. Widespread in winter, with influx of birds from farther north.

61. *Falco femoralis* Temminck. Aplomado Falcon. Before 1890 a fairly common summer (or permanent?) resident in the southeast; since then virtually extinct in the state, with only two credible records since about 1910: near McNeal, Cochise Co., 13 Nov. 1939, and St. David, 7 Oct. 1940. Sight records since 1940 are all unsubstantiated, and the bird's status in Arizona now must be characterized as "extinct."

62. *Falco columbarius* Linnaeus. Merlin. Uncommon transient and winter resident virtually statewide, scarcer in mountains, many records from in or about towns and cities. Summer reports unsubstantiated.

Arizona specimens are about equally divided between two races, the medium dark northwestern *F. c. bendirei* Swann and the very pale *F. c. richardsonii* Ridgway of Canada's prairie provinces. A Grand Canyon specimen (GCN, McPhearson) is probably *F. c. suckleyi* Ridgway.

63. *Falco sparverius* Linnaeus. American Kestrel. Common resident and transient, abundant in some areas in migration; uncommon to sparse in winter in the higher mountains, and in summer in western Arizona.

Arizona birds are largely *F. s. sparverius* Linnaeus; *F. s. peninsularis* Mearns probably occurs in at least the Yuma-lower Gila area; better specimens are needed. Kestrels from the Gila River Indian Reservation appear to be intermediates (A.M. Rea).

FAMILY TETRAONIDAE: GROUSE AND PTARMIGAN

64. *Dendragapus obscurus* (Say). Blue Grouse. Fairly common resident of boreal zones of the White Mountains region, less common along the North Rim of the Grand Canyon and in the Chuska Mountains of northern Apache Co. Recently introduced in the San Francisco Mountains. Highly dubious are records of one seen on the east side of the Chiricahua Mountains, 24 May 1979 (M.S. Eltzroth et al.), and, in the same area, two about 1973 (W.S. Spofford) and one 13 July 1979 (L. Jones).

[*Centrocercus urophasianus* (Bonaparte). Sage Grouse. Hypothetical. One seen near Nixon Spring, Mount Trumbull region, 29 July 1937.]

FAMILY PHASIANIDAE: QUAILS, PHEASANTS, AND PEACOCKS

65. *Colinus virginianus* (Linnaeus). Bobwhite. Extinct in the wild in Arizona for many years; formerly (mainly before 1890) common in tall grass-mesquite plains from Baboquivari Mountains east to upper Santa Cruz Valley. Grazed out of existence by early 1900s. Reintroduction attempts have been underway in the Altar Valley since 1970, using stock from adjacent Sonora and their descendants; results as of 1980 are encouraging. Records for Huachuca and Whetstone Mountains are not well-founded, though repeated in the A.O.U. Check-list.

Arizona birds were the Masked Bobwhite, *C. v. ridgwayi* Brewster.

66. *Callipepla squamata* (Vigors). Scaled Quail. Common to abundant resident of grassy plains in southeastern and south-central Arizona, west and northwest to Baboquivari and Quinlan Mountains, south-central Pinal Co., and east of San Carlos. A male was seen and heard about 30 km (19 mi) southwest of Sells, 24 May 1973 (D.E. Brown). Occurs locally in upper Little Colorado River drainage, perhaps by introduction. The wandering proclivities of this quail are exhibited by a covey of six or seven seen on the *main ridge* of the Baboquivari Mountains near the head of Sabino Canyon, 29 Nov. 1980 (J. Levy). Hybrids with the following species have been found occasionally since about 1950, chiefly in the vicinity of Antelope Peak southwest of the confluence of the Gila and San Pedro Rivers.

The Arizona population belongs to *C. s. pallida* Brewster.

67. *Callipepla gambelii* (Gambel). Gambel's Quail. Abundant resident in all areas where mesquite occurs, including the Grand Canyon, locally higher (along foot of Mogollon Plateau, Juniper and Santa Maria Mountains, Big Lue Mountains, Oracle, etc.) and scarcer in extreme deserts of the southwest. Native occurrence in northern Arizona not substantiated; known to have been introduced in various places in the northern part of the state (including Pipe Spring National Monument, Moenave in the western Navajo Indian Reservation), for the most part unsuccessfully.

The paler nominate race is found in all parts of the state, except at the foot of the Mogollon Plateau and possibly in the vicinity of the Chiricahua Mountains, where it is replaced by the darker, browner, more richly colored *C. g. fulvipectus* (Nelson).

68. *Cyrtonyx montezumae* (Vigors). Mearns' (Montezuma) Quail. Common to locally abundant resident of grassy open woods of the mountains of southeastern and central Arizona, west to the Baboquivari Mountains (and possibly Morena Mountain on the Papago Indian Reservation west of the Baboquivaris, where a pair was seen 23 May 1972 by D.E. Brown) and north and northwest to southwest of Camp Verde, *10 May 1970* (ARIZ, R. L. Todd), 53 km (33 mi) south-southeast of Flagstaff, *15 Dec. 1966* (MNA, H.G. Shaw), and the Blue region. Also found in the White Mountains region, including to 3050 m (10,000 ft) on White Mountain Baldy; near Greer, 5 Oct. 1978 (K. Kaufman, S. Terrill et al.); and not uncommon near Eagar (F. Fanning). Principally found in the Upper Sonoran Zone.

United States birds belong to the race *C. m. mearnsi* Nelson.

[*Phasianus colchicus* Linnaeus. Ring-necked Pheasant. Has been introduced repeatedly in agricultural areas, without continued success; it persists only by artificial replenishment. The statement (A.O.U. Check-list) that it is established in southeastern Arizona is without any basis.]

69. *Alectoris chukar* (Meisner). Chukar. Firmly established on the North Rim of Grand Canyon and below the west and south sides of the Kaibab Plateau from releases made in 1958–60 by the Arizona Game and Fish Department, using wild-trapped birds from California and Nevada. They seem most common in tributaries of Snake Gulch and along Hack Canyon and Kanab Creek (including Jump Up) and on Fishtail Mesa. However, not known to persist in areas to the east and southeast (D.E. Brown).

FAMILY MELEAGRIDIDAE: TURKEYS

70. *Meleagris gallopavo* Linnaeus. Turkey. In early days, abundant resident of virtually all forested parts of the state (including the Baboquivari Mountains) except Hualapai (and Galiuro?) Mountains and Kaibab Plateau, descending in winter to some of the valleys. By 1920 shot out except in San Francisco and White Mountains regions. Since then restocked over much of former range and elsewhere (including Kaibab Plateau) with varying degrees of success. A small population in the Guadalupe Mountains in the extreme southeast may have been maintained by birds dispersing from the Sierra San Luis in adjacent Mexico; recent sight records there are of escaped domestic Turkeys, however. Stray Turkeys have been seen in the bottom of the Grand Canyon, 9 Aug. 1970 (S.H. Levy) and near the junction of Davidson Canyon and Cienega Creek, southeast of Tucson, 8 Nov. 1973 (Monson). Seven were noted in dense cottonwoods along the San Francisco River in New Mexico but near the Arizona line, 3 June 1976 (R. Glinski). Due care must be exercised to be sure that Turkeys observed are not feral domestic birds.

Arizona Turkeys supposedly belong to *M. g. merriami* Nelson, except for birds of the Guadalupe and Peloncillo Mountains, which perhaps are of the race *M. g. mexicana* Gould, but there are no specimens from most parts of its former range.

FAMILY GRUIDAE: CRANES

[***Grus americana*** (Linnaeus). Whooping Crane. A banded adult with Sandhill Cranes at the south end of the Willcox Playa, 26 Dec. 1980 (D. Perkins) and 29 Dec. 1980 (Perkins, D.E. Brown) was one of the Whooping Cranes reared by foster Sandhill Cranes from eggs imported from Canada to Grays Lake, Idaho.]

71. *Grus canadensis* (Linnaeus). Sandhill Crane. Abundant in the Kansas Settlement area of the Sulphur Springs Valley (up to 7900 in 1979–80), and along the lower Colorado River below Parker (up to 1500 in 1976–77) and at Cibola National Wildlife Refuge (up to 1000 in 1978–79); also in northern Sulphur Springs Valley (about 400 in Jan. 1980). Known almost solely as a winter resident in irrigated tracts where waste grain and roosting sites are both available. Lesser numbers have been found in winter in the Topock region, at Gila Bend, and at Arlington in Maricopa Co. These modern-day concentrations began taking place in the 1960s, following an unknown number of decades of comparative scarcity. Other than wintering flocks, the only recent records are of one at Phoenix, 12 Oct. 1969 (R. Witzeman), two near Benson, 16 Mar. 1974 (P. Edgell), two at Painted Rock Reservoir, 7 Nov. 1974 (S. Terrill et al.), one at Gillespie Dam, 20 Feb. 1978 (P. Burch, D. Stejskal), and one at St. David, 8 Oct. 1978 (Monson). Prior to 1936, a few northern Arizona records, including summer occurrences. Virtually unknown as a migrant in recent years. "Abundant" below Yuma, 9 Apr. 1862.

Most Arizona birds are thought to belong to *G. c. canadensis* (Linnaeus), the "Lesser" Sandhill Crane, but the "Greater" Sandhill Crane, *G. c. tabida* (Peters) also occurs and is the only race which would be found in summer.

FAMILY RALLIDAE: RAILS, GALLINULES, AND COOTS

72. *Rallus longirostris* Boddaert. Clapper Rail. Before 1940, known only from cattail marshes in the Yuma region, but since then has advanced upstream along the Colorado River to become a more or less common summer resident in cattails north to the

Topock Marsh, arriving at Topock in the mid-1960s.
Since 1969, extremely small numbers have been
located in cattail marshes at Tacna on the lower Gila
River; since 1975, along the Salt River above and
below Phoenix and (intermittently?) at Picacho
Reservoir (R.L. Todd et al.). An unknown percentage
of the population winters, at least in the area from
Imperial Dam downstream. About 900 were censused
from Yuma to Topock in May 1973 (Todd et al.).
   Our subspecies is *R. l. yumanensis* Dickey, the Yuma
   Clapper Rail.

73. *Rallus limicola* Vieillot. Virginia Rail. Summer
resident of marshes in the White Mountains region
down to adjacent Upper Sonoran Zone. May breed
in other marshes in southern Arizona, such as at San
Bernardino Ranch and near St. David in Cochise Co.
and along the lower Salt and Gila Rivers. A downy
young was captured in a marsh adjacent to the Gila
River near Tacna, Yuma Co., 4 May 1970 (R.
Hernbrode, Jr., R.L. Todd). In the Bill Williams
Delta, young were found for the first time 29 Mar.
1978 (K.V. Rosenberg), and the species likely nests
along the lower Colorado River south to Mittry Lake
below Imperial Dam. In the north, it has also nested
at Pipe Spring National Monument in 1974 (R.
Wilt). Locally a common migrant, at least along
Colorado Valley and formerly at Tucson, and even
may be seen at desert water holes. Common during
winter in suitable places in the south, being abundant
at Tavasci Marsh at Clarkdale and along Salt River
near Phoenix; has been found as high as McNary,
Apache Co., 22 Jan. 1950 (H. Tvedt).

74. *Porzana carolina* (Linnaeus). Sora. Breeds
commonly at marshes in northern Arizona; also
probably in central Arizona, one record of adult with
young near Chandler, 25 Aug. 1974 (S. Terrill). Ten
or more were heard at Picacho Reservoir, 20 June

1952. Common transient in grassy, reedy, or weedy moist areas statewide. Winters commonly at unfrozen marshes, including isolated small cattail patches; recorded twice from frozen marshes in southern Navajo Co. Supposed possible breeding birds seen in July in southern Arizona could be early returning migrants; it is believed that they may return in the south as early as the first week in July.

75. *Coturnicops noveboracensis* (Gmelin). Yellow Rail. One caught alive near Sacaton, Gila River Indian Reservation, *28 Mar. 1909,* the only substantiated record, although not improbably a sparse winter visitant. Phillips heard what he suspects was a Yellow Rail at the old Binghamton Pond in Tucson, 14 Jan. 1940.

76. *Laterallus jamaicensis* (Gmelin). Black Rail. Summer resident beginning in 1969 (first found at small marsh on California side between Laguna and Imperial Dams, 15 June 1969, G. McCaskie, A. Craig), locally common in certain *Scirpus* marshes along a short stretch of the Colorado River in Yuma Co., from Mittry Lake north to above Martinez Lake. One photograph, at Mittry Lake, *30 May 1970* (ARIZ, R.L. Todd). Up to 80 individuals were "detected" in the Mittry Lake area from 6 to 17 May 1980 (Todd). Also found on California side of river in same district, especially at West Pond below Imperial Dam. Black Rails may be resident in these same areas, as the "growl" call peculiar to this species has been heard at least in Dec. (Todd, K. Kaufman et al.). Unconfirmed sight records at Tucson; near Casa Grande; at Quitobaquito, 24 Sept. 1972 (J. Mann) and 7 or 8 Apr. 1973 (D. Stejskal); and Willcox, 18 to 19 Apr. 1977 (P.M. Walters et al.). One reported heard in Bill Williams Delta, 18 Apr. 1979 (J. Bean, A. Laurenzi).
    The race occurring in Arizona is presumably *L. j. coturniculus* Ridgway. There are no specimens.

77. ***Porphyrula martinica*** (Linnaeus). Purple Gallinule. Casual to sparse summer visitant (*July* to *Sept.*), mainly to the Tucson area, where there are a number of records; also, one record for Montana Lake, near Oro Blanco, western Santa Cruz Co., *2 Aug. 1909,* one caught alive in Arizona near Rodeo, New Mexico, June 1935, one seen at St. David, 24 Aug. 1972 (P. Norton), and one seen near Willcox, 7 Aug. 1975 (D. Pearson).

78. *Gallinula chloropus* (Linnaeus). Common Gallinule. Common to fairly common resident locally across the southern and western parts of the state where cattails or tules are associated with shallow streams, ponds, or canals, north as far as Chino Valley, Yavapai Co. (at least in 1976, C.S. Tomoff). Occasional migrant or winter resident in less favorable spots in above range. Casual at Pipe Spring National Monument, 8 and 9 June 1974 (R. Wilt) and at Phantom Ranch, bottom of the Grand Canyon, 17 to 18 May 1977 (L. Simpson, S. Stockton). Has been recorded as resident in southwestern Utah (R. Wauer, R.C. Russell).

79. *Fulica americana* Gmelin. American Coot. Common summer resident, and common to abundant migrant, of water areas with cattail–tule margins. Winters commonly to abundantly wherever open water is present, abundantly along lower Colorado River.

FAMILY HAEMATOPODIDAE:
OYSTERCATCHERS

[*Haematopus bachmani* Audubon. Black Oystercatcher. Hypothetical. One alongside highway near Picacho Peak, Pinal Co., 13 Sept. 1972 (H.E. Gaither).]

FAMILY RECURVIROSTRIDAE:
AVOCETS AND STILTS

80. *Himantopus mexicanus* (Müller). Black-necked Stilt. Breeds locally along lower Colorado River and at Phoenix; also nested near Chandler in 1975 (S. Burge), at Painted Rock Reservoir in 1978 (according to J. Witzeman), and at Tucson in 1979 (L.A. Hill) and 1980 (H. Fetter et al.); formerly nested on San Pedro River. Otherwise a fairly common to common migrant in southern and western Arizona, common in fall along lower Colorado River. The only records for the northern part of the state are for Pipe Spring National Monument in June 1974 and Sept. 1973 (R. Wilt); there are unsubstantiated reports for the Grand Canyon area. Has wintered in some numbers at Phoenix (1971–72 and 1975–76); also two records for that season in lower Gila River Valley, 11 Dec. 1921 and *17 Feb. 1940.*

81. *Recurvirostra americana* Gmelin. American Avocet. Has been found breeding regularly in Willcox area since 1965, and at Phoenix from 1969 to 1977; also has bred at Parks Lake, extreme southeastern Graham Co. (June 1968, S.H. Levy), at Tucson (May 1972, H. Fetter), and near Chandler (May 1975, S. Burge). Otherwise, a common to fairly common migrant statewide; sometimes occurs in large flocks in fall along lower Colorado River. Occasionally winters along lower Colorado River (six to ten in Bill Williams Delta, 1948–49, Monson) and at Phoenix; also possibly at Willcox, where two seen 24 Feb. 1952 (S.H. Levy) and three 27 Feb. 1975 (Monson); one near Douglas to 31 Dec. 1980 (A. Moorhouse). Five seen (one collected) near Anita, Coconino Co., *1 Dec. 1935* (GCN, C. Wheeler).

FAMILY CHARADRIIDAE: PLOVERS

82. *Charadrius semipalmatus* Bonaparte. Semipalmated Plover. Uncommon transient along open shorelines throughout the state. One June record (Willcox, 10 June 1975, Monson). One observed at West Pond, California side of Colorado River below Imperial Dam, 22 June 1968 (G. McCaskie et al.).

83. *Charadrius vociferus* Linnaeus. Killdeer. The ubiquitous water-bird of the state, found year long anywhere at open water. Abundant at times in migration, and in irrigated areas (including golf courses) in winter. Downy young may be found as late as 28 Oct. (Tucson, 1974, H. Fetter).

84. *Charadrius alexandrinus* Linnaeus. Snowy Plover. Breeding at Willcox at a recently constructed pond and nearby smaller alkali ponds since 1972; also bred twice at Painted Rock Reservoir, Maricopa Co., in 1974 and again in 1980. Otherwise a fairly common to uncommon transient in southern Arizona north to Prescott vicinity; the only records for the north are from ponds along the South Rim of the Grand Canyon, 30 Apr. 1967 (L. Bancroft, B. Ford) and 7 Apr. 1977 (R. Euler). Winters sparingly along lower Colorado and Gila Rivers. Two winter records at Phoenix, 28 Dec. 1963 (Christmas Bird Count), and at Willcox, 31 Dec. 1976 (Monson, E. Willis); also one at Tucson, 3 Dec. 1971 (Monson).

The only Arizona specimen is *C. a. nivosus* (Cassin).

85. *Charadrius montanus* (Townsend). Mountain Plover. Sparse to uncommon; in small numbers in fall in the western part of the state, and as wintering flocks on barren desert flats and fallow fields in the Florence, Phoenix–Chandler, and Yuma–Gila Bend–Parker regions; found one year in Avra Valley, Pima Co. (1965, D. Prentice). No recent records farther east, but 14 were taken in the Sulphur Springs Valley west of the Chiricahua Mountains, *23* to *24 Feb. 1915* (VPI, A.J. van Rossem). About 50 seen near Cerro Colorado crater in the Sierra Pinacate of Sonora, Mexico less than 30 km (20 mi) from Arizona, 22 Nov. 1973 (S.M. Russell, D. Lamm). Several flocks seen northeast of Springerville in Aug. 1914 suggest breeding, especially in view of a nesting pair found within 11 km (7 mi) of Arizona in New Mexico (about 37 km or 23 mi east of Springerville) 12 and 13 June 1978 (T.B. Johnson, B. Spicer).

86. *Pluvialis dominica* (Müller). American Golden Plover. A very sparse fall migrant, and an even rarer spring migrant (about 16 fall records, only five spring records; all single birds), with records across southern Arizona from Willcox to Nogales west to near Parker and Prescott.

The race of the only Arizona specimen is *P. d. dominica* (Müller).

87. *Pluvialis squatarola* (Linnaeus). Black-bellied Plover. Uncommon transient probably statewide, but only one record for the north: five at Ganado Lake, Navajo Indian Reservation, 21 Oct. 1978 (K. Kaufman, G. Rosenberg). Most records are from south-central Arizona, and along the lower Colorado River; reported eastward to Willcox (twice in 1976) and near Douglas (17 Aug. 1979, A. Moorhouse); mostly in ones or twos, but 16 at Painted Rock Reservoir, Maricopa Co., 5 Oct. 1974 (several observers). One winter record, Yuma, 30 Dec. 1940. One at Poston, Yuma Co., 28 May 1980 (M. Kaspryzk), would seem to be extraordinarily late, although ten were seen at Willcox, 22 May 1976 (D. Stotz et al.).

FAMILY SCOLOPACIDAE: SANDPIPERS, TURNSTONES, PHALAROPES, AND OTHERS

88. *Limosa haemastica* (Linnaeus). Hudsonian Godwit. Casual. One at Willcox, 14 to *16 May 1976* (ARIZ, photo, J. Witzeman); first seen by M. Hansen and B. Jones. Another reported from Willcox, 28 Apr. 1978 (D. Reilly). Five were seen, two of them collected, at Las Vegas Wash, Nevada, on Lake Mead, *15 May 1976* (University of Nevada Museum of Biology, Las Vegas, C.S. Lawson).

89. *Limosa fedoa* (Linnaeus). Marbled Godwit. Sparse to uncommon spring transient (but 180 at Topock, 29 Apr. 1952, Monson) and fairly common fall transient, with hardly any records from the northeast. Five June records: two at Lake Havasu, 29 June 1950 (Monson), one at Willcox, 22 June 1975 (J. and R. Witzeman), one near Sonoita, 14 June 1976 (S. Alden), and three and two from lower Colorado River: Cibola National Wildlife Refuge and Martinez Lake, Yuma Co., 9 and 25 June 1977, respectively (according to K.V. Rosenberg). One winter record, San Pedro River east of Santa Catalina Mountains, 27 Jan. 1886.

90. *Numenius phaeopus* (Linnaeus). Whimbrel. Until 1970, recorded only sparsely, along the lower Colorado River. Since then the species has been recorded every year except 1972 and 1974, as many as seven records being obtained in 1978. The records come almost entirely from the lower Colorado River Valley, exceptions being records from Painted Rock Reservoir (including one *14 June 1980,* (ARIZ, photo, K.V. Rosenberg et al.), Phoenix, and curiously, Nogales (two records in 1978, 16 Apr., P.A. Buckley, and 6 May, C. Meaker et al.) and Willcox (1 Sept. 1973, S. Speich).

The only Arizona specimen is of the race *N. p. hudsonicus* Latham.

91. *Numenius americanus* Bechstein. Long-billed Curlew. Uncommon transient statewide, more common in lower Gila and Salt River Valleys and along lower Colorado River, sometimes in large flocks in fields (124 south of Mesa, 3 Apr. 1952, Monson; 135 in same place, 12 Mar. 1964, W.C. Royall). Sparse in winter in the south, when it has even occurred in the bottom of the Grand Canyon; occasional along lower Colorado River throughout summer, when it has also been found in the north, also at Phoenix, one in June–July 1975 (many observers); at St. David, one 6 June 1975 (Monson); and along Verde River east of Phoenix, two 16 June 1979 (R. Sells).

Both subspecies (*N. a. americanus* Bechstein and *N. a. parvus* Bishop) are found in Arizona.

92. *Bartramia longicauda* (Bechstein). Upland Sandpiper. A few old transient records from the southeast (Pima, Cochise, and Graham Cos.), the last in *May 1887*. Since then, two sight records: three near Mesa, 17 to 18 Oct. 1961 (W.C. Royall, Jr., S. Demaree et al.) and one near Chandler, 5 Oct. 1974 (S. Terrill et al.). One seen on California side of Lake Havasu, 11 Sept. 1952.

93. *Tringa melanoleuca* (Gmelin). Greater Yellow-legs. Rather common migrant statewide on shore lines, muddy or sandy flats, or shallow water, mostly in small numbers; winters along Colorado River and in south, when sparse except in the Yuma and Phoenix regions and at the Willcox Playa. Sometimes occurs in early and mid-June along the lower Colorado River, and some returning fall migrants recorded as early as the first few days in July.

94. *Tringa flavipes* (Gmelin). Lesser Yellowlegs. In same habitats as the preceding, a common fall transient in the north and southeast. Rather uncommon migrant over Arizona, otherwise, particularly scarce westward. Has been reported at Phoenix and Tucson (unverified sight records) in winter. This and the preceding species are readily confused.

95. *Tringa solitaria* Wilson. Solitary Sandpiper. Fairly common to uncommon transient statewide, except in Yuma, where it is unusual; spring records scarce in west and north. One seen near Yuma in winter, 26 Dec. 1950; also one at Guevavi Ranch, Santa Cruz Co., 3 Dec. 1978 (K. Kaufman). No winter specimens, so subspecies unknown.

Available Arizona specimens are all *T. s. cinnamomea* (Brewster).

96. *Catoptrophorus semipalmatus* (Gmelin). Willet. Fairly common to uncommon migrant statewide, particularly along the lower Colorado River. Sometimes occurs in June, usually along the lower Colorado River, with at least 67 at Painted Rock Reservoir, 17 June 1978 (R. and J. Witzeman). One winter sight record, of three birds at Phoenix, 27 Dec. 1969 (Christmas Bird Count). Exhausted birds have been found on the open desert—four at the King of Arizona Well, Yuma Co., 14 Apr. 1954 (R.L. Means), and one on the Tule Desert, Yuma Co., 8 Sept. 1961 (Monson).

97. *Actitis macularia* (Linnaeus). Spotted Sandpiper. Breeds along lakes and streams of Mogollon Plateau and just below, sparser northward, but *not* breeding on San Francisco Mountains. Juveniles following two adults were found at the bottom of the Grand Canyon, 11 July 1973 (R.R. Johnson). Common transient statewide, and winters more or less commonly along the Colorado River and in southern Arizona, east to Santa Cruz Valley and north irregularly to Camp Verde.

98. *Heteroscelus incanus* (Gmelin). Wandering Tattler. Casual. One at Phoenix, *18 Sept.* to *9 Oct. 1971* (ARIZ, photos, R. Witzeman).

99. *Arenaria interpres* (Linnaeus). Ruddy Turnstone. Very sparse migrant, only 13 records, from Sierra Vista and Nogales west to the Colorado River. Also two records from the California side of Lake Havasu. No specimens, but photographs of two birds at Phoenix *24* and *25 Sept. 1966* (ARIZ, R. Witzeman).

[*Arenaria melanocephala* (Vigors). Black Turnstone. One was seen on the California side of Lake Havasu, 21 May 1948.]

100. *Phalaropus tricolor* (Vieillot). Wilson's Phalarope. Common to fairly common transient statewide, often locally abundant; occasional birds linger through June. Birds seen after mid-June are likely returning fall migrants. No acceptable winter records.

101. *Phalaropus lobatus* (Linnaeus). Northern Phalarope. Common to uncommon fall transient statewide, scarce some years; sparse to uncommon in spring. One at Tucson, 4 June 1969 (J.A. Tucker), another there 7 June 1978 (Monson). One winter record, Phoenix, 18 Dec. 1976 (Christmas Bird Count).

102. *Phalaropus fulicarius* (Linnaeus). Red Phalarope. Sparse to uncommon fall transient, never more than two at a time, through southern Arizona to lower Colorado River; migration usually late but prolonged, from July (even one at Picacho Reservoir, 30 June 1964, B. Harrison) to early December. Has been recorded twice in spring: Tucson, 5 Apr. 1976 (R. and F. Steffens) and Bill Williams Arm of Lake Havasu, 2 Apr. 1978 (E. Cook et al.). Four winter records: tank south of Sierritas, Pima Co., *3 Jan. 1959;* Tucson, 29 to 30 Dec. 1966 (B. Harrison, R. Norton); Phoenix, 28 Jan. 1968 (R. Norton); and near Nogales, 6 Feb. 1976 (M. King, D. Stotz). A record for northern Arizona, one at Springerville, *5*

Oct. 1978 (ARIZ, photo, S. Terrill, first seen by J. Witzeman).

[*Scolopax minor* (Gmelin). American Woodcock. Hypothetical. One reported in South Fork, Cave Creek Canyon, Chiricahua Mountains, 16 Feb. 1976 (L. and R. Duncan).]

103. *Gallinago gallinago* (Linnaeus). Common Snipe. Fairly common to common transient throughout state along streams and canals, at ponds, and in marshy or springy places, wintering generally at unfrozen waters. Breeds near Springerville. One photographed near Poston, Yuma Co., 18 July 1979 (K.V. Rosenberg) was probably a bird that for some reason had failed to migrate.

Arizona birds are *G. g. delicata* (Ord).

104. *Limnodromus griseus* (Gmelin). Short-billed Dowitcher. Often "sighted" in Arizona, but actually far outnumbered by the Long-billed Dowitcher. Definite records are all of immatures in *Sept.,* across southern Arizona and north to near Phoenix and at Springerville. Careful observations indicate it is a sparse to uncommon transient along the lower Colorado River (K.V. Rosenberg, S. Terrill et al.). There is no basis for the statement (A.O.U. Check-list) that it winters all through the southwestern United States.

A specimen from 16 km (10 mi) north of Douglas, *4 Sept. 1964* (US, S.H. Levy) was identified by F.A. Pitelka as *L. g. hendersoni* Rowan, and other Arizona specimens may be the same.

105. *Limnodromus scolopaceus* (Say). Long-billed Dowitcher. Common to fairly common migrant statewide; winters sparingly in southern Arizona and along the lower Colorado River, generally in flocks. Rare in late May and June, on the basis of unverified sight records, some of which could pertain to the preceding species. June specimens are badly needed.

106. *Calidris canutus* (Linnaeus). Red Knot. Sparse fall transient in the south, from Willcox (10 Sept. 1975, P. Norton) and Nogales (9 Sept. 1973, S. Speich) west to Colorado River. Two were observed at Ganado Lake, Navajo Indian Reservation, 23 Sept. 1979 (S. Terrill, K.V. Rosenberg et al.). One near Davis Dam, 28 Nov. 1975 (C.S. Lawson), was very late. Only 16 records in all, with a specimen at Topock, *23 July 1952.*

107. *Crocethia alba* (Pallas). Sanderling. A mostly sparse transient across southern Arizona to the lower Colorado River and north to Prescott, where six seen 9 Sept. 1978 (C.S. Tomoff); to Ganado Lake, where two seen 23 Sept. 1979 (S. Terrill et al.); to Lake Mary near Flagstaff, where one seen 3 Oct. 1979 (W.C. Hunter, J. Andrews); and to Chinle, Navajo Indian Reservation, where two seen 14 Sept. 1980 (K. Kaufman et al.).

108. *Ereunetes pusillus* (Linnaeus). Semipalmated Sandpiper. Known definitely only from four specimens: near Sasabe, *23 Apr. 1957;* near Bapchule, Gila River Indian Reservation, *27 Apr. 1969* (DEL, A.M. Rea); Picacho Reservoir, *15 Aug. 1974* (ARIZ, Monson); and Phoenix, *21 Aug. 1980* (ARIZ, S. Terrill). However, may really be considerably more common due to difficulty in separating it from other species. Statement (A.O.U. Check-list) that it has been found as a rare transient, both spring and fall, in the intermountain region rests largely or wholly on misidentifications.

109. *Ereunetes mauri* Cabanis. Western Sandpiper. Common to abundant transient statewide, especially in fall. Very small numbers winter irregularly (?) in western and central Arizona east to Tucson; birds identified as this species recorded from Nogales, 18 Dec. 1971 and 30 Dec. 1978 (Christmas Bird counts); Sierra Vista, 16 Dec. 1978 (Christmas Bird Count); near Douglas, 18 Feb. 1979 (A. Moorhouse); and Willcox Playa, 23 Feb. 1979 (Monson).

110. *Erolia minutilla* (Vieillot). Least Sandpiper. Common to abundant transient statewide, especially in fall; winters more or less commonly in south from western to central Arizona, uncommonly to sparsely east to San Pedro Valley. One reported on Grand Canyon Christmas Count, 20 Dec. 1969 (A. Hill); one at Springerville, 24 Dec. 1979 (G. Rosenberg). One seen near Parker, 20 June 1977 (K.V. Rosenberg).

[*Erolia fuscicollis* (Vieillot). White-rumped Sandpiper. Hypothetical. One seen, and calls recorded, at Willcox, 4 June 1977 (K. Kaufman, E. Cook, D. Stotz).]

111. *Erolia bairdii* (Coues). Baird's Sandpiper. Sparse to uncommon spring migrant in southeast (Willcox, Tucson); also records at Jose Juan Tank, Growler Valley, 17 to *18 Mar. 1960* (US, Monson), and at Pipe Spring National Monument, 20 and 28 Apr. 1974 (R. Wilt). Common to fairly common fall transient statewide. One at Willcox, 28 June 1977 (K. Kaufman, Monson). At least 250 at Willcox, 5 Sept. 1976 (D. Stotz, M. Robbins). Spring records for central Arizona cited in A.O.U. Check-list are based on specimens of *Ereunetes mauri.*

112. *Erolia melanotos* (Vieillot). Pectoral Sandpiper. Uncommon fall migrant in small numbers across Arizona, probably more numerous in the lower Colorado Valley. Records in the north few. Since 1977, six spring records, from Willcox and the lower Colorado Valley. One winter record, Martinez Lake above Imperial Dam, 30 Dec. 1957. Unverified winter sight records at Phoenix.

113. *Erolia acuminata* (Horsfield). Sharp-tailed Sandpiper. One near Chandler, *15* to *17 Oct. 1972* (ARIZ, photos, R. Witzeman).

114. *Erolia alpina* (Linnaeus). Dunlin. Fairly common transient and mostly sparse winter visitant in western Arizona, scarcer to the east where unrecorded in winter east of Tucson. Unrecorded in the north.

> Arizona specimens from the Colorado River are *C. a. pacifica* (Coues); one from Willcox Playa, *29 Apr. 1968* (US, S.H. Levy) is *C. a. hudsonia* Todd. Specimens from Phoenix and Picacho Reservoir are very close to typical *pacifica*.

115. *Micropalama himantopus* (Bonaparte). Stilt Sandpiper. Uncommon to sparse transient statewide, except in lower Colorado River Valley where unrecorded. All northern Arizona records are in the fall.

116. *Philomachus pugnax* (Linnaeus). Ruff. One at Phoenix, 10 Nov. 1974 to 17 Feb. 1975 (photo, *15 Nov. 1974,* ARIZ, J. Witzeman); bird first identified by R. Norton and D. Danforth.

FAMILY STERCORARIIDAE: JAEGERS AND SKUAS

117. *Stercorarius pomarinus* (Temminck). Pomarine Jaeger. Three records: near Flagstaff, *late Oct.* or *early Nov. 1927;* lower Lake Havasu, *26 Sept. 1950;* and Lake Havasu, 3 to *4 Sept. 1977* (ARIZ, photo, R. Witzeman; first seen by K. Kaufman et al.).

118. *Stercorarius parasiticus* (Linnaeus). Parasitic Jaeger. Five records: Bill Williams Delta, *13 Oct. 1947;* lower Lake Havasu, *19 Sept. 1953;* Phoenix, 7 to 20 *Sept. 1970* (*date?* ARIZ, photo, R. Witzeman); Lake Havasu, *4 Sept. 1977* (ARIZ, photo, R. Witzeman); and adult, Lake Havasu, *14 Sept. 1977*

(ARIZ, photo, S. Cardiff, J. Dunn). Immature jaegers thought to be of this species seen at Painted Rock Reservoir, 22 to 29 Aug. 1974 (Monson et al.), at Davis Dam, 17 to 19 Sept. 1976 (C.S. Lawson), at Lake Havasu, 27 Aug. 1977 (G. Gregg, D. Stotz et al.), at Painted Rock Reservoir, 23 Aug. 1980 (R. Bradley et al.), and at Lake Havasu, 31 Aug. 1980 (K.V. and G. Rosenberg).

119. *Stercorarius longicaudus* Vieillot. Long-tailed Jaeger. Two adults at Lake Havasu, *14 Sept. 1977* (ARIZ, photos, R. Witzeman), also one seen next day (K. Kaufman et al.). An immature jaeger identified as this species observed in same locality, 14 Sept. 1977 (photo, J. Dunn, S. Cardiff). An adult was observed at Tucson, 7 Sept. 1980 (Kaufman).

FAMILY LARIDAE: GULLS AND TERNS

[*Larus hyperboreus* Gunnerus. Glaucous Gull. An immature was photographed *30 Nov. 1972* at Boulder Beach, Lake Mead, in Nevada, less than 8 km (5 mi) from Arizona (Museum of Biology, University of Nevada, Reno, C.S. Lawson).]

120. *Larus glaucescens* Naumann. Glaucous-winged Gull. Two specimens: lower Lake Havasu, *24 Feb. 1954,* and Colorado River about 13 km (8 mi) above Imperial Dam, *17 Nov. 1956.* Immature gulls of this species cannot be safely identified in the field; sometimes they are hard to identify in the hand.

121. *Larus occidentalis* Audubon. Western Gull. Two records: one immature, Parker Dam, *12 Dec. 1946,* and one adult, Painted Rock Reservoir, 18 July 1979 (D. Stotz). One in Boulder Beach, Nevada, area of Lake Mead, *winter 1980–81* (ARIZ, photo, C.S. Lawson). Some of the large immature gulls observed in winter along the Colorado River may be

Westerns, but it is believed they are chiefly, if not all, Herring Gulls.

The specimen is *L. o. occidentalis* Audubon, as determined by A.J. van Rossem. The July adult at Painted Rock Reservoir was thought to be a "Yellow-footed" Gull, *L. o. livens* Dwight, but leg color was not discernible.

122. *Larus argentatus* (Pontoppidan). Herring Gull. Uncommon winter visitant (and migrant?) along lower Colorado River; sparse elsewhere, only five specimens, one from Yuma, *12 Feb. 1903,* three in fall from Tucson, and one from Phoenix, 6 Nov. 1963, found dead *8 Nov. 1963* (ARIZ, S. Demaree). Sight records are mostly of immatures, hence open to question; adult records include one at Lake Mary near Flagstaff, 15 Apr. 1973 (R. Bradley), one at Tucson, 21 Nov. 1975 (M. King), four at Davis Dam and Lake Mohave, winter of 1975–76 (C.S. Lawson et al.), and two at Davis Dam, 9 Feb. 1979 (B. Whitney). A summer third-year immature reported at Painted Rock Reservoir, 22 July 1979 (K. Kaufman et al.).

123. *Larus thayeri* Brooks. Thayer's Gull. Three specimens: Lake Havasu, *13 Dec. 1946,* Marshall Lake near Flagstaff, *22 Oct. 1966* (MNA, A. Jones), and fresh road-kill near Bowie, Cochise Co., *1 Dec. 1968* (WNMU, D. Zimmerman). A gull thought to be Thayer's was collected at Lake Mary, near Flagstaff, *30 Nov. 1980* (ARIZ, D.R. Pinkston, K.V. Rosenberg). There are several winter sight records of immatures from Lake Mohave and Davis Dam, beginning in Dec. 1974, but immatures cannot be safely identified in the field. No records of adults.

124. *Larus californicus* Lawrence. California Gull. Fairly common to uncommon migrant, chiefly in spring, along the lower Colorado River, where it also occurs in some numbers at Davis Dam and Lake Mohave in winter. Elsewhere (as at Phoenix and Willcox) rather uncommon to sparse. Occasional summer records along lower Colorado River and at Painted Rock Reservoir. Scarce in north, where reported only in the fall except for ten near Kayenta, Navajo Indian Reservation, 7 May 1980 (C. Sexton). Some immatures may be confused with small immature Herring Gulls.

125. *Larus delawarensis* Ord. Ring-billed Gull. Common to abundant transient and winter visitor along the lower Colorado River, frequent at same seasons elsewhere in the south but much less common. Also a common transient on larger lakes of the Lake Powell, Flagstaff, St. Johns, and White Mountains regions, but generally scarce to uncommon elsewhere in north. As many as 50 to 70 may be found in groups in summer along the lower Colorado River and at Painted Rock Reservoir; usually rather uncommon elsewhere in summer.

126. *Larus canus* Linnaeus. Mew Gull. Two adults and two immatures at Davis Dam, *19 Mar. 1979* (ARIZ, photos, B. Whitney). Another immature at same place, 31 Mar. to 21 Apr. 1979 (Whitney et al.). Also a gull identified as this species at Lake Mohave, 25 Jan. 1978 (K.V. Rosenberg).

127. *Larus atricilla* Linnaeus. Laughing Gull. One specimen, near Imperial Dam, *3 Sept. 1960*. One at Davis Dam, 17 to *20 Mar. 1979* (ARIZ, photo, B. Whitney); first seen by J. Bean and A. Laurenzi. Unverified sight records from various places in southern Arizona, mostly from Phoenix but also Picacho Reservoir, Tucson, and Willcox.

128. *Larus pipixcan* Wagler. Franklin's Gull. Rather scarce migrant, more common in spring, throughout state except along lower Colorado River where it is even less common. A few birds "summer over" in some years, with records mainly from Willcox and Phoenix. The only specimens are two in *Oct.* from the lower Colorado River. Eighteen at Firebird Lake south of Phoenix, 7 Nov. 1979 (S. Terrill, G. Rosenberg) were an unprecedentedly large number. Some, if not most, sight reports of Laughing Gulls belong here.

129. *Larus philadelphia* (Ord). Bonaparte's Gull. Uncommon transient throughout state, usually in numbers less than seven to ten; sparse in winter in south from Tucson and Nogales westward. Scattered summer records from Willcox, Phoenix, and lower Colorado River; also one at Sierra Vista, Cochise Co., 30 June 1979 (D. Stotz, S. Parker, G. Rosenberg). One flying in cold weather high in Santa Catalina Mountains, 12 Nov. 1913 (T.G. Pearson).

130. *Larus heermanni* Cassin. Heermann's Gull. Scattered records of individuals or twos (only exception: eight in Phoenix area during storm, 28 Nov. 1975, J. and R. Witzeman, S. Terrill) from southern Arizona, in Tucson and Nogales areas westward; also Colorado River north to Davis Dam (17 Sept. 1976, C.S. Lawson), and Lake Mohave (12 Oct. 1975, W. Prange). Records from Sept. through May; one record from Tucson, 19 June 1977 (Monson et al.). The only specimens are two from Tucson, *7 Nov. 1970* and *27 Nov. 1970* (ARIZ, L.N. Huber).

131. *Rissa tridactyla* (Linnaeus). Black-legged Kittiwake. Very sparse late fall and winter visitor, except in late *1980,* when nine were found in four localities: Painted Rock Reservoir, 17 to 30 Nov. (five on 22 Nov., G. and K.V. Rosenberg et al.); along Arizona Hwy. 83 about 5 km (3 mi) south of Interstate Hwy. 10, one freshly dead, *16 Nov.* (ARIZ, G. Brailey); upper Lake Havasu, two in late Nov. to *5 Dec.* (ARIZ, M. Kaspryzk et al.); and one

below Parker Dam, 21 Dec. (Rosenbergs). Eleven
were counted on Las Vegas Bay, Lake Mead,
Nevada side, in early Dec. 1980 (C.S. Lawson).
Previous records were: a specimen from Roosevelt
Lake, *12 Dec. 1965* (US, shot by hunter, recovered
by F. Thompson, prepared by S.H. Levy); a single
bird during the winter of 1975–76 at Davis Dam plus
one there *17* to *20 Feb. 1975* (ARIZ, photos,
Lawson); a sight record with sketch from Martinez
Lake above Imperial Dam, 24 Nov. 1973 (T.
Danielson, T. and J. Heindel); and one (possibly
two?) in area of Bill Williams Arm of Lake Havasu
and Parker Dam, 11 to 20 Nov. 1978 (D. Stotz et
al.), including ARIZ, photo, [date?] *1978* (B. Whitney).

The Roosevelt Lake specimen is unidentifiable as to
race. The 1980 specimen is of the Pacific *R. t.
pollicaris* Ridgway.

132. *Xema sabini* (Sabine). Sabine's Gull. Sparse
fall transient throughout state; only one record in the
northeast, Many Farms Lake, Navajo Indian Reservation, 15 Oct. 1979 (G. Rosenberg et al.). The only
spring records are: flock of seven at Martinez Lake
above Imperial Dam, 13 Apr. 1956; one at same
locality, 27 Apr. 1956; and one east of Tacna, Yuma
Co., 16 Apr. 1960.

Arizona specimens are referable to the nominate race.

133. *Gelochelidon nilotica* (Gmelin). Gull-billed
Tern. Two acceptable records: one specimen from
two seen, Colorado River about 53 km (33 mi) above
Imperial Dam, *24 May 1959;* and one at Nogales,
24 Apr. 1976 (B. Harrison et al.).

The Arizona specimen is *G. n. vanrossemi* Bancroft.

134. *Sterna forsteri* Nuttall. Forster's Tern. Common to fairly common transient in lower Colorado
Valley, elsewhere generally scarce. Sparse in mid-
and late June on lower Colorado River, and one at

Phoenix after 16 June 1977 (several observers).
Four winter records, all singles: Martinez Lake
above Imperial Dam, 23 Dec. 1960 (Monson); on
Tucson Valley Christmas Bird Count, 28 Dec.
1969; at Green Valley, Pima Co., 16 to 17 Feb.
1973 (H.E. White); and below Patagonia Lake, 30
Dec. 1978 (D. Stotz, S. Parker).

135. *Sterna hirundo* Linnaeus. Common Tern.
Fairly common to uncommon fall transient along
lower Colorado River and in northern Arizona;
elsewhere uncommon to sparse. Due to difficulty of
separating breeding plumage adults from adults of
the foregoing, it could occur more often than sus-
pected, including during the spring (when two acceptable records, Nogales, 6 May 1978, and Ganado
Lake, Navajo Indian Reservation, 29 May 1979,
both K. Kaufman et al.).

136. *Sterna paradisaea* Pontoppidan. Arctic Tern.
Two specimens (both ARIZ) from Tucson, *4 Sept.
1965* (W. Bulmer) and *4 Oct. 1968* (D.L. Burckhal-
ter) are the only known records. Both occurred after
storms in the Gulf of California.

137. *Sterna albifrons* Pallas. Least Tern. A sparse
visitant across the southern part of the state east to
Willcox (where one seen 6 June 1976, D. Stotz, S.
Allen), all records (less than a dozen) falling from
May to September; also one record for the north,
flock of four or five at Mormon Lake, 4 to 9 Sept.
1933. One specimen, lower Lake Havasu, *18 June
1953.* Three photographed at Painted Rock Reservoir,
8 to *10 July 1974* (ARIZ, R. Witzeman). A published
record for Big Lake, Apache Co., really pertains to
the Black Tern.

138. *Sterna caspia* (Pallas). Caspian Tern. Fairly
common transient along lower Colorado River,
uncommon transient at Painted Rock Reservoir,

almost casual east to Phoenix, and one record for
Patagonia Lake, 7 Aug. 1976 (D. Danforth et al.);
also, about ten seen at Sullivan Lake, north of
Prescott, 30 Apr. 1936, two at Ganado Lake,
Navajo Indian Reservation, *17 Aug. 1980* (ARIZ,
photo, K.V. Rosenberg et al.), and there are fall sight
records from Mormon and Long Lakes in the Flagstaff
area. Records along lower Colorado River span the
summer. Three winter records, from Martinez Lake
above Imperial Dam: one 30 Dec. 1961 (Monson),
and four 23 Dec. 1974 and one 16 Dec. 1978
(Christmas Bird Counts).

139. *Chelidonias niger* (Linnaeus). Black Tern.
Common transient along lower Colorado River, and
fairly common (sometimes common locally) over
rest of state, especially in fall. No positive breeding
record, though records span the summer.

FAMILY RYNCHOPIDAE: SKIMMERS

140. *Rynchops niger* Linnaeus. Black Skimmer.
Photographs of individual birds, Colorado River 18
km (11 mi) above Imperial Dam, *12 June 1977*
(ARIZ, J.F. Drake) and at upper end of Lake
Havasu, *3 Sept. 1977* (ARIZ, R. Witzeman). Lake
Havasu bird first seen 1 Sept. (P. Lehman et al.).

FAMILY ALCIDAE: AUKS, MURRES, AND PUFFINS

[*Synthliboramphus antiquus* (Gmelin). Ancient
Murrelet. One observed and photographed in Las
Vegas Bay, Lake Mead, Nevada, *24* to *26 Mar.
1974* (Museum of Biology, University of Nevada,
Las Vegas, F. Long; other observers included V.
Mowbray, P. Long). The locality is about 11 km (7
mi) from Arizona.]

FAMILY ANATIDAE:
SWANS, GEESE, AND DUCKS

141. *Olor columbianus* (Ord). Tundra (Whistling) Swan. Winters uncommonly and in small numbers in lower Colorado Valley; now sparse fall migrant and winter visitant elsewhere. The only spring records are of individuals: at desert tank halfway between Flagstaff and Winslow, 13 May 1934; at Lees Ferry, 14 Mar. 1970 (M.M. Riffey); and near Lees Ferry, early Mar. 1977 (J. Craighead et al.).

142. *Branta canadensis* (Linnaeus). Canada Goose. Winters commonly to abundantly in southwestern and central Arizona and along the Virgin River, sparsely to uncommonly elsewhere. Uncommon migrant in northern Arizona. There are only three records, of crippled birds, remaining into summer in the lower Colorado Valley (two in Topock Marsh, 10 and 29 Aug. 1951, Monson; two in Topock Marsh, 27 May 1952, Monson; and one at Martinez Lake above Imperial Dam, June 1977, S. Furness). There is also a report of a single bird summering at the bottom of the Grand Canyon, 7 July to 14 Aug. 1977 (G. Fuller, W. Ranney). A resident flock at Alpine, Apache Co., originated from introduced birds. A pair was reported to have produced young at Little Bear Lake, White Mountains, in 1977 (C. and E. Wolfe).

> Arizona specimens are chiefly the subspecies *B. c. moffitti* Aldrich, and we also have some specimens of *B. c. parvipes* (Cassin). It is believed *B. c. leucopareia* (Brandt) also occurs, although there are no specimens.

143. *Branta hutchinsii* (Richardson). Cackling Goose. This is not yet recognized by the A.O.U. Check-list as a species, but as a subspecies of the preceding. Apparently very sparse in Arizona, it has been taken at Topock, *15 Dec. 1949* (photo, confirmed by J. Delacour) and *14 Nov. 1953.* One was also shot at Picacho Reservoir in the early 1950s (photo unfortunately lost, S.H. Levy).

The Arizona specimen and the 1953 photo are of the race *B. h. minima* Ridgway, which nests along the coast of western Alaska.

144. *Branta bernicla* (Linnaeus). Brant. Since *1965,* when one was photographed *28–29 May* (ARIZ, M.B. Brownlee) on the Colorado River about 77 km (48 mi) above Yuma, a sparse straggler to the lower Colorado Valley from the Topock area south. Other substantiated records are one at Mittry Lake below Imperial Dam, *23 Dec. 1970* (ARIZ, photos and wing, C. Wood), and one about 32 km (20 mi) above Blythe, California, *14 Apr. 1978* (ARIZ, photo, K.V. Rosenberg). As many as three found on Cibola National Wildlife Refuge, 16 Feb. 1979 (B. Whitney). One dead bird was examined but not retained at Picacho Reservoir about Nov. 1941 or 1942; one was shot near Arlington, 6 Jan. 1975 (according to T. Stejskal); and one was seen at Tucson, 29 to 30 Dec. 1972 (H. Fetter et al.).

It is presumed birds found in Arizona are the Black Brant *B. b. nigricans* (Lawrence), but the specimen or photo material is inconclusive as to subspecies, except for the Wood photo, which is of an immature *nigricans*.

145. *Anser albifrons* (Scopoli). White-fronted Goose. Formerly common, now uncommon, fall transient, and sparse in winter, in the Colorado Valley. Sparse in fall and winter in south-central and southeastern Arizona. Formerly occurred in flocks along the lower Colorado River in spring. Two records for northern Arizona: seven at Mormon Lake, 16 Sept. 1940 (Phillips) and four at White Mountain Lake near Show Low, 16 Sept. 1977 (Monson).

Arizona specimens are of the subspecies *A. a. frontalis* Baird.

146. *Anser caerulescens* (Linnaeus). Snow Goose. Formerly abundant winter visitor to lower Colorado and Gila Valleys, in the last decade much reduced in numbers; still winters uncommonly on lower Colorado River, about 200 in a wheat field south of Bullhead City, 5 Feb. 1980 (R. Martin) being unusual. Flocks are seen occasionally flying over southeastern Arizona, and small numbers are transients or winter visitants elsewhere in the south. In the north, formerly an occasional transient, but since *1941* only six records: one shot at St. Johns, 11 Jan. 1951; several in bottom of Grand Canyon, 17 Apr. 1976 (S. Tesch, G. Gerhart); several at Springerville, 7 Nov. 1976 (D. Stotz, J. and R. Witzeman); two at Springerville, 11 Dec. 1977 (Monson) to 30 Dec. 1977 (K. Kaufman); five at Springerville, 24 Nov. 1980 (Kaufman); and three at Ganado Lake, Navajo Indian Reservation, 25 Nov. 1980 (Kaufman et al.). The dark morph of this species, the "Blue Goose," has been found at Topock, 20 to 31 Jan. 1950 and 29 Dec. 1953; at Benson, *11 Nov. 1961* (MNA, L.L. Hargrave); at Willcox, 10 Jan. to 6 Feb. 1972 (R. and B. Smith et al.); at Martinez Lake above Imperial Dam, 21 Nov. 1976 (Yuma Audubon Society); at Cibola National Wildlife Refuge, 9 Dec. 1978 (refuge personnel); and again at Topock, *6 Dec. 1980* (ARIZ, photo, K.V. Rosenberg, A. Higgins).

The nominate race, or "Lesser" Snow Goose, is the one found in Arizona.

147. *Anser rossii* Cassin. Ross' Goose. Sparse winter visitor in southern Arizona, east to Camp Verde, Tucson, and upper San Pedro Valley, usually solitary, but as many as four at Martinez Lake above Imperial Dam in 1960, eight at Topock in 1973 (S. Burr), six and seven at Cibola National Wildlife Refuge in 1978–79 and 1979–80 (according to B. Whitney and R. Martin, respectively) and five south

of Bullhead City, Mohave Co., 5 Feb. 1980 (Martin).
Unrecorded between *1887* and *1948*.

148. *Dendrocygna autumnalis* (Linnaeus). Black-
bellied Whistling-Duck. Common to fairly common
in summer in southeastern and central Arizona, east
to Elfrida in the Sulphur Springs Valley (1973, B.
Swarbrick) and northwest to the Phoenix area. Has
nested at Tucson, near Nogales, at Hereford, near
Peoria, Maricopa Co., in 1969 (R.R. Johnson, J.C.
Barlow), at St. David in 1976 (D. Danforth), and at
Mammoth, lower San Pedro Valley, in 1979 (Monson). Seldom seen after Nov. and before Mar.; five
spent the winters of 1979–80 and 1980–81 at
Tucson. Nested at Pima, 1969 (D. Wingfield).

149. *Dendrocygna bicolor* (Vieillot). Fulvous
Whistling-Duck. Now very sparse from early summer
to early winter, seldom seen in spring, in southern
and western Arizona; recent records are almost
entirely of singles or pairs. Formerly a fairly common
winter resident at Yuma. No breeding record. The
only recent substantiated flocks were at Martinez
Lake above Imperial Dam: 15 on *24 Apr. 1956* and
27 on *16 Nov. 1961* (ARIZ, photos, Monson).

150. *Anas platyrhynchos* Linnaeus. Mallard.
Common to uncommon, but sometimes abundant,
transient and winter resident wherever there is open
water. Breeds on high mountain lakes in the north,
locally in the lower Colorado Valley and (formerly)
near Phoenix, and probably in the Sulphur Springs
Valley. This applies to the typical Mallard, *A. p.
platyrhynchos.*

A female-plumaged race, the "Mexican Duck,"
A. p. novimexicana Huber (*Anas diazi* Ridgway of
the A.O.U. Check-list), is locally resident in southeastern Arizona, nesting from the San Bernardino
Ranch east of Douglas and the San Simon Cienega

(in New Mexico part only) west to near Willcox and the Willcox Playa (at least since 1968; S.H. Levy et al.). Also found nesting at Centerfire Bog, Catron Co., New Mexico, near the Arizona boundary east of the White Mountains, in 1975 (J.P. Hubbard). A straggler west to the San Rafael Valley, Santa Cruz Co., *21 Nov. 1971* (a mounted specimen, J. Engelmann and R. Small), and to Stewart Mountain Lake on the Salt River about *1943.*

Subspecific status is as indicated above. The extent of hybridization between the two races in Arizona is unknown.

[**Anas rubripes** Brewster. Black Duck. Hypothetical. A "typical" bird was present at Papago Park in Phoenix from 6 to 12 Jan. 1980 (S. Terrill et al.). The bird was wild in behavior and did not associate with other ducks at the Park.]

151. Anas strepera Linnaeus. Gadwall. Fairly common to common transient statewide. Common to abundant winter visitant along low river valleys, and at open lakes and ponds except in north, where uncommon. Nests on high mountain lakes, and locally elsewhere in the north (near Pipe Spring National Monument, 1974, R. Wilt), formerly locally and irregularly (?) in very small numbers in the lower Colorado Valley (at Topock in 1949 and 1951, Monson; 1970, B.D. Graves). Non-breeding individuals occasional in summer.

152. Anas acuta Linnaeus. Pintail. Abundant to common migrant, winters on open waters; rather uncommon spring migrant in central and western Arizona. Nests on lakes of the Mogollon Plateau. Nested at least once near Willcox Playa (duck with ten newly-hatched young, 21 May 1974; B. Swarbrick), and in Prescott region in 1976 (C.S. Tomoff). Non-breeding birds may be seen elsewhere in summer, sometimes as many as 75 (Walker Lake at north end of Imperial National Wildlife Refuge, California side, 17 June 1961, Monson).

153. *Anas crecca* Linnaeus. Green-winged Teal. Abundant to common transient and winter resident on open waters, including creeks. Nests sparsely on lakes of the Mogollon Plateau, and possibly nested near Buckeye, Maricopa Co., in 1973 (according to A.M. Rea). A few non-breeders remain through the summer in the south.

> The American race is *A. c. carolinensis* Gmelin. A male of the European subspecies, *A. c. crecca* Linnaeus, was observed at Picacho Reservoir, 18 Jan. 1953 (R.R. Johnson et al.).

154. *Anas discors* Linnaeus. Blue-winged Teal. Spring transient throughout state, numbers and dates variable from year to year, but migration generally beginning in Jan. (as early as 1 Jan. 1967 at Nogales, B. Harrison). Fall status uncertain, but recorded to *31 Oct.* in northern Arizona and (sparingly) into Nov. and Dec. in southern Arizona; teals with blue wings are common to abundant migrants statewide. Seen not infrequently in summer, mostly in the south, and quite possibly nests at Mogollon Plateau lakes. Young were reported from the Chino Valley, Yavapai Co., 1 July 1980 (C.S. Tomoff). We do not know the source of the A.O.U. Check-list statement that it breeds in southeastern Arizona.

155. *Anas cyanoptera* Vieillot. Cinnamon Teal. Common to abundant migrant in spring, and probably likewise in fall (especially early fall), although status uncertain then because difficult to separate from *A. discors* with any certainty. Small numbers sometimes winter in southern and central Arizona. Spring migration begins in Jan. Breeds commonly on lakes of the Mogollon Plateau, and sparsely in southern

Arizona (near Buckeye, 1948, W.M. Pulich; at Topock, 1966, J.M. Welch, and 1970, B.D. Graves; in Phoenix region, 1971 and 1977, R.L. Todd; near Poston and in Dome Valley east of Yuma, 1979, according to S. Goldwasser; at Arivaca, 1979, B. Harrison, Monson; and near Willcox Playa, 1979, Monson).

[*Anas penelope* Linnaeus. European Wigeon. Hypothetical. A male seen at Topock, 18 Dec. 1947. One at Phoenix in Mar. 1966 (C. Tolinen, M. Bonnewell) and another there Jan. to Feb. 1979 (photo, R. Witzeman) and again in the following two winters (many observers). A possible hybrid with the following found at Mammoth, 6 and 7 May 1979 (G. Rosenberg, S. Terrill; photo, K.V. Rosenberg), and another hybrid there, 3 Feb. 1980 (D. Stotz). A male observed at Ganado Lake, Navajo Indian Reservation, 6 Oct. 1979 (G. Rosenberg et al.). The possibility that these records all represent escapes rules out the species' admission to a list of Arizona birds.]

156. *Anas americana* Gmelin. American Wigeon. Common migrant, wintering commonly to abundantly, on open waters; a few non-breeding birds may be seen in summer statewide. Prior to 1929 nested at least on occasion on lakes of the White Mountains, while three broods were found in the summer of 1979 (Nutrioso Reservoir, Sunrise Lake) by L. Piest.

157. *Anas clypeata* Linnaeus. Northern Shoveler. Common to abundant transient and winter visitant on open waters, including small ponds. Non-breeding birds or transients may be seen during summer statewide, in small numbers (usually one or two). No positive nesting record.

158. *Aix sponsa* (Linnaeus). Wood Duck. Sparse, found almost throughout state, mostly in fall and early winter, and seldom more than one or two at a time (but 18 near Prescott, 5 to 8 Nov. 1980, C.S. Tomoff). About five June records, from lower Colorado Valley, Prescott (26 June 1977, Tomoff), and near Nogales (5 June to 11 July, Monson et al.). No definite records in the south, east of the Santa Cruz Valley. A popular bird in aviaries, it is believed that some records are those of escapes or releases.

159. *Aythya americana* (Eyton). Redhead. Fairly common to abundant transient and winter visitor on open waters, especially on the Mogollon Plateau and at Cholla Lake, Navajo Co. Has nested locally in the lower Colorado Valley, on the Mogollon Plateau, and at Picacho Reservoir. A few non-breeding birds may be seen in summer.

160. *Aythya collaris* (Donovan). Ring-necked Duck. Fairly common migrant, especially in fall; locally common to abundant in winter on open waters. Fairly common as a nesting bird locally in White Mountains; a few non-breeding birds may be seen elsewhere in summer.

161. *Aythya valisineria* (Wilson). Canvasback. Fairly common to uncommon migrant, and winters in some numbers, even abundantly, locally on open waters; sometimes abundant in fall on mountain lakes. There are scattered summer records of singles, chiefly in the south.

162. *Aythya marila* (Linnaeus). Greater Scaup. Because of increasing numbers of sight records (mostly of drakes) by competent observers, it is believed this duck is more common and widespread than the only four specimen records would indicate: one from near Clarkdale, *8 Dec. 1887,* a partial skeleton found at Picacho Reservoir, *31 Jan. 1953,* one 16 km (10 mi) southeast of Arivaca, *3 Dec. 1961,* and one south of Parker, *3 Jan. 1977* (ARIZ, B. Anderson). Also one reported from lower Colorado Valley (in Baja California).

163. *Aythya affinis* (Eyton). Lesser Scaup. Common to abundant migrant, especially in fall; winters fairly commonly wherever there is open water, even on Mogollon Plateau lakes. A few non-breeding birds may be seen throughout the summer, at least in the south.

164. *Bucephala clangula* (Linnaeus). Common Goldeneye. Sparse to uncommon winter visitant on unfrozen lakes and rivers, chiefly those of central and western Arizona; usually considerable numbers below Davis and Parker Dams, where wintering flocks may number up to 1000 or more. Sparse fall migrant on Mogollon Plateau and north. Individuals or pairs may remain until May along the Colorado River.

165. *Bucephala islandica* (Gmelin). Barrow's Goldeneye. Present in numbers up to 60 since winter of 1973–74 just below Davis Dam, from late Nov. through most of Feb., and even to 3 Apr. 1979 (Monson); two were collected there, *3 Feb. 1975* (YALE, W. Martin). A drake seen near Tucson, 29 Mar. 1973 (C. Corchran, D. Lamm); another drake at Willow Lake near Prescott, 22 Mar. 1977 (H. and A. Gaither). Since 1977–78 also has appeared (as many as 12) at Parker Dam each year (G. McCaskie et al.); at Parker, *Jan.–Feb. 1979* (ARIZ, photo, K.V. Rosenberg); at Cibola National Wildlife Refuge, 14 Feb. 1978 (T. Brush); at Prescott, 15 to 21 Feb 1979 (C.S. Tomoff et al.); and at Imperial Dam, California side, 31 Jan. 1980 (S. Terrill).

166. *Bucephala albeola* (Linnaeus). Bufflehead. A fairly common to common transient; in winter common, abundant locally, in lower Colorado Valley but less common eastward and in the north when waters ice-free. On occasion may be seen on very small mountain ponds, as two at High Tank 8, Kofa Mountains, 10 Apr. 1952 (M.C. Nelson), and a male at John Hands and Herb Martyr "Lakes,"

Chiricahua Mountains, 11 to 15 Feb. 1975 (M. Cutler, S. Spofford et al.). Usually numerous in winter at Patagonia Lake. An occasional bird remains until late May. Casual near Phoenix, 20 June 1943; at Willcox, 1 July 1976 (Monson); at Patagonia Lake, 14 July 1976 (J. Levy); and at Nogales, 12 July 1977 (Monson).

167. *Clangula hyemalis* (Linnaeus). Oldsquaw. Sparse fall and winter visitant, recorded south to Willcox, Nogales, Phoenix, and near Yuma, but only twice in the north, 62 km (39 mi) north of Williams, *5 Dec. 1960* (US, S.H. Levy), and at Lake Mary, near Flagstaff, 30 Nov. 1978 (J. Coons). All records of single birds except at Davis Dam, where up to eight were seen, 20 Jan. 1977 (C.S. Lawson). One summer record, a male reported at Davis Dam, 6 July 1975 (V. Mowbray, J. O'Connell).

168. *Melanitta deglandi* (Bonaparte). White-winged Scoter. One male taken at Ashurst Lake near Flagstaff, *16 Nov. 1963,* a female at Tucson, *27 Oct. 1969* (ARIZ, E.L. Smith), and an immature male (one of two birds taken) at a stock tank near Corona de Tucson, north of the Santa Rita Mountains, Pima Co., *16 Nov. 1980* (YALE, G. Wooters, specimen prepared by S.H. Levy). Since 1969 has occurred sparsely from Davis Dam and Lake Havasu east to Nelson Reservoir, Apache Co., in late Oct. and Nov., exceptionally below Supai, 20 Dec. 1955, and at California side of Imperial Dam, 22 to 23 Apr. 1977 (A. Higgins, K.V. Rosenberg, D. Wells).

169. *Melanitta perspicillata* (Linnaeus). Surf Scoter. Sparse late fall migrant statewide, occurring usually as singles or twos. However, a total of 62 was seen during a storm on 28 Nov. 1975, including a flock of 27, in the Chandler–Phoenix area (S. Terrill, J. and R. Witzeman, S. Majlinger). One spring record, at Willcox, a male photographed *16 May 1976* (ARIZ, J. Witzeman). Specimens from near Prescott and at Lake Havasu.

170. *Melanitta nigra* (Linnaeus). Black Scoter. Casual to very sparse, two records for *1975:* one at Tucson, 3 Nov. (P. Norton et al.) and three at Phoenix, 4 to 12 Nov. (photographed 5 Nov., ARIZ, J. Witzeman). One reported from Guevavi Ranch near Nogales, 30 Dec. 1978 (R. Norton et al.); another at Lake Mary near Flagstaff, 28 Nov. 1980 (G. and K.V. Rosenberg).

171. *Oxyura jamaicensis* (Gmelin). Ruddy Duck. Common to abundant transient statewide, less common to eastern Arizona. Winters fairly commonly almost wherever there is open water, abundantly at some ponds and lakes. Breeds on Mogollon Plateau, locally along lower Colorado River, and sparsely elsewhere (including Phoenix region; Arivaca Jct., 1974, P. Meyers and E. Rose; east of Tucson, 1977, P.M. Walters and D. Lamm; and near Pipe Spring National Monument, 1974, R. Wilt). Fairly common non-breeder in summer in southern Arizona.

172. *Lophodytes cucullatus* (Linnaeus). Hooded Merganser. Winter resident in very small numbers (but 13 at Topock, 12 Jan. 1950, Monson) in southern Arizona, principally in lower Colorado Valley above Parker Dam. Possibly transient in the Grand Canyon, where one seen 29 Oct. 1932 (E.D. McKee). Earliest fall record is at Lake Mohave, 25 Oct. 1976 (W. Prange). One summer record: Santa Cruz River near Calabasas (located formerly at the meeting of the Santa Cruz River and Sonoita Creek), *1 June 1890* (if correctly re-labeled—possibly *6 Jan.?*).

173. *Mergus merganser* Linnaeus. Common Merganser. Common to abundant winter resident on larger bodies of open water, uncommon elsewhere (including in the Grand Canyon). Uncommon fall transient on lakes of Mogollon Plateau. Breeds in small numbers along streams below Mogollon Plateau and White Mountains, also on the Gila River in New Mexico within 45 km (28 mi) of Arizona. Occasional individuals may stay summer-long in the Colorado Valley (usually a small flock to be found below Parker Dam).

174. *Mergus serrator* Linnaeus. Red-breasted Merganser. Irregular transient in lower Colorado Valley, sometimes common; elsewhere decidedly uncommon to sparse, especially in the north. Occasional individuals may remain summer-long in lower Colorado Valley; as many as eight at Topock, 24 June 1949 (Monson). A male seen at Cholla Lake, Navajo Co., 16 Aug. 1973 (Monson). Winters uncommonly in lower Colorado Valley and sparsely elsewhere. Formerly wintered abundantly on Roosevelt Lake, and a few wintered at Lakeside, Navajo Co., in 1936.

FAMILY COLUMBIDAE: PIGEONS AND DOVES

175. *Columba fasciata* Say. Band-tailed Pigeon. Common summer resident of mountains, northwestern to southeastern Arizona. Uncommon and irregular in extensive tracts of pure ponderosa pine, and in winter in southeast only (but up to 400 in Prescott area, winter of 1976–77, C.S. Tomoff). Squab still in the nest in Huachuca Mountains on 10 Oct. 1949 (C. Wallmo). Casual transient and migrant as single birds on desert, straggling to Big Sandy Valley; Ajo and Growler Mountains; and even lower Colorado River Valley below Lake Havasu. Five or six seen on Summit Plateau of Carrizo Mountains, 5 Sept. 1978 (J.T. Marshall), and one in Kofa Mountains (20 Aug. 1979, R. Furlow). About ten observed at Teec Nos Pos, Navajo Indian Reservation, 27 to 30 May 1979 (K. Kaufman et al.). Range and occurrence determined to some extent by the availability and amount of some seasonal foods (i.e., mast, elderberries). Statement that it winters on Verde River (A.O.U. Check-list) not based on any valid record known to us.

Arizona birds are of the nominate race.

[*Columba livia* Gmelin. Rock Dove. Although breeding commonly in cities and towns in a semi-domesticated state, not known to nest in Arizona under natural, wild conditions.]

176. *Zenaida asiatica* (Linnaeus). White-winged Dove. Abundant summer resident in Sonoran zones in southern and central Arizona, and along Colorado River below Davis Dam. This range includes the area east of the Hualapai Mountains and the Prescott region, in which places it is much less common; has nested as far north as west of Valentine in Mohave Co. Has been a summer resident in southwestern Utah and adjacent Arizona since 1960 (W.H. Behle, R. Wauer). Mostly sparse and irregular in winter, although sometimes locally common even as far east as Douglas (in 1978–79, A. Moorhouse). It has increased its range and numbers since the 1870s. Birds are often seen and heard as early as Feb., at least in Tucson and Phoenix, where it formerly (up to 1950s) was not found in spring until Apr.

Arizona birds are *Z. a. mearnsi* (Ridgway).

177. *Zenaida carolinensis* (Linnaeus). Mourning Dove. Common resident in valleys of southern, central, and most of western Arizona, abundant in farmlands. Common summer resident in the north, where it is generally sparse and local in winter.

[*Streptopèlia risoria* (Linnaeus). Ringed Turtle Dove. Though present in the wild state at Tucson since at least 1964, recently at Phoenix and Tempe, and taken at Yuma, *2 Sept. 1961* (ARIZ., hunter-killed), satisfactory evidence of its continuing nesting in the state has not been obtained.]

178. *Columbina passerina* (Linnaeus). Ground Dove. Resident in better-watered valleys of southern and central Arizona (including the San Bernardino Ranch of Cochise Co.), especially common in summer, but much less common in winter. Does not breed in Sulphur Springs Valley, where only one record, two at Kansas Settlement, 12 July 1979 (Monson), or in upper Gila Valley, where two seen near Thatcher, Feb. to Mar. 1974 (J. and L. Goodhew). Occasionally seen to north, even to Prescott, 22 to 26 Nov. 1975 (V. Miller), to near Mormon Lake, 19 Aug. 1963 (F.A. Thompson), to Flagstaff, 30 Oct. 1931, and to Grand Canyon Village, 22 to 23 Oct. 1930; also in southern Nevada and southern Utah (near Paria River, Kane Co., 25 Aug. 1963, J.. Meyers). Occasionally wanders into foothills or desert near resident range, e.g., birds visited feeders at Portal, Cochise Co., in Jan. to Feb. 1974 and Oct. to Dec. 1975 (according to S. Spofford).

179. *Scardafella inca* (Lesson). Inca Dove. Common resident of cities and towns, and at some ranch-yard situations, in Lower Sonoran Zone of central and central-southern Arizona; also breeds and resident at Douglas, Bisbee, Yuma, Parker, California side of Parker Dam, and Sonoyta, Sonora, Mexico. Since about 1970 it has nested at Needles, California; Bullhead City, Mohave Co.; Globe; and Camp Verde. One seen at Willcox, 1 Nov. 1978 (Monson). Early records do include three at Camp Verde, *Oct. 1885,* where it was not found again until 1972 (Christmas Bird Count)! Has straggled to various mountain canyons in southeast and to Organ Pipe Cactus National Monument headquarters (R.L. Cunningham et al.), and casually to Eagar (one seen), 13 Oct. 1979 (K. Kaufman et al.), Flagstaff, 21 June 1963 (F.A. Thompson), and the Grand Canyon, 25 Sept. 1956 (J.H. Riffey) and June 1976 (R.R. Johnson); also recorded twice in southwestern Utah (according to W.H. Behle) and several times in southern Nevada (according to C.S. Lawson).One wintered at 1530 m (5000 ft) in Ramsey Canyon, Huachuca Mountains, 1973–74 (J. and C. Peabody).

FAMILY PSITTACIDAE: LORIES, PARROTS, AND MACAWS

180. *Rhynchopsitta pachyrhyncha* (Swainson). Thick-billed Parrot. Formerly erratic visitant, mainly in winter, to southeastern Arizona, chiefly in mountains. The last reliable reports were in 1935 and 1938, the last being a flock seen in Rhyolite Canyon, Chiricahua Mountains (F. Fish, National Park Service). The last major flight was in 1917–18; rumors to 1945. Possibly ranged north centuries ago to the Verde Valley.

FAMILY CUCULIDAE: CUCKOOS, ROADRUNNERS, AND ANIS

181. *Coccyzus americanus* (Linnaeus). Yellow-billed Cuckoo. Breeds commonly along wooded streams of Sonoran zones, chiefly of southern and central Arizona and extreme northwest; uncommon transient on desert and in towns. Transients pass north through southern Arizona in last third of June, probably even into July.

Arizona specimens are of the dubious western form, *C. a. occidentalis* Ridgway.

[***Coccyzus erythropthalmus*** (Wilson). Black-billed Cuckoo. Hypothetical. Two fall sight records

by experienced observers: Peña Blanca Lake northwest of Nogales, 11 Oct. 1966 (R. Sutherland,
according to S.M. Russell); and Patagonia, 26 Aug.
1972 (M. Robbins).

182. *Geococcyx californianus* (Lesson). Road-
runner. Common resident in Sonoran zones (chiefly
Lower Sonoran) of southern, central, and western
Arizona; scarce in Upper Sonoran Zone in north-
central part and even scarcer in northeast, where still
no nesting records (but a female near laying taken 32
km [20 mi] east of St. Johns, *30 July 1937,* CAN,
H.H. Poor, Phillips). Wanderers appear in high
mountains occasionally, as at top of Mt. Lemmon,
Santa Catalina Mountains, 19 Aug. 1979 (M.W.
Larson).

183. *Crotophaga sulcirostris* Swainson. Groove-
billed Ani. A straggler from Mexico, more or less
regular recently but with only one or two records per
year, the maximum number of birds per occurrence
being 12 to 15 at Arivaca, fall of 1978 (B. Harrison
et al.). Records distributed throughout the four
seasons, but only one spring report, Pinal-Maricopa
county line south of Chandler, 13 May 1974 (A.M.
Rea). Has been found in southern Arizona from the
New Mexico boundary west to Quartzsite, Yuma
Co., and north to Phoenix. Two records for northern
Arizona: Lyman Lake, Apache Co., 24 Oct. 1967
(B. White, Arizona Game and Fish Department),
and one photographed at Deer Creek Falls, Grand
Canyon, *3 July 1975* (ARIZ, C. Palsgrove, H.
Messamer et al.). Records for 1888 and 1932 cited
in the A.O.U. Check-list are not presently confirm-
able, but are possible.

FAMILY TYTONIDAE: BARN OWLS

184. *Tyto alba* (Scopoli). Barn Owl. Fairly common
resident throughout most of the open Sonoran zones

except in the deserts of the southwest (where, however, one seen in Growler Wash, western Pima Co., 14 Oct. 1959, Monson). Apparently local, but ranging into lower Transition Zone, in the northeast; also found at times in mountain canyons in Upper Sonoran Zone. No winter records north of Lake Mohave, Salome, and Camp Verde.

FAMILY STRIGIDAE: TYPICAL OWLS

(contributed by Joe Marshall)

185. *Otus kennicottii* (Elliot). Western Screech Owl. Common to abundant resident throughout open woods and saguaro areas of the Sonoran zones except in northeast, where it is scarce; even occurs in residential and farmland areas. Four specimens have been obtained in the Transition Zone at Flagstaff, one each in *Apr.* and *Oct.* and two in *Nov.* (NAU, R.P. Balda). These are regarded as wanderers.

O. k. aikeni (Brewster), large, gray, with coarse bold pattern of black marks, is found on the Mogollon Plateau of northeastern Arizona south to Granville, Greenlee Co. The Flagstaff specimens are of this race. *O. k. cineraceus* (Ridgway), smaller than *aikeni,* occurs in southeastern Arizona from the Gila River and Pinaleno Mountains to the Santa Rita, Patagonia, Huachuca, Dragoon, Chiricahua, and Peloncillo Mountains and intervening valleys. *O. k. gilmani* (Swarth), gray similar to the two above, but more finely marked, is found in deserts and foothills of central and southwestern Arizona, nesting and roosting commonly in saguaro holes. *O. k. yumanensis* (Miller and Miller), with dorsum gray having a pinkish cast in fresh fall plumage; streaks narrow; ventral crossbars fine and regularly arranged and closely set; occurs along the lower Colorado and Big Sandy Rivers, extending northward up the Virgin River into Utah.

186. *Otus trichopsis* (Wagler). Whiskered Owl. Common resident in the southeast west to the Baboquivari Mountains and north to the Peloncillo and Santa Catalina Mountains, in heavy Upper Sonoran Zone woodlands.

Arizona birds are *O. t. aspersus* (Brewster), gray with no red phase.

187. *Otus flammeolus* (Kaup). Flammulated Owl. Common summer resident in most of Transition Zone and possibly higher, particularly where oaks are present. Not sparse as a spring transient in lowlands of south, and recorded once at bottom of Grand Canyon, *11 May 1929.* Apparently a common fall transient at Flagstaff, where as many as 16 were caught in mist nets from *6 Sept.* to *12 Oct.* (NAU, R. P. Balda). A very few fall records from non-breeding areas, including one near Tuseral Tank, Tule Mountains, Yuma Co., 26 Oct. 1980 (S.H. Levy). One winter record, at Phoenix, *16 Feb. 1949.* One reported heard along lower Bill Williams River, 9 Mar. to 18 Apr. 1979 (T. Brush, K. Kaufman, K.V. Rosenberg, S. Terrill et al.), and one calling in lowland mesquite along the Santa Maria River (county unknown), 22 to 24 Jan. 1980 (B. Millsap et al.).

An as yet unnamed population occurs from the Hualapai Mountains eastward throughout the forests of the Mogollon Plateau and the Bradshaw Mountains east to the New Mexico line north of the Gila River. It is dark gray, boldly marked with black. Some of the black streaks on chest and flanks are so thick as to appear almost square. The nominate race occupies the mountains of the southeast, west to the Santa Ritas and north to the Pinal, Pinaleno, and Chiricahua Mountains. Its plumage has a lighter gray background, with finer black marks, and with a lot of rufous trim.

188. *Bubo virginianus* (Gmelin). Great Horned Owl. Fairly common resident statewide, except in densest forests.

Arizona specimens all appear to be *B. v. pallescens* Stone.

[*Nyctea scandiaca* (Linnaeus). Snowy Owl. Hypothetical. A record of three seen in a snowstorm about 32 to 40 km (20 to 25 mi) south of Seligman, Yavapai Co., 23 Dec. 1970 (R.C. and R.L. Jolly) seems doubtful. One was taken on or about *1 Dec. 1929* at Indian Springs, Clark Co., Nevada, only about 90 km (56 mi) from Arizona (A.J. van Rossem, 1939, *Pac. Coast Avif.* 24). Collector unknown; specimen is at University of California in Los Angeles.]

189. *Glaucidium gnoma* Wagler. Pygmy Owl. Generally fairly common resident of coniferous forests and locally of Upper Sonoran Zone woods west to Pajaritos and Santa Catalina Mountains, Prescott, near Ash Fork, and South Rim of Grand Canyon. The only record for the Chuska Mountains is of one seen near Roof Butte, 6 Oct. 1937 (Monson). Has reached lowest edge of Upper Sonoran Zone in the Santa Catalina Mountains, *21 Jan. 1950,* and in the Galiuro Mountains, *7 Apr. 1950.*

The nominate race occupies oak woodlands of the southeastern mountains. It is a smaller form than the following, with the calls delivered mostly in twos. *G. g. pinicola* Nelson is found in the rest of the state. Calls of the style associated with this form have been heard in the Santa Catalina Mountains.

190. *Glaucidium brasilianum* (Gmelin). Ferruginous Owl. A seldom seen owl; local and sparse resident of Lower Sonoran Zone in saguaros and along desert washes and in riparian trees of central-southern and central Arizona, from mouth of Verde River, Superior, and Tucson (and possibly Sonoita Creek below Patagonia, where reported 6 June 1975 by G.S. Mills) west to desert ranges of southern Yuma Co. (at least to Cabeza Prieta Tanks, 10 Apr. 1955, Monson). Has declined considerably in numbers (and range?) since about 1950 to the point in 1980 of being absent except possibly in the Organ Pipe Cactus National Monument region.

The race found in Arizona is *G. b. cactorum* van Rossem.

191. *Micrathene whitneyi* (Cooper). Elf Owl. Common summer resident in southern Arizona lowlands, scarcer north of Gila Valley in central Arizona, ranging up into evergreen oak belt and in riparian timber in most of the mountains. Scarce to sparse in Colorado Valley, where it has been found in cottonwoods since the 1960s on the Nevada and California sides of the river south of Davis Dam to near Needles, California, and, after 1977, in the Bill Williams Delta region.

Arizona Elf Owls belong to the nominate race.

192. *Athene cunicularia* (Molina). Burrowing Owl. Generally an uncommon and rather local resident in Sonoran zone grasslands and fallow or abandoned farmlands, except in farm areas about Phoenix and Yuma, where common. Also sparse fall transient, mainly in northeast and on southwest deserts; one record on Mogollon Plateau (White Mountains, 9 Oct. 1937). Somewhat less common in winter, at least in southeast where in most winters it is almost entirely absent east of the San Pedro Valley and in the north, where only two records: Snowflake, *22 Dec. 1947* and Springerville, 8 Jan. 1959. A bird seen in the north Growler Valley west of Ajo, 10 Feb. 1949 (A.F. Halloran) was probably unusual.

193. *Strix occidentalis* (Xantus). Spotted Owl. Uncommon resident of deep, shady ravines of forested mountains and high mesas, west in the south to the Pajaritos Mountains (Sycamore Canyon). Sparse in lowlands not far from mountains, perhaps chiefly in winter. Nested near Tucson, *1872;* one seen there in Mar. and found dead, *2 Apr. 1975* (ARIZ, A.M. Rea). Two seen in mesquite near Supai, Havasupai Indian Reservation, 7 Sept. 1970 (W. Hill).

S. o. *huachucae* Swarth is the Arizona subspecies, paler than *S. o. lucida* (Nelson).

194. *Asio otus* (Linnaeus). Long-eared Owl. Quite uncommon winter resident at various points throughout the state. A sparse summer nesting bird (entirely in Sonoran Zones?), perhaps nomadic, or moving into a locality in fair numbers for a few years, then disappearing again. Has nested as far southwest as Bates Well, Organ Pipe Cactus National Monument, *June 1932.* Several nests have been found in saguaros. Birds taken, freshly dead, from upper Lake Havasu, *9 July 1948* (!) and from highway a few km west in California, *7 May 1952.* Observed on Bill Williams Mountain in the summer of 1980 (C.S. Tomoff). Winter flocks may number up to 50 birds; this includes 20 to 30 along Centennial Wash near Wenden, Yuma Co., 6 Feb. 1980 (B. Millsap).

Arizona birds are of the race *A. o. tuftsi* Godfrey.

195. *Asio flammeus* (Pontoppidan). Short-eared Owl. Sparse, but locally more common (sometimes in flocks), winter visitant in open grassland, marshes, swales, and fields of southern and western Arizona, also records for extreme desert: one south of Mohawk, Yuma Co., 27 Nov. 1942; several in eastern Yuma and western Pima Cos., 1959–60 (Monson). Sparse in migration in north. One seen near Sunrise Lake,

White Mountains, 9 June 1978 (E. Cook, K. Kaufman). A report of numbers on the Colorado River is perhaps erroneous. About 50 found along Santa Cruz River below Tucson, 15 Feb. 1965 (S.M. Russell).

196. *Aegolius acadicus* (Gmelin). Saw-whet Owl. Sparse breeding bird of mountain forests throughout Arizona; sparse at these and almost casual in lowland localities in winter. Extreme records include one at Puerto Peñasco, Sonora, *12 Nov. 1977* (ARIZ, found freshly dead). Nomadic or colonial. Irruptions in some winters bring large numbers to a region, where they may stay for a few years and nest. Common some years in pinyon-juniper woodlands (R.R. Johnson); such irruptions in the Grand Canyon area have been coordinated with abundance in New Mexico (J.P. Hubbard). Status poorly known.

FAMILY CAPRIMULGIDAE: GOATSUCKERS

197. *Caprimulgus vociferus* Wilson. Whip-poor-will. Common summer resident of densely wooded timber in southeastern mountains in Transition and adjacent Upper Sonoran Zones and more recently in central Arizona to the White Mountains; ranges west to Pajaritos Mountains, and northwest less commonly to Bill Williams Mountain, Coconino Co. (C.S. Tomoff et al.) and the Hualapai Mountains. Two fall lowland records: near Roosevelt, *4 Nov. 1952,* and Tucson, 6 Oct. 1953. Has been seen as late as 30 Nov. 1976 in Ramsey Canyon, Huachuca Mountains (R. and C. Yutzy et al.). Some birds winter, as indicated by two records: one at Blue Point cottonwoods, Maricopa Co., 20 Jan. to 17 Mar. 1973 (R.R. Johnson, J. Simpson) and one in lower Finger Rock Canyon, Santa Catalina Mountains, *19 Feb. 1977* (ARIZ, J. Porter).

Specimens are all *C. v. arizonae* (Brewster) with the exception of the Roosevelt bird,which is of the eastern nominate race.

198. *Caprimulgus ridgwayi* (Nelson). Préstame-tu-cuchillo; Ridgway's Whip-poor-will; Buff-colored Nightjar. First found in Arizona in Guadalupe Canyon in the extreme southeast, *12 May 1960;* it has been found there irregularly ever since. One heard along Sonoita Creek below Patagonia, 3 and 4 July 1971 (R. Rowlett). From *19 May* to *17 July 1978* one to two birds present in Sutherland Wash north of the west part of the Santa Catalina Mountains (many observers; calls taped by E.L. Smith). On 5 June 1980, one heard at the mouth of Aravaipa Canyon (S. Umland, D. Laush); in July at least three in same locality (K.V. Rosenberg) and still present 18 Aug. (G.S. Mills); one seen at Cooks Lake, near confluence of Aravaipa Creek and San Pedro River, 28 Aug. (Monson).

199. *Phalaenoptilus nuttallii* (Audubon). Poor-will. Common in summer about slopes, hills, and rocky outcrops of Sonoran zones (rarely higher, as at Phelps Cabin, White Mountains, *26 Oct. 1936,* and at Alpine, Apache Co., 23 Aug. 1971, Monson) throughout state, less common in desert southwest. Hibernates. Winters in small numbers through southern Arizona. Large numbers seen sometimes in spring are probably transients, and unknown numbers undoubtedly pass through in fall as well.

Only the nominate race is found in Arizona.

200. *Chordeiles minor* (Forster). Common Night-hawk. Common summer resident, and abundant in migration, in open parts of Upper Sonoran Zone and above, in central and northern Arizona; less common and local summer resident of elevated grasslands of southeast from west side of Mule

Mountains west to Pajaritos Mountains; also one (migrant?) seen near Apache, Cochise Co., 18 July 1965 (J.D. Ligon, R.P. Balda). Possibly bred formerly in the Chiricahua Mountains: *21 June 1921* (VPI, J.E. Law); several "booming" birds in Pinery Canyon in summers of 1919 and 1921 (Law); at least three "booming" in Pinery Canyon, July 1978 (D. Stotz, G.S. Mills, W. Roe). Probably a migrant over mountains of southeast, as at top of Mt. Lemmon, Santa Catalina Mountains, 8 June 1976 (Monson). Extremely sparse transient in Lower Sonoran Zone (no specimens) in Tucson Valley; near Tempe, 26 Sept. 1977 (S. Terrill); one seen near Phoenix, 22 Sept. 1978 (K. Kaufman et al.); and one at Painted Rock Reservoir, 1 Sept. 1980 (L. Terrill, G. Rosenberg). One reported at Flagstaff, 7 Nov. 1980 (J. Coons) was exceptionally late. Unknown elsewhere in Lower Sonoran Zone closer than Indian Springs, southern Nevada.

The breeding race is the rufescent, moderately dark *C. m. henryi* Cassin. The most common migrant race is the more blackish *C. m. hesperis* Grinnell. A road-killed specimen of the even darker nominate race was found 68 km (42 mi) north of St. Johns, *10 Sept. 1956.* A young bird from near Prescott *24 Aug. 1931* seems referable to the pale *C. m. howelli* Oberholser, as do two specimens from the Chiricahua Mountains, *27* and *28 May 1915* (VPI, A.J. van Rossem), according to J.P. Hubbard.

201. *Chordeiles acutipennis* (Hermann). Lesser Nighthawk. Common to abundant summer resident in Lower Sonoran Zone valleys of southern and western Arizona, except in most of Yuma Co. away from the Colorado and Gila Valleys. Sparse in summer near the Grand Canyon in the Grand Wash Cliffs area and in the Toroweap Valley (Upper Sonoran Zone grassland?). Also has been reported recently in summer from the Upper Sonoran Zone at Wupatki National Monument in 1975 (R.P. Balda), and in southeastern Utah near Hanksville, Wayne Co., about 155 km (95 mi) north of Arizona, *8 July 1961* (UU, Behle et al.). It is also recorded from near St. George, Utah, 10 June 1963 (D.L. Carter et al.). There are a number of recent winter records in the south ranging from Tucson west to the Colorado River north as far as Parker, but only one winter specimen, Phoenix, *27 Dec. 1897.*

FAMILY APODIDAE: SWIFTS

[*Cypseloides niger* (Gmelin). Black Swift. Hypothetical. Probably transient through state, but no specimens or photos. One old specimen (AMNH) labeled "Arizona," without further data. Of a handful of sight records, the following are considered most valid: flock of about 35 seen over pond south of Pima, Graham Co., 30 May 1953; one at the same place, 17 Aug. 1954; flock of about 12, upper Cave Creek Canyon, Chiricahua Mountains, 11 July 1964 (B.K. Harris, J.P. Hubbard, J.D. Ligon), and one in same locality, 27 Aug. 1977 (D. and M. Wolfe, D. DeKeyzer); two over Globe, 28 Sept. 1965 (L.L. Hargrave); one along Santa Maria River, Yavapai Co., 11 May 1980 (J. Zook); one 9 May 1977 about 16 km (10 mi) south of Ehrenberg, Yuma Co. (A. Higgins, M. Lange); and three cruising around a north slope of the Hualapai Mountains, 3 May 1979 (B. Millsap). Two sight records in fall at Flagstaff, one of which is apparently the basis of statement in A.O.U. Check-list that it migrates through Arizona. Also seen twice by Mearns in 1880s (once on 6 May 1887 atop "Squaw Peak, Verde Mountains"). Two specimens were taken along the Gila River south of Cliff in adjacent New Mexico, *31 May 1967* (DEL, US, J.P. Hubbard).

Also, a record of at least six seen in Virgin River bottomlands near St. George, Utah, 10 June 1963 (D.L. Carter et al.), and a dying bird found at Zion National Park, Utah, *2 Aug. 1960* (UU, G. Musser).]

202. *Chaetura pelagica* (Linnaeus). Chimney Swift. Only one documented record: non-breeding pair at Tucson, 30 May to *mid-June 1952.* As many as five to eight individuals judged to be this species on the basis of call-notes have been present on and near the University of Arizona campus in Tucson in summers probably since 1973, with outside dates ranging from 21 May 1977 (D. Stotz) to 29 Aug. 1975 (R. Russell). Numerous records of genus not determined to species. A transient reported from Colorado River above Yuma, *6 May 1930* (SD, L.M. Huey).

203. *Chaetura vauxi* (Townsend). Vaux's Swift. Fairly common to common, but irregular, migrant in central-southern and western Arizona, east to Santa Catalina and Huachuca Mountains, with a few uncertain reports as far east as the Chiricahua Mountains. A report of 200 in a large flock of White-throated Swifts at Davis Dam in early Feb. is dubious. Single *Chaetura* swifts have been seen near Searchlight, Nevada, 29 Aug. 1947 (Monson); at Ganado Lake, Navajo Indian Reservation, 30 May 1978 (S. Terrill); at Chinle, Navajo Indian Reservation, 31 Aug. 1980 (D. Stejskal, K. Kaufman); and at confluence of Little Colorado River with its South Fork, west of Springerville, 10 Sept. 1980 (B. Jones).

Regular migrants belong to the pale northern nominate race. One specimen of the darker *C. v. tamaulipensis* Sutton from Fort Huachuca, *14 May 1950.*

204. *Aeronautes saxatilis* (Woodhouse). White-throated Swift. Common breeding bird at cliffs in the mountains and mesas except in the southwest, where it nests only at Parker Dam, and perhaps (sparingly) in the Kofa and Castle Dome Mountains of Yuma Co. Occasional over low country in summer. Found in winter, often in large numbers, in southern and western Arizona (but not in southern Yuma Co. east of the Colorado River Valley), usually at lower elevations than in summer, and in Mar. as far up the Colorado River as Pierces Ferry, Lake Mead (16 to 22 Mar. 1974, A.M. Rea). One reported at St. George, Utah, 3 Jan. 1979 (S.E. Hedges).

Only the nominate race has been taken in Arizona.

FAMILY TROCHILIDAE: HUMMINGBIRDS

205. *Calothorax lucifer* (Swainson). Lucifer Hummingbird. Status indefinite, but has appeared with some regularity in the southeast since 1971 (Guadalupe Canyon, *14 July 1971*, ARIZ, photos, A. Myerfeld). Two old records, Ft. Bowie, Cochise Co., *8 Aug. 1874*, and "Arizona" (*date?*; old specimen in US). A male was seen in Guadalupe Canyon, 22 July 1963 (S.H. Levy), and a female was reported from a ranch feeder in the southeastern Chiricahua Mountains, 17 June to 1 July 1965 (R.P. Balda). Nest found in Guadalupe Canyon, 20 May 1973 (T. Parker), but record not documented. Valid records (dates ranging from 2 Apr. 1979, Portal, to 6 Oct. 1976, Portal) mainly from near Portal, Cochise Co., and Ramsey Canyon, Huachuca Mountains, where there are numerous feeders, but also once west to Pajaritos Mountains (California Gulch, female, 3 June 1978, S.M. Russell). Records of females (males also!) often pertain to the following species, whose bill has the appearance of being slightly down-curved.

206. *Archilochus alexandri* (Bourcier and Mulsant). Black-chinned Hummingbird. Common summer resident in certain deciduous associations of Sonoran zones, including low mountain canyons, cities, and along Colorado River; generally absent from deserts. Migrates across the Mogollon Plateau, at least in the fall, and the southwestern deserts in spring. Scarce in western Arizona after mid-June. Sparse numbers may sometimes remain in the south into Dec. when, in lack of specimens, even records of adult males can hardly be credited. The latest specimen taken was on *2 Oct. 1947.*

207. *Calypte costae* (Bourcier). Costa's Hummingbird. Breeding, post-breeding, and winter ranges quite complicated. It is a common breeding bird in the desert regions of central and western Arizona, north to Lake Mead area and Florence region, and east generally to Santa Rita, Tucson, and Picacho Mountains. Does *not* nest in Huachuca Mountains. Also nests (irregularly?) in Guadalupe Canyon in extreme southeast, including the New Mexico portion; at Patagonia Lake; at Nogales; and in the Grand Wash Cliffs of the extreme northwest (*1974,* REA, A.M. Rea). Disappears from its breeding range almost completely by early July; reappears in southwestern Arizona in Oct., and in Phoenix and Tucson regions starting in late Jan. It was characterized as uncommon in spring in the general Aravaipa Canyon region, Pinal and Graham Cos., in 1979–80 (G.S. Mills). In 1979–80 a number of birds appeared through June in canyons of the Santa Catalina Mountains, and young birds have remained as late as *10 Aug. 1884* on the east foot of the same mountains. Aside from the general Yuma Co. region, it evidently does not normally occur between early Aug. and late Jan., contrary to the statement (A.O.U. Check-list) that it "winters over most of breeding range," including "Williams River" (i.e., Big Sandy River). There are scattered sparse records of adult males through the Aug.–Jan. period, mostly at Phoenix and Tucson and once at Portal, usually at feeders; a female was taken in a mist net and released after examination east of Tucson, *1 Dec. 1977* (S.M. Russell, C. Corchran). Non-specimen records of females cannot be safely credited. An adult male was caught in a mist net at Bear Wallow (2440 m or 8000 ft) in the Santa Catalina Mountains, 9 July 1976 (D. Lamm, J. Luepke). One (sex?) seen in Gardner Canyon north of Sonoita, 5 Feb. 1972 (G. McCaskie, T. Parker), and one was collected at Clifton, *9 Mar. 1936.* Two males reported from St. George, Utah, 27 Apr. 1966 (R. Wauer).

208. *Calypte anna* (Lesson). Anna's Hummingbird. Until the 1960s migrated in rather small numbers into Lower Sonoran Zone of southern Arizona in Sept. and early Oct. and wintered there until Dec. and rarely to early Mar. Some birds now remain to breed in deciduous associations from Yuma north to Lake Havasu in lower Colorado River Valley and east as far as the Santa Catalina Mountains foothills; most nests have been found in urban situations. First nesting was at Yuma in *Mar. 1962* (ARIZ, photo, Monson). Some nesting birds may be resident, as beginning at least in *1971* (*13 July,* Tucson, ARIZ, photo, E.M. Read) scattered birds are being seen throughout the summer. Fall birds may occur at feeders in the Transition Zone in southern Arizona; one at Flagstaff, *27 Oct. 1980* (NAU, R.P. Balda). No records east of Tucson and the Huachuca Mountains between late Dec. and late Aug.; occurs as far north as Globe through the winter, and individuals have been found as far north as Prescott (23 to 26 Nov. 1973, S. Harris) and the Hualapai Mountains, *19 July 1959.* Wintering birds are found into the Upper Sonoran Zone in the Santa Catalina Mountains. Young have left the nest as early as 31 Dec. 1968, at Phoenix (S. Demaree). A male found at 3300 m (10,800 ft) in the San Francisco

Mountains, *26 June 1971* (NAU, R.P. Balda) was quite extraordinary!

209. *Selasphorus platycercus* (Swainson). Broad-tailed Hummingbird. Common summer resident throughout boreal and Transition zones, and among deciduous trees along streams in adjacent Upper Sonoran Zone. Migrates uncommonly through lower country between or adjacent to breeding territories, principally in spring and in cool and wet weather; has been seen as far west as Quitobaquito, Organ Pipe Cactus National Monument, 12 Apr. 1967 (R.L. Cunningham). A male still at Pipe Spring National Monument, 12 June 1974 (R. Wilt). One seen in cold weather at 2135 m (7000 ft) in Mazatzal Mountains, Maricopa Co., 22 Feb. 1976 (S. Terrill, R. Witzeman et al.). We have no fall records in the lowlands of northwestern Arizona, and reports in the adjacent Nevada lowlands would seem to require specimen support. No verified winter records. Hybrid with *Calypte costae* reported from Rincon Mountains.

210. *Selasphorus rufus* (Gmelin). Rufous Hummingbird. Common spring migrant from west slope of Baboquivari Mountains and Phoenix region westward south of the Gila River almost to Colorado River, mid-Feb. to Apr.; rather sparse farther east, chiefly at feeders, early Mar. to early May, and casual in the north (one record, Flagstaff, about *25 Apr. 1952*). Abundant fall migrant in northern and eastern Arizona, occurring in smaller numbers in central and southwestern Arizona, arriving as early as 26 June 1969 in Ramsey Canyon, Huachuca Mountains (J. Peabody, R.A. Hudgins et al.). A few early winter records at feeders in southeastern Arizona, but none beyond *14 Jan. 1951* at Tucson and *8 Jan. 1976* at Portal (ARIZ, S. Spofford). A male supposedly spent the winter of 1976–77 at a Tucson golf course, but record not definite. *Selasphorus* records, probably of this species, at Safford, 12 Dec. 1978 (Monson), near Phoenix, 20 Dec. 1978 (R. Bradley), and near Yuma, 11 Feb. 1979 (B. Whitney et al.).

211. *Selasphorus sasin* (Lesson). Allen's Hummingbird. Rather uncommon early fall transient (chiefly in July) in the mountains of central southern Arizona, east occasionally to the Mule Mountains (at Bisbee) and Benson. Once north to the south end of the Bradshaw Mountains, *8 Aug. 1957* (ARIZ, J.T. Bialac). Two verified spring records: Heart Tank, Sierra Pinta, Yuma Co., *18 Feb. 1955,* and east side of Baboquivari Mountains, *20 Feb. 1979* (ARIZ, E.J. Fisk); also one southwest of Sonoyta, Sonora, *22 Feb. 1955.* Owing to confusion with Rufous Hummingbird may be more commonly seen than records indicate.

Arizona specimens are, to date, the smaller nominate form.

212. *Selasphorus heloisa* (Lesson and Delattre). Heloise's Hummingbird. Accidental: two female specimens, Ramsey Canyon, Huachuca Mountains, *2 July 1896.*

These specimens are the types of the pale northwestern race *S. h. morcomi* (Ridgway), of which *S. h. margarethae* (Moore) is a synonym.

213. *Stellula calliope* (Gould). Calliope Hummingbird. Uncommon to sparse spring migrant (late Mar. to early May) in southwestern Arizona, chiefly from Tucson Mountains westward; a few records at feeders from Portal west to Madera Canyon, Santa Rita Mountains. Common fall transient in mountains of northern and eastern Arizona (early July to Sept., a few later); occasional in lowlands in north and east. A male at Portal, 13 to 17 June 1974 (S. Spofford). Reports from Ramsey Canyon, Huachuca Mountains, on 1979 and 1980 Christmas Bird Counts are dubious.

214. *Eugenes fulgens* (Swainson). Rivoli's Hummingbird. Fairly common summer resident in mixed Upper Sonoran and Transition Zones of mountains of southeastern Arizona, north to Pinalenos and Santa Catalinas; recently (since about 1973) has been found north and west to Greer, White Mountains (female, 14 May 1973, Monson), plus other records there in 1978 and 1979 (according to B. Jones), and west to Flagstaff (female, *13 June 1974,* ARIZ, photo, R.P. Balda, plus other records), and, in fall, to Prescott (26 Sept. to 1 Oct. 1976, B. Burns, C.S. Tomoff; and 25 Oct. to 1 Nov. 1980, Tomoff). There is a record of a male noted on the South Rim of the Grand Canyon east of Desert View, 5 June 1976 (B.T. Brown). This hummingbird now remains at feeders in mountains of southeast until Nov. and Dec., and sometimes through the winter, as at Ramsey Canyon, Huachuca Mountains, for three winters beginning in 1965–66 (J. Peabody); at Portal, 1974–75 and 1975–76 (S. Spofford); and at Madera Canyon, Santa Rita Mountains, 1976–77 (R. Newcomer et al.). No verified lowland records. Recorded several times in extreme southwestern Utah (according to W.H. Behle et al.).

Arizona birds are nominate *E. f. fulgens,* of which *E. f. aureoviridis* van Rossem is a synonym.

215. *Lampornis clemenciae* (Lesson). Blue-throated Hummingbird. Uncommon summer resident of moist canyons in the Chiricahua, Huachuca, and Santa Rita Mountains; also a specimen from Santa Catalina Mountains, *14 May 1884,* plus sight records including two or three at Summerhaven feeders, June to July 1977 (W. Roe) and again until at least 1980. Unverified sight records from Oak Creek Canyon south of Flagstaff, and the Pinal and

Peloncillo Mountains. One over-wintered at Portal,
1973–74 (I. Hicks, S. Spofford); three in the unusually
cold winter of 1978–79 (Spofford); two in the
winter of 1980–81 (Spofford); and one remained in
Ramsey Canyon, Huachuca Mountains, to 12 Jan.
1971 (J. Peabody). No verified records at "lower
elevations," where said to winter by A.O.U. Check-
list; an earlier report from "Tucson" is an error, but a
male was at a feeder in east Tucson from late Nov.
1967 to 26 Jan. 1968 (J. Coston).
> The Arizona race is *L. c. bessophilus* (Oberholser), if
> distinguishable from the nominate race.

216. *Heliomaster constantii* (Delattre). Plain-
capped Starthroat. Accidental at feeders recently:
one at Nogales, 20 to 30 *Sept. 1969* (Bill Harrison et
al., ARIZ, photo by R. Witzeman); one at Patagonia,
15 to 22 July 1978 (S. Larson et al.); and one at
Phoenix, 17 *Oct.* to 28 Nov. *1978* (J. Yoba et al.,
ARIZ, photo by G. Metson). One flycatching near
Hereford, Cochise Co., 28 June 1980 (K.V. Rosenberg, T. Brush), was not at a feeder.

217. *Amazilia beryllina* (Lichtenstein). Berylline
Hummingbird. A very sparse visitor and sometime
breeder in mountains of southeast. One identified in
Madera Canyon, Santa Rita Mountains, June 1964
(R. Stallcup et al.). One at Ramsey Canyon, late
June to early *Aug. 1967* (ARIZ, photo, J.M. Shep-
pard et al.); another at Cave Creek Canyon, Chirica-
hua Mountains, 30 June to 1 Aug. *1971* (ARIZ,
photo, H. Snyder et al.); plus sight records at
Ramsey Canyon in 1975, 1977, and 1978. Nested
unsuccessfully at Cave Creek Canyon, 1976 (nest at
AMNH, V. Roth), but young fledged from nest at
Ramsey Canyon, 1978 (photo of nest, ARIZ, J.O.
Anderson). One observed in upper Carr Canyon,
Huachuca Mountains, 30 June 1979 (D. Danforth).

218. *Amazilia violiceps* (Gould). Violet-crowned Hummingbird. Found uncommonly in summer from Guadalupe Canyon in extreme southeast west to Santa Rita Mountains and Patagonia regions; nests have been discovered only in Guadalupe Canyon and the Chiricahua and Huachuca Mountains. Also records from Arizona-Sonora Desert Museum, 22 Oct. 1972 (Monson) and from near Prescott, 11 to 19 *Oct. 1975* (ARIZ, photo, V. Miller). Seen as late as 7 Dec. 1978 at Nogales (R. Madding) and at Ramsey Canyon, Huachuca Mountains (according to D. Danforth), and one was at a north Tucson feeder from 24 Nov. 1970 until late Feb. 1971 (B. and F. Weideman). Only two reports prior to *1948*.

Arizona birds are the green-tailed *A. v. ellioti* Berlepsch.

219. *Hylocharis leucotis* (Vieillot). White-eared Hummingbird. Sparse summer visitant (still no nests) to southeastern mountains, north to Santa Catalinas and west to Huachucas; no verified records as yet for Santa Ritas. A female was taken in the South Fork of Cave Creek Canyon, Chiricahua Mountains, *25 June 1940* (CM, A.C. Twomey). Otherwise, no authenticated records between *1933* and *1961* (one identified as this species seen in Molino Basin, Santa Catalina Mountains, 10 July 1952, R. Smart et al.). Supposed winter date listed in A.O.U. Check-list is an error.

220. *Cynanthus latirostris* Swainson. Broad-billed Hummingbird. Common summer resident in mesquite-sycamore associations from the Guadalupe Mountains west along border, locally, to the west side of the Baboquivari Mountains, and north to the Galiuros and Santa Catalinas. A pair in courtship display noted along Verde River northeast of Phoenix, 16 May 1976; a young bird fallen from its nest in Phoenix, *18 Apr. 1980,* turned out to be of this species (both K. Ingram). One female or immature on lower Trout Creek, Big Sandy Valley, Mohave Co., 18 Aug. 1977 (Monson); recent records from the lower Colorado River Valley (five reports, including two in the Blythe, California vicinity; a male at Ehrenberg, Yuma Co., Feb. 1976, A. Higgins; a male in the Dome Valley east of Yuma, 6 to 8 Sept. 1979, S. Goldwasser; and a female on the lower Bill Williams River, 30 Sept. 1979, K.V. Rosenberg, V. Hink); some sight records, mainly in spring, from the Pinal Mountains and the Boyce Thompson Arboretum near Superior. Occurs uncommonly around Tucson (including Tucson Mountains) during migrations and recently at feeders in winter; sparse in Phoenix region in late summer, fall, and winter since 1969–70. Has wintered at Nogales, also. One photographed at Springdale, southwestern Utah near Zion National Park, 1 Oct. to 25 Nov. 1978 (R. Fesler et al.).

The race found in Arizona is the relatively small and green-breasted *C. l. magicus* (Mulsant and Verreaux).

FAMILY TROGONIDAE: TROGONS

221. *Euptilotis neoxenus* (Gould). Eared Trogon. At least three and apparently four present in South Fork of Cave Creek Canyon, Chiricahua Mountains, *23 Oct.* to *3 Dec. 1977* (ARIZ, photos, A. Clay, B. Schaughency et al., first identified by R.Taylor); also one seen in Ramsey Canyon, Huachuca Mountains, 1 to 3 Dec. 1977 (B. Jones et al.). One seen and a dropped tail feather collected, lower Cave Creek Canyon, *5 Nov. 1978* (L. Kiff et al.). A male observed in upper part of South Fork of Cave Creek Canyon, 12 to 13 Aug. 1979 (Taylor et al.) and again 22 Oct. 1979 (A. McCallum).

222. *Trogon elegans* Gould. Coppery-tailed Trogon. Fairly common summer resident of well-wooded canyons of the Huachuca, and, since the 1930s, the Santa Rita and, still later, the Chiricahua Mountains.

Not more than four records between 1963 and 1980 in Guadalupe Canyon in the extreme southeast, but has been recorded in the Pajaritos and Atascosa Mountains almost annually since 1972 (first found there in spring of 1966, D.E. Brown). A few winter records beginning in 1973–74 (but one male in Cave Creek Canyon, Chiricahua Mountains, 17 Jan. 1965, H. Cole, M. Chandler), mainly from the Huachucas, but also from below Patagonia, the Pajaritos, near Tucson, *17 Jan. 1953,* and Brown Canyon, Baboquivari Mountains, the first week of Dec. 1977 (J. Goodman). Extralimital records aside from those in winter include one in Posta Quemado Canyon, Rincon Mountains, 9 Sept. 1974 (H. Coss), one along Sonoita Creek southwest of Patagonia, 28 June 1979 (D. Stotz et al.), and one near Lewis Springs, upper San Pedro Valley, 30 June 1979 (S. Parker).

Arizona birds are *T. e. canescens* van Rossem.

FAMILY ALCEDINIDAE: KINGFISHERS

223. *Megaceryle alcyon* (Linnaeus). Belted Kingfisher. Fairly common to common transient wherever there are permanent fish-inhabited waters, and winters where these do not freeze; also sometimes appears at temporary waterholes on desert. Some individuals tend to stay until early June, and to return in late July, in southern Arizona. Although there are summer records for central and northern Arizona, particularly along the Black and Verde Rivers, the only good evidence of nesting in the state in the present century is provided by a nest with nestlings found in late May 1980 on Spring Creek near Cottonwood, Yavapai Co. (S. Emslie). Bendire says "nests" found in "southern Arizona" in 1890s, and A.M. Rea (Ph.D. dissertation, University of Arizona, 1977) presents evidence that the Belted Kingfisher nested along the Gila River near Komatke, Gila River Indian Reservation, within this century. One reported on lower Gila River, 19 June 1979 (G. Robinson).

We consider the species monotypic.

224. *Chloroceryle americana* (Gmelin). Green Kingfisher. Sparse straggler into Santa Cruz drainage (Tucson and above) and San Pedro Valley (Benson and above) in fall and winter, sometimes (less than five records) in summer. No authentic record west of Arivaca (*23 Dec. 1960*) and Pajaritos Mountains (25 Dec. 1966, E. Willis); Coues' records for the Colorado River (1865) are very much open to question. Though called "casual" in A.O.U. Check-list, there are specimens from Fairbank, Nogales, Arivaca, Patagonia, and Tucson, and valid sight records from Hereford, St. David, and Benson as well. A specimen was obtained on Arroyo Cajón Bonito in extreme northeast Sonora in *July 1892* or *Sept. 1893* (US, E.A. Mearns).

Arizona birds are *C. a. hachisukai* (Laubmann).

FAMILY PICIDAE: WOODPECKERS AND WRYNECKS

225. *Colaptes auratus* (Linnaeus). Common Flicker. Common resident throughout wooded parts and in saguaro deserts, except along lower Colorado River where it is chiefly a winter visitant. Winters almost anywhere.

C. a. luteus Bangs, the Yellow-shafted Flicker in part, is a sparse transient and winter visitant, recorded in all parts of the state except the extreme northwest; northern Arizona specimens only at Cedar Ridge and Grand Canyon Village, both Coconino Co. Dates range from 3 Oct. 1974 (Cape Royal, Grand Canyon, Monson) to *7 May 1947*. We include here as a synonym *C. a. borealis* Ridgway.

C. a. canescens Brodkorb, a form of the Red-shafted
Flicker, is a common resident of forested mountains, as
well as of adjacent riparian sites even sometimes into
the Lower Sonoran Zone in cottonwood groves. Winters
commonly in areas with trees and large desert shrubs
and cacti, below and in the Transition Zone. Intergrades
with *C. a. luteus* appear very rare; intergrades with *C.
a. mearnsi* occur in upper San Pedro and upper Santa
Cruz Valleys, along the Verde and Agua Fria Rivers
above the Phoenix region, and apparently in the Mayer
and (in present century) Camp Verde areas, as well as
along Beaver Dam Wash in the extreme northwest
(*May 1966,* ZION, R. Wauer). *C. a. collaris* Vigors, a
more brownish coastal red-shafted race, also winters in
Arizona, but is less common and widespread.

C. a. mearnsi Ridgway, a form of the Gilded Flicker,
is a common resident in the wooded Lower Sonoran
Zone, including saguaros, from San Pedro Valley west;
scarcer in Yuma Co. and along the Colorado River,
where it ranged 120 years ago up to Fort Mojave. A
juvenile was taken in Carr Canyon, Huachuca Mountains, *18 June 1940* (CM, A.C. Twomey).

[*Dryocopos pileatus* (Linnaeus). Pileated Woodpecker. Hypothetical. Found once, near Point Imperial
on North Rim of the Grand Canyon, where one was
seen 30 Aug. 1935 and workings photographed. The
record, however, was not substantiated, though it is
cited in the A.O.U. Check-list. One was collected at
Bluff, San Juan Co., Utah, about 30 km (19 mi) from
Arizona, *21 May 1892* (AMNH, C.P. Rowley).]

[*Melanerpes carolinus* (Linnaeus). Red-bellied
Woodpecker. Erroneously reported on the basis of
two specimens in a collection, examined, doubtless
erroneously labeled.]

226. *Melanerpes uropygialis* Baird. Gila Woodpecker. Common resident throughout Lower Sonoran
Zone of southern and western Arizona; rather local

in extreme southeast. Mysteriously absent from Arivaca area. Winters fairly commonly in adjacent Upper Sonoran Zone, uncommonly in other parts of the Upper Sonoran Zone in southeast, casually reaching the lower edge of Transition Zone. Occurs occasionally in Prescott region; one was taken about 16 km (10 mi) west of town, *16 Sept. 1940* (CM, A.C. Twomey). There are winter sight records north to near Pierce Ferry, Mohave Co., and one was seen at Eagar, 26 Nov. 1978 (K. Kaufman, B. Jones).

Gila Woodpeckers in Arizona are the nominate race, from which *M. u. albescens* (van Rossem) is not satisfactorily separable (A.M. Rea, MS.).

227. *Melanerpes erythrocephalus* (Linnaeus). Red-headed Woodpecker. Casual: one taken *about June 1894* in the Chiricahua Mountains (location of specimen unknown); one seen repeatedly in Phoenix from Mar. to May 1959 (many observers); and one photographed in lower Ash Canyon, Huachuca Mountains, *3* to 10 *Mar. 1974* (ARIZ, D. Danforth et al.) after being first seen 15 Feb. 1974 (T. Miller).

228. *Melanerpes formicivorus* (Swainson). Acorn Woodpecker. Common resident among large oaks in mountains throughout Arizona. Straggles from breeding range at all seasons except early spring (but mainly in fall), in some years as far as the lower Colorado River and Organ Pipe Cactus National Monument.

The Arizona race is the slender-billed *M. f. aculeatus* Mearns.

229. *Melanerpes lewis* (Gray). Lewis' Woodpecker. Fairly common resident of certain open Transition Zone "parks" in San Francisco Mountains, and in the vicinity of Lakeside, Navajo Co.; more sparse and local northward and eastward of these areas. More or less uncommon (in most years) as a transient and winter visitant in open Upper Sonoran and low Transition woody areas. Occasionally winters in moist lowlands, commonly so in flight years, often found in pecan groves.

230. *Sphyrapicus varius* (Linnaeus). Yellow-bellied Sapsucker. Nests in Canadian Zone of mountains along and north of the Mogollon Plateau, and irregularly (?) in the Bradshaw (1975–76, C.S. Tomoff) and Hualapai Mountains. Quite sparse except in parts of White Mountains, Blue Range, Promontory Point on the Mogollon Rim, and Kaibab Plateau. Common transient for long periods throughout most of state but sparse in driest open desert areas. Common in winter (except in north where very sparse) in Sonoran Zone deciduous trees and somewhat less common in Upper Sonoran evergreen oaks and junipers. A hybrid with *S. thyroideus* reported from the Huachuca Mountains.

S. v. varius (Linnaeus), the eastern form, is a sparse and irregular winter resident in southeastern Arizona and casual northwestward to the Colorado River. *S. v. nuchalis*, the "Red-naped Sapsucker," is the race commonly found and breeding in Arizona. *S. v. ruber* (Gmelin), the "Red-breasted Sapsucker," is sparse in winter in southeastern Arizona. *S. v. daggetti* Grinnell, paler and with a greater amount of white spotting on the back than *ruber*, has been taken only at Sacaton, in the Hualapai Mountains, and in the lower Colorado River and the Bill Williams Delta. It appears in winter, although the Hualapai specimen was taken in *July*. Intermediates between *nuchalis* and this or the preceding race have been taken in southern Arizona.

231. *Sphyrapicus thyroideus* (Cassin). Williamson's Sapsucker. Nests in aspens from Mogollon Rim northward, including Bill Williams Mountain, San Francisco Mountains, Kaibab Plateau, and White Mountains, more or less commonly. Winters in Transition and (sparingly) high Upper Sonoran Zones south and west of Mogollon Rim, rarely on Mogollon Plateau, and once at Grand Canyon Village. Has been recorded in fall west to Kaibab Indian Reservation and Pipe Spring National Monument (Sept. 1974, R. Wilt). Irregular and sparse winter visitant in the Lower Sonoran Zone, usually near mountains but west casually to Colorado River (two sight records), and including Tucson Mountains, 15 Aug. 1961. A female recorded at Barfoot Park, Chiricahua Mountains, 25 June 1976 (E. and S. Cardiff) and 13 July 1976 (S. Terrill et al.).

Arizona birds belong to the small-billed Rocky Mountains race *S. t. nataliae* (Malherbe).

232. *Dendrocopos villosus* (Linnaeus). Hairy Woodpecker. Common to fairly common resident of coniferous woodlands (including pinyon-juniper in the north); locally resident in some Upper Sonoran deciduous woodlands in north, south to riparian situations below Mogollon Rim (including along Little Colorado River near Joseph City, Navajo Co., where seen 16 Aug. 1973, Monson, and at Mocassin, Mohave Co., 1 Oct. 1974, Monson and R. Wilt). Formerly descended in winter to adjacent valleys, even to Lower Sonoran as at Tucson, but no recent record at any distance from conifers except sight records at Phoenix, 20 Nov. 1966 (S. Demaree) and 24 Feb. to 15 Mar. 1975 (P. Burch et al.), and at Whitlow Dam near Florence Jct., Pinal Co., 22 Nov. 1980 (R. Dummer).

D. v. orius (Oberholser) is the race found southward to the Pinaleno Mountains; *D. v. leucothorectis* (Oberholser) is included here. *D. v. icastus* (Oberholser) is found from the Santa Catalina Mountains southward.

233. *Dendrocopos pubescens* (Linnaeus). Downy Woodpecker. Sparse resident in deciduous trees of Transition and Canadian Zones from the Blue

Range, White Mountains (where less uncommon), Sierra Ancha, and San Francisco Mountains northward, including the Navajo Indian Reservation. Apparently less rare in winter, when it reaches the Upper Sonoran Zone. Casual in southern Arizona: near Kelvin, Gila Co., *Apr. 1882;* Pinery Canyon, Chiricahua Mountains, *10 Apr. 1928* (VPI, F. Hands); Pinaleno Mountains, 20 Oct. 1935 and 9 May and 27 Aug. 1936; Tucson, *13 Mar. 1954;* and Phoenix, 3 to 15 Jan. 1976 (several observers).

Arizona birds belong to the race *D. p. leucurus* (Hartlaub).

234. *Dendrocopos scalaris* (Wagler). Ladder-backed Woodpecker. Common resident throughout the Lower Sonoran Zone, more sparingly in open parts of Upper Sonoran Zone except in northeast (east of Kaibab Plateau) where absent.

The Arizona subspecies is *D. s. cactophilus* (Oberholser), of which *D. s. yumanensis* van Rossem is a synonym.

235. *Dendrocopos nuttallii* (Gambel). Nuttall's Woodpecker. Accidental, specimen taken at Phoenix, *24 June (or Jan.?) 1901* (MCZ). Breninger, the collector, never published his record; there is some possibility of a *lapsus* in labeling, since some specimens retained in his Phoenix Museum proved to be mislabeled as to dates.

236. *Dendrocopos stricklandi* (Malherbe). Arizona Woodpecker. Common resident of evergreen oaks of southeastern Arizona, west and north to the Baboquivari, Santa Catalina, and Pinaleno Mountains. Rare in some winters in adjacent lowlands. Old specimens labeled "Portal" and "San Bernardino" were probably taken at higher places.

Arizona birds are the large brown-backed *D. s. arizonae* (Hargitt).

237. ***Picoides tridactylus*** (Linnaeus). Northern Three-toed Woodpecker. Fairly common to uncommon resident in boreal zones, sparse in Transition Zone, from White to San Francisco Mountains and on the Kaibab Plateau. Two males observed at Pine Flat, Oak Creek Canyon, Coconino Co., 6 July 1978 (G. Rosenberg, T. Brush), and one seen in Chuska Mountains, 5 July 1980 (L. and S. Terrill, G. Rosenberg).

The white-backed *P. t. dorsalis* Baird is the race found in Arizona.

FAMILY COTINGIDAE: COTINGAS

238. ***Pachyramphus aglaiae*** (Lafresnaye). Rose-throated Becard. Local and fluctuating summer resident along Sonoita Creek below Patagonia, Santa Cruz Co.; in recent years near Arivaca, Pima Co., and along Sycamore Canyon, Pajaritos Mountains. In Guadalupe Canyon in the extreme southeast and near Tucson, inactive nests were found in 1957 and 1958–59, respectively. Strays have been reported from Box Canyon, north end of Santa Rita Mountains, 16 June 1973 (E. and S. Cardiff), Madera Canyon in the Santa Ritas, 16 to 18 May 1979 (pair) (J. and R. Barnett et al.), and upper Aravaipa Canyon east of Graham Co. line, 6 July 1979 (G.S. Mills). A report from the Chiricahua Mountains lacks solid basis. Before *1947* at Patagonia, only one accidental record: Huachuca Mountains, *20 June 1888.*

Arizona birds are the pale gray *P. a. albiventris* (Lawrence), of which *richmondi* van Rossem is a synonym.

FAMILY TYRANNIDAE: TYRANT FLYCATCHERS

239. ***Tyrannus tyrannus*** (Linnaeus). Eastern Kingbird. Sparse to uncommon summer visitant in northeastern Arizona; even more sparse transient in late summer and early fall in southern Arizona west to the lower Colorado River (including one at Davis Dam, 16 Aug. 1976, R. Stallcup). No Arizona nest yet recorded. Found at Phantom Ranch in Grand Canyon, 19 May 1929; at Flagstaff, *19 June 1938;* along Beaver Dam Wash in the extreme northwest, 21 July 1966 (R. Wauer); at Granite Park east of the Grand Canyon on the Hualapai Indian Reservation, 16 June 1974 (S.W. Carothers); and at the bottom of the Grand Canyon about 18 km (11 mi) below Toroweap Valley, 19 July 1973, and at Deer Creek, downstream from Tapeats Creek, 9 June 1980 (R.R. Johnson). One seen near Tucson in Mar. 1943 and also 10 June 1979 (K. Kaufman); one near Cascabel, lower San Pedro Valley, 25 June 1979 (D. Stotz); and one at Patagonia, 13 July 1980 (Stallcup).

240. *Tyrannus verticalis* Say. Western Kingbird. Common summer resident in open associations below the Transition Zone (local in northern Arizona); and common transient (especially in fall) elsewhere in unforested areas, up to the Transition Zone. No authentic records between Oct. and Mar., except 13 Nov. 1974 (T.B. Johnson) on the Santa Rita Range Reserve, Pima Co.; *6 Nov. 1977* (collected but lost [?], A. Higgins et al.) south of Parker; and 2 Nov. 1978 (K. Kaufman) at Tucson.

241. *Tyrannus vociferans* Swainson. Cassin's Kingbird. Common summer resident in Upper Sonoran and highest Lower Sonoran Zones, openings in ponderosa pines, and along major wooded streams except lower Colorado and lower Salt and Gila Rivers, where it is a sparse transient; has been found throughout the summer at Tucson, including two nests. Late stragglers in early winter at Tucson and in Pajaritos Mountains, and perhaps at the east base of the Santa Rita Mountains. One present at San Simon Cienega, Hidalgo Co., New Mexico, 9 Dec. 1979 (according to S. Spofford). No Jan. or Feb. records.

Arizona birds are of the nominate race.

242. *Tyrannus crassirostris* Swainson. Thick-billed Kingbird. First found (and nesting) in 1958 in Guadalupe Canyon in extreme southeastern Arizona, then at Patagonia in 1961 (*not* 1962). Nested at Madera Canyon, Santa Rita Mountains, Pima Co., 1963 to 1965 (H.L. Crockett et al.). By 1972 it was in the Nogales vicinity, by 1975 at Arivaca, and by 1977 and 1978 it was found in the Pajaritos Mountains region (three localities) and even in Brown Canyon, east side of the Baboquivari Mountains (G.S. Mills, W. Roe). An adult with two fledglings was observed at Cooks Lake, in the San Pedro Valley near the mouth of Aravaipa Creek, 28 Aug. 1980 (Monson, M.W. Larson); an individual was noted there 18 July 1979 (Monson, R. Glinski). Summer strays have been reported from Portal, 17 to 20 May 1972 (R. Gordon) and 3 May 1978 (S. Spofford), in Huachuca Canyon, Huachuca Mountains, 3 June 1978 (B. Harrison), and near the Boyce Thompson Southwestern Arboretum, 25 May 1979 (R.L. McKernan) west to Quitobaquito, Organ Pipe Cactus National Monument, on or about 1 June 1976 (R. Stallcup) and the lower Colorado River (both sides) about 14 km (9 mi) north of Blythe, California, 5 Aug. to 16 Sept. 1978 (S. Clark et al.). The only records in winter are from Laguna Dam, Yuma Co., *17 Dec. 1972* to 4 Jan. 1973 (ARIZ, photo, R.L. Todd et al.); from near Parker, *2 Dec. 1977* (ARIZ, A. Higgins et al.); and on Lost Lake, California, Colorado River below Parker, *20 Dec. 1979* (ARIZ, photo, K.V. Rosenberg et al.).

We consider the species monotypic.

243. *Tyrannus melancholicus* Vieillot. Tropical Kingbird. Has nested locally, usually in open cotton-woods, in Santa Cruz Valley (including Sopori Wash, 21 June 1980, G.S. Mills) from Tucson south to Yerba Buena Ranch east of Nogales; along Salt River east of Phoenix; in lower San Pedro Valley; and presumably at the San Bernardino Ranch in Cochise Co. where seen in summers of 1976 through 1980 (D. Danforth et al.). However, it is only in the section of the Santa Cruz Valley south of Green Valley (Canoa Ranch) that it now nests persistently; it has not nested in the Tucson vicinity since 1970, and was not noted at Cooks Lake until 1975. Birds also seen in Avra Valley, Pima Co., in 1973 (Monson) and at Arivaca in 1977 and 1978 (B. Harrison). Wanders rarely in summer and fall to Colorado River, north to Topock (1 Oct. 1947) and northeast to Pomerene, San Pedro Valley (*11 Sept. 1953*). One casually at Imperial-Riverside Co. line, California side of Colorado River, 22 Mar. 1957, and one at Pima, Graham Co., 10 Apr. 1955. One present at Rodeo, New Mexico, 14 to 21 *Dec. 1980* (New Mexico Ornithological Society files, photo, J. Schatz, Jr.).

The race found in Arizona is *T. m. satrapa* (Cabanis and Heine), of which *T. m. occidentalis* Hartert and Goodson is a synonym.

244. *Muscivora forficata* (Gmelin). Scissor-tailed Flycatcher. Very sparse summer visitant generally, but unrecorded in northwest, and only two records from the northeast: Kayenta, *8 July 1934,* and near Little Colorado River about 29 km (18 mi) north-east of Snowflake, 4 Oct. 1975 (D.H. Ellis). Extreme dates are 20 Apr. 1977 in Calabasas Canyon near Nogales (Monson), and 13 Oct. 1974, Gila River near Wellton, Yuma Co. (G. Robinson) and 13 Oct. 1980, northwest of Poston, Yuma Co. (L. Abbott et al.). Always seen singly. In the summer of 1979, one paired with a Western Kingbird at Needles, California, but two nesting attempts failed (S. Cardiff).

245. *Pitangus sulphuratus* (Linnaeus). Kiskadee Flycatcher. Accidental, two records: northeast Tucson Valley, 15 to 29 Mar. 1978 (M. Sheldrick et al.), and Canoa Ranch near Green Valley, Pima Co., 27 Dec. *1979* to 6 May 1980 (ARIZ, photo on *29 Dec.,* S. Terrill).

246. *Myiodynastes luteiventris* Sclater. Sulphur-bellied Flycatcher. Fairly common summer resident of sycamore-walnut canyons in southern Arizona, from the Chiricahua Mountains west to the Pajaritos Mountains, and apparently now regularly in Bear Canyon, Santa Catalina Mountains. Has been reported from Wet Canyon, Pinaleno Mountains (June–July 1951 and June 1952, J.T. Marshall); from Guadalupe Canyon in the extreme southeast (27 June 1971, T. Manolis, and 15 May 1977, L.C. Goldman); as well as on the east side of the Baboquivari Mountains (10 June 1978, G.S. Mills and W. Roe) and in the Sierra Ancha (12 and 16 June 1977, R.R. Johnson, and 25 June 1978, S. Terrill). May also occur along Eagle Creek, Greenlee Co. (heard, 8 July 1977, H. and N. Snyder, and one seen, 21 May 1980, R. Dummer). "Lowland" records come from the Santa Cruz River 32 km (20 mi) north of Nogales, *27 May 1917,* and Sonoita Creek several km below Patagonia at least twice in the late 1970s (according to G.S. Mills).

247. *Myiarchus crinitus* (Linnaeus). Great Crested Flycatcher. Casual; one in Huachuca Mountains, *3 June 1901,* and one identified near Kayenta, Navajo Indian Reservation, 9 Oct. 1980 (D. Stotz, S. Parker).
    The specimen is of the nominate race, of which *M. c. boreus* Bangs is a synonym.

248. *Myiarchus tyrannulus* (Müller). Wied's Crested Flycatcher. Common summer resident of saguaro, cottonwood, willow, and sycamore associations north to central Arizona (including Oak Creek Canyon), much less common toward Colorado River, where it is found locally north to the southern tip of Nevada, and even to Beaver Dam Wash in extreme northwestern Arizona (*5 May 1966,* UU, R. Wauer, plus other later records) and extreme southwestern Utah (*18 May 1966,* UU, R. Wauer, and *24 May 1968,* UU, W.H. Behle). At Yuma has apparently nested in the city. No valid winter records, or spring records earlier than *12 Apr.*

The race found in Arizona is the large *M. t. magister* Ridgway.

249. *Myiarchus cinerascens* (Lawrence). Ash-throated Flycatcher. Common summer resident throughout all but the densely wooded parts of the Sonoran zones, occasionally straggling higher. Winters in mountains of Yuma Co., and sparsely to uncommonly along lower Colorado River, east to Phoenix and Casa Grande areas, and even more sparsely to Tucson, Nogales, and Patagonia Lake.

Arizona birds are of the nominate race.

250. *Myiarchus nuttingi* Ridgway. Nutting's Flycatcher. Accidental; one record, near Roosevelt Lake, *8 Jan. 1952.*

The specimen is *M. n. vanrossemi* Phillips.

251. *Myiarchus tuberculifer* (Lafresnaye and D'Orbigny). Olivaceous Flycatcher. Common local resident of denser evergreen oaks from Guadalupe Canyon to the Baboquivari Mountains, and in high Lower Sonoran riparian associations of Santa Cruz River drainage; now ranges north increasingly, locally and in fluctuating numbers, to the Pinaleno and Pinal Mountains. Has also been found exceptionally on

Mitchell Peak, south end of White Mountains, *8 July 1951;* at Sells, Papago Indian Reservation, *8 July 1918;* in the Superstition Mountains, Maricopa Co., 30 May 1976 (R. Norton et al.); on Christopher Creek 24 km (15 mi) northeast of Payson, 19 May 1978 (S. Terrill, G. Rosenberg); and along the Colorado River at Cibola, Yuma Co., *14 Nov. 1977* (ARIZ, A. Higgins, first seen by P. Mack). Has been reported in spring migration below the Huachuca Mountains; near San Xavier Mission; at Tempe, 11 to 14 May 1980 (K.V. Rosenberg et al.); and on Bonita Creek near Safford, 12 to 13 May 1980 (T. Clark).

The Arizona race is the pale *M. t. olivascens* Ridgway, including the Colorado River specimen.

252. *Sayornis phoebe* (Latham). Eastern Phoebe. Sparse fall transient and winter visitor in southern Arizona, chiefly in the southeast but recorded west to the Colorado River. Records span the period from *16 Aug. 1919* (Dickey Collection, University of California, Los Angeles, H.H. Kimball, Paradise, east side of Chiricahua Mountains) to 21 Mar. 1977 (K.V. Rosenberg, Bill Williams Delta). Two northern records: a bird reported southwest of Springerville, 19 to 26 May 1978 (S. Terrill, G. Rosenberg), and one seen at Beaver Dam in extreme northwest, 19 May 1966 (R. Wauer).

253. *Sayornis nigricans* (Swainson). Black Phoebe. Breeds commonly along permanent streams and some canals of central and southeastern Arizona; also breeds uncommonly and locally in the bottom of the Grand Canyon, in western Arizona, on the north slope of the White Mountains (as high as Greer, 2620 m or 8600 ft), and even up into the Transition Zone. Winters at water throughout Lower Sonoran Zone valleys, including the Colorado and Virgin

Rivers and Grand Canyon, sparingly so east of San
Pedro Valley. An astonishing winter record is of a
bird below the confluence of the Little Colorado
River and its South Fork, west of Springerville, 24
Dec. 1979 (R.L. Todd). On migration, which may
begin in spring as early as mid-Feb., apt to occur at
any water hole or cattle trough, even in the northeastern part of the state (and in the northwest, as at
Pipe Spring National Monument, 23 July 1973, R.
Wilt) and up into the ponderosa pine zone. Not
"resident" as stated in A.O.U. Check-list.

Arizona birds are of the race *S. n. semiatra* (Vigors).

254. *Sayornis saya* (Bonaparte). Say's Phoebe.
Fairly common breeding bird about cliffs and struc-
tures throughout less densely wooded parts of the
Sonoran Zone, and locally higher. Winters south
and west of the Mogollon Rim in Sonoran zones,
sparingly north to the Navajo Indian Reservation
and inside the Grand Canyon. During fall migration
may be found on Kaibab and Mogollon Plateaus
away from breeding areas. A post-breeding migration
carries most of the birds out of the south-central and
southwestern part of the state, where virtually absent
in July and August.

The taxonomy of Say's Phoebe has not been adequately
worked out, but for the present it seems that all Arizona
birds are the nominate race.

255. *Empidonax fulvifrons* (Giraud). Buff-breasted
Flycatcher. Summer resident, now found only in
openings of the Transition Zone of the Huachuca
Mountains. Observed in Cave Creek Canyon, Chiricahua Mountains, from 1965 (J.D. Ligon and R.P.
Balda) to 1971 (according to S. M. Russell), and in
Rose Canyon, Santa Catalina Mountains, 4 May
1980 (D. Stotz et al.). Before 1920, was found,
perhaps in small numbers, as far north as Prescott
(one pair, *1865*) and Fort Apache (*1876*), and also

in the Santa Catalina, Rincon, Santa Rita, Chiricahua, and Patagonia Mountains. Common in the Sierra de San Luis, Chihuahua, just a few km south of New Mexico, May 1976 (J.P. Hubbard, Monson). In spring migration has occurred at the foot of mountains, even to Sonoita Creek and west to the Pajaritos Mountains, but not since *1947*.

256. *Empidonax wrightii* Baird. Gray Flycatcher. Common summer resident of pinyon-juniper areas from Mogollon Plateau northward; also westward to at least the Juniper Mountains and southward to Fort Apache. Winters sparingly in mesquite associations, usually near water, in southern and central Arizona, north to Topock, Salome, and Wickenburg, and east to San Pedro Valley and casually to the Chiricahua Mountains. Common transient in more open parts of state, except in southeast, where uncommon. Found casually in Upper Sonoran evergreen oaks of Patagonia Mountains, *21 Feb. 1948*.

257. *Empidonax oberholseri* Phillips. Dusky Flycatcher. Locally common summer resident of Canadian Zone willows of White and (very locally) San Francisco Mountains, and possibly also Chuska Mountains and the Kaibab Plateau. Winters casually to sparsely along lower Colorado and Salt Rivers and in Chiricahua Mountains, more regularly near Tucson and Patagonia, where not exceptional. Though said by A.O.U. Check-list to winter "casually" in Arizona, nine specimens have been taken near Tucson in the period between 20 Nov. and 10 Mar. of eight different winters; four in two years at Patagonia; three in three years at Nogales; four near Phoenix; two on the lower Colorado River; and one or two in the Chiricahua Mountains. Uncommon but widespread spring migrant throughout wooded areas of state but perhaps only casual along lower Gila and Colorado Rivers (where, however, taken near Needles,

California, *19 Feb. 1910,* Museum of Vertebrate Zoology, Berkeley, J. Grinnell, and near Bard, California, *25 Apr. 1930* and *25 Sept. 1925,* SD, L.M. Huey; and two specimens taken, but not examined by us, on lower Bill Williams River, *9 Apr. 1977,* ARIZ, K.V. Rosenberg, and north of Ehrenberg, Yuma Co., *16 Jan. 1981,* ARIZ, M. Kaspryzk). Common fall migrant in extreme southeast, uncommon elsewhere, but possibly only casual in southwestern and central Arizona.

258. *Empidonax hammondii* (Xantus). Hammond's Flycatcher. Common generally in migrations, except in northeast in spring, when status unknown. Winters regularly in small numbers in the Nogales-Patagonia area, less commonly at Tucson, and has also occurred in winter (more or less casually) in the Chiricahua and Santa Catalina Mountains, as well as near Phoenix and at Salome. One taken in the Bill Williams Delta, *21 Mar. 1977* (ARIZ, A. Higgins), was under observation since Jan. A pair with nest found in Chuska Mountains, 4 July 1980 (K.V. Rosenberg, J. Rice et al.), but no specimen obtained; photographed, and call notes heard.

259. *Empidonax pusillus* (Swainson). Least Flycatcher. A rare fall migrant in western Arizona, only one spring record: three in Big Sandy Valley, *20 Oct. 1951;* one from the Tule Mountains, Yuma Co., *29 Sept. 1956;* one from Salt River and 91st Ave., Maricopa Co., *12 Apr. 1978* (REA, A.M. Rea); also one from Boulder City, Nevada, *6 Sept. 1950.* Sight records based on calls are unsatisfactory and unacceptable until and unless unmistakable criteria are scientifically developed.

260. *Empidonax difficilis* Baird. Western Flycatcher. Common summer resident in boreal zones throughout southeastern Arizona, and in the northeast, west to Kayenta region and San Francisco

Mountains; breeds down into more shady parts of Transition Zone locally. Absent as a breeder from northwestern and central Arizona and the Grand Canyon. Common transient in southwestern and central Arizona, sparse in the north (fall records only) and extreme east, and unknown in northeast. A late bird identified as this species at Sunrise, White Mountains, 12 Oct. 1980 (D. Stotz) was in breeding area. Winters sparsely in the lower Colorado River Valley from the Bill Williams Delta south; there are a number of winter sight records from along the Salt River near Phoenix, but no specimens. Also, sight records of one at Cooks Lake in San Pedro Valley near mouth of Aravaipa Creek, 20 Nov. 1978 and 23 Jan. 1979 (Monson) and (date?) Feb. 1979 (K.V. Rosenberg); one at the same place, 3 Feb. 1980 (Stotz). There are two specimen winter records from central-northern Sonora near the Arizona line and sight records from Nogales and the Pajaritos Mountains. Records of transients nearly span the summer.

The breeding race is *E. d. hellmayri* Brodkorb; it is also a scarce transient. *E. d. difficilis* Baird has been found in the north only twice, in the fall, but it is a common migrant in southern Arizona, when and where it far outnumbers *hellmayri*. The Baja California race *E. d. cineritius* Brewster, pale and with rounded wing, has been taken once, *13 Dec. 1950,* in the Bill Williams Delta. *E. d. insulicola* Oberholser, from islands off the coast of southern California, is represented from Arizona, in typical form, by a single specimen, taken in the Bill Williams Delta, *12 Apr. 1948,* and in intermediate form by various others.

261. ***Empidonax flaviventris*** (Baird and Baird). Yellow-bellied Flycatcher. Accidental, one specimen: Tucson, *22 Sept. 1956.*

262. ***Empidonax virescens*** (Vieillot). Acadian Flycatcher. Accidental, one specimen: Tucson, *24 May 1886.*

263. *Empidonax traillii* (Audubon). Willow Flycatcher. Breeds very locally in dense willow association and button bush swamps of Sonoran zones throughout the state; and in the Transition Zone in dense willows at Alpine, Apache Co., and at confluence of Little Colorado River and its South Fork. No nests found since before 1970, however. Singing solitary birds are sometimes found in willows in midsummer anywhere in state. Transient throughout state, being especially common in southwest, but possibly only a fall casual in the northeast. Migrants pass through the south chiefly in first half of June and during Aug. and Sept.

> The breeding race is the pale *E. t. extimus* Phillips. Only two typical specimens of the Great Basin race *E. t. adastus* Oberholser have been taken. The Pacific Coast race *E. t. brewsteri* Oberholser is the abundant transient through southern Arizona, occasional in the northeast.

264. *Contopus musicus* (Swainson). Coues' Flycatcher. Common summer resident of Transition Zone of southeastern and central Arizona, northwest to Prescott and north sparingly to Bakers Butte (Mogollon Rim) and south and west slopes of Blue Range and White Mountains. On migration sometimes found in adjacent Upper Sonoran Zone; exceptionally in lower Whetstone and Baboquivari Mountains, at San Xavier Mission (27 Sept. 1974, D. Stotz), and even along Salt and San Pedro Rivers. A very sparse winter resident, chiefly in deciduous trees, from Patagonia and Tucson west to Yuma and Parker Dam along the Colorado River, north to Wickenburg; and even one singing in the upper Santa Catalina Mountains, 30 Dec. 1950.

> The nominate race is found in Arizona and western and central Mexico. *C. m. pallidiventris* Chapman is apparently a synonym.

265. *Contopus mesoleucus* (W. Deppe). Olive-sided Flycatcher. Fairly common summer resident in extensive boreal zone forests, less common in adjacent ponderosa pine-Gambel oak associations, of northeastern Arizona, west to Kaibab Plateau and south to the entire Mogollon Plateau and (irregularly?) the Sierra Ancha. Fairly common migrant over entire state, less common toward west side.

The breeding race is *C. m. majorinus* (Bangs), but most migrants are the smaller nominate race.

266. *Contopus virens* (Linnaeus). Eastern Wood Pewee. One specimen record: near Tucson, *7 Oct. 1953.* One reportedly was seen and heard singing repeatedly at Guevavi Ranch, Santa Cruz Co., 15 Oct. 1972 (T. Parker et al.); another singing at Phoenix, 14 Sept. 1975 (D. Stejskal); and a third heard at Springerville, early Sept. 1979 (S. Terrill et al.). We seriously doubt that voice identification is reliable unless the bird is in full song, which means SPRING—and even then it should be collected.

267. *Contopus sordidulus* (Sclater). Western Wood Pewee. Common summer resident throughout the Transition Zone, in heavy pinyon stands, in walnut-ash-sycamore associations, and locally near water down to cottonwoods of upper part of Lower Sonoran Zone; also at Pipe Spring National Monument, 1973 (R. Wilt). Breeds west to Baboquivari and Hualapai Mountains. Common transient throughout state.

C. s. "veliei Coues" is the breeding subspecies. The darker northwestern *C. s. saturatus* Bishop migrates over most of Arizona.

268. *Pyrocephalus rubinus* (Boddaert). Vermilion Flycatcher. Common to abundant summer resident in mesquites, willows, and cottonwoods (always near water in the lower, western valleys), in southern and central Arizona north to Globe region, but rather local along the Salt and Colorado Rivers, including the bottom of the Grand Canyon (in recent years) and the Virgin River drainage in the extreme north-west. Also nests locally in sycamore-ash-cottonwood associations. Sparse in spring in Transition Zone, as on Natanes Plateau, Graham Co., 15 Apr. 1937; at Flagstaff, 17 May 1972 (G. Foster); and near Mormon Lake, Coconino Co., 30 Apr. 1975 (Monson). Casual at Snowflake, Apr. 1964 (pair). Two adults and a young male taken 13 km (8 mi) north of Prescott, *10 Sept. 1940* (CM, A.C. Twomey). Winters in moister valleys of most of breeding range, particularly at lower elevations, sparingly or not at all in extreme southeast except at San Bernardino Ranch. An immature male at Eagar, Apache Co., 25 Dec. 1980 (G. Rosenberg), was astonishing. Observed in Washington Co., Utah, 11 Dec. 1963 (W.C. Royall), and 28 Dec. 1965 and 21 Feb. 1966 (R. Wauer). Uncommon transient at or near water in southwestern deserts.

269. *Camptostoma imberbe* Sclater. Beardless Fly-catcher. Fairly common summer resident in cotton-wod, heavy mesquite, canyon hackberry, and even sycamore-evergreen oak-mesquite associations, north to the mouth of the San Pedro River (exceptionally to Verde River east of Phoenix, 4 June 1975 and 21 May 1976, S. Terrill), and from New Mexican border to west side of Baboquivari Mountains (but east of the San Pedro drainage only in Guadalupe Canyon in the extreme southeast and at San Bernar-dino Ranch; also, recorded as "rare" in Cave Creek Canyon, Chiricahua Mountains, Mar. to July 1965, R.P. Balda). Winters in small numbers in the Tucson region, on the east side of the Baboquivaris, in the vicinity of Nogales, and locally along the San Pedro River (including upper Aravaipa Canyon, Graham Co., 1979–80, G.S. Mills, J. Luepke).

FAMILY ALAUDIDAE: LARKS

270. *Eremophila alpestris* (Linnaeus). Horned Lark. Nests in open grasslands throughout the state, and in some farmlands; thus absent during the breeding season in open areas without grass, except irregularly in creosote bush areas in the southwest following wet winters. Winters commonly in same areas, also in fields, parks on the plateaus, and sometimes on barren shores of rivers and lakes and in above-mentioned creosote bush areas. Absent from all brushy or wooded areas. Casual above timberline in the White Mountains.

Subspecies found in Arizona: 1. *E. a. enthymia* (Oberholser) winters fairly commonly in the northeast, less commonly to sparsely elsewhere. *E. a. utahensis* (Behle) is not considered separable. 2. *E. a. lamprochroma* (Oberholser) has been found only in winter and only from Tucson and the Aquarius Mountains of Mohave Co. 3. *E. a. actia* (Oberholser) is hypothetical. Reported at Fort Huachuca, but specimens not locatable by us. Has occurred on Colorado River at Fort Yuma, California. 4. *E. a. ammophila* (Oberholser) has been found once, at Tucson. 5. *E. a. leucansiptila* (Oberholser) is the race of southwestern Arizona, east to the Phoenix region and north to Salome and Congress Junction. Unusual east to Safford. 6. *E. a. occidentalis* (McCall) is the breeding race of central and northern Arizona, south to the Gila Valley. It spreads in winter statewide. We include here *E. a. leucolaema* Coues. 7. *E. a. adusta* (Dwight) is the race of southeastern Arizona, breeding west to Ventana Ranch, Papago Indian Reservation, and north beyond Tucson. Many specimens of Horned Lark exhibit intermediate characters as clines separating the breeding subspecies of Arizona.

FAMILY HIRUNDINIDAE: SWALLOWS

271. *Tachycineta thalassina* (Swainson). Violet-green Swallow. Common summer resident in most of Transition and Canadian Zones, and locally in Upper Sonoran cliffs in the Baboquivari-Quinlan Mountains and near water in the northeast. There are isolated Lower Sonoran Zone colonies in Havasupai Canyon, near Camp Verde, and along the Colorado River (nests on the California side) at Parker Dam. Common throughout state on migration, but irregular and sparse in west in fall. The early return of some birds in late Jan. and Feb. gives an erroneous impression of wintering. A very few mid-winter sight records, from as far east as Tucson and Nogales, in Dec. and early Jan.; mid-winter records of as many as 50 at Phoenix and 150 in the Yuma area surely represent, in large part if not entirely, misidentified Tree Swallows. The statement (A.O.U. Check-list) that it winters up the Colorado River to Needles, California, is erroneous.

Except for one specimen of the small *T. t. brachyptera* Brewster taken at Flagstaff, Arizona birds are of the race *T. t. lepida* Mearns. Colorado River breeding birds may approach *brachyptera,* but almost no material is available.

272. *Tachycineta bicolor* (Vieillot). Tree Swallow. Winters commonly along the lower Colorado River, and occasionally eastward as far as Phoenix and even to Picacho Reservoir in Pinal Co. Generally distributed during migration, usually along streams or at lakes or ponds; reappears in the fall migration as early as the end of June. It has been recorded throughout June at Topock, and has been found nesting on the Kaibab Plateau, *July 1973* (ARIZ, photos, R. and M. Wilson). A nest was found and other adults were carrying nest material at Lee Valley Reservoir, White Mountains, 28 May 1978, and a pair was noted feeding young in the nest at Crescent Lake, also in the White Mountains, 15 July 1979 (D. Stotz et al.). A nest with eggs was found at Cliff in southwestern New Mexico about 40 km (25 mi) from Arizona, 27 June 1968 (J.P. Hubbard). One was seen in the Chuska Mountains, 4 July 1980 (K.V. Rosenberg et al.). Generally, the Tree Swallow is absent from Arizona between mid-May and early July.

273. *Riparia riparia* (Linnaeus). Bank Swallow. Fairly common (sometimes locally abundant in northeast in fall) to uncommon transient at lakes, ponds, irrigated fields, etc., throughout Arizona. One winter record, a single bird over the Colorado River about 15 km (9 mi) below Parker, 23 Dec. 1977 (G. McCaskie).

Arizona birds are of the nominate race.

274. *Stelgidopteryx serripennis* (Audubon). Rough-winged Swallow. Common summer resident in dirt banks of streams throughout Sonoran zones of state, irregular in Transition Zone at Flagstaff. Rather common transient at and along waters; spring southern Arizona arrivals are in late Jan. and early Feb. Winters (irregularly?) in small numbers along Colorado River and at Phoenix (171 counted along Colorado River near Parker on Christmas Bird Count, 23 Dec. 1977!); also recorded sparsely in mid-winter from Tucson and Nogales.

The breeding race (except probably in northeast) is *S. s. psammochrous* Griscom. *S. s. serripennis* (Audubon), of which *S. s. aphractus* Oberholser is a synonym, migrates throughout the state.

275. *Hirundo rustica* Linnaeus. Barn Swallow. Local summer resident in eastern Arizona towns and ranches from San Bernardino Ranch west to Nogales, and north to Willcox and Continental, Pima Co., and

again in the Show Low–Holbrook–St. Johns–Springerville region. It has nested at least once at Mayer,
Yavapai Co. Common in migration at and along
waters and over fields throughout state, dates nearly
spanning the summer. Almost casual in early winter
at Parker, where six seen 20 Dec. 1979 (D. Stotz),
eight on 14 Dec. 1980 (K.V. Rosenberg), and four
on 22 Dec. 1980 (K. Kaufman); at Imperial Dam,
Colorado River, 18 Dec. 1973 (R. Erickson, T.
Schulenberg); and at Phoenix, 26 Dec. 1971 (R.
Witzeman).

276. *Hirundo albifrons* Rafinesque. Cliff Swallow.
Nesting colonies are found almost throughout the
state in the vicinity of water, mainly on cliffs, dams,
bridges, and culverts, but occasionally on buildings,
even in cities (as on buildings of the University of
Arizona campus in recent years). Common transient
at rivers, lakes, fields, etc. statewide, and southward
migration apparently starting in late June. Occasionally seen in the last half of Feb. and in Mar., rarely in
first part of Feb. (near Tucson, *10 Feb. 1948,*
probably wintering). Casual in winter, when it is
normally in South America, at Phoenix (individuals
23 Dec. 1973, B. Burch, and 22 Jan. 1975, R.
Norton).

Arizona subspecies are: 1. The nominate race is perhaps
the breeding bird in the northeast, also a migrant there
as well as in other parts of the state. 2. *H. a. hypopolia*
(Oberholser) is apparently a sparse migrant in both
southern and northern Arizona. It and *H. a. lunifrons*
Say and *H. a. albifrons* Rafinesque are probably
synonyms. 3. *H. a. tachina* (Oberholser) is the breeding
race over most of the state except in the extreme northeast and in the southeast, and is a migrant throughout
Arizona. It is the race that colonized Tucson in the
1960s. 4. *H. a. melanogaster* (Swainson) breeds in the

southeast. *H. a. minima* (van Rossem and Hachisuka) is a synonym.

277. *Hirundo fulva* Vieillot. Cave Swallow. One with Cliff Swallows on the University of Arizona campus, Tucson, *11 May* to about 7 June 1979. First found by D. Stotz, photographed by D. Cook (ARIZ). Found at same place the next year, 11 Apr. to 27 May (Stotz).

278. *Progne subis* (Linnaeus). Purple Martin. Breeds in Transition Zone of open parts of the entire Mogollon Plateau region, and even to such areas as Williams, Mount Trumbull, the Natanes Plateau, the Sierra Ancha, the Prescott region, and (sparsely) the Hualapai Mountains; also in the Chiricahua Mountains, but absent as a breeding bird from Transition Zone in the other mountains of southern Arizona and in the northeast (flocks of unknown origin may be seen in breeding season over the Santa Catalina Mountains). Occurrence on Kaibab Plateau unverified. Also breeds patchily or locally in saguaro associations of south-central Arizona east to the Pajaritos Mountains, west to Organ Pipe Cactus National Monument (since 1967), and north to Wickenburg (K. Kingsley); Picacho, Pinal Co.; Florence; Roosevelt Lake; and the lower San Pedro Valley. Nested away from saguaros in this region only once, at Arivaca in *June 1952.* Sparse outside of breeding ranges, but strays occasionally even to the lower Colorado River on migration and one seen on Beaver Dam Wash, extreme southwestern Utah, 7 May 1964 (D.L. Carter, R.W. Russell). Nineteen were observed in stormy weather at Ganado Lake, Navajo Indian Reservation, 26 May 1979 (K. Kaufman et al.), and a male was seen there 17 May 1980 (H. Richard, M.W. Loder). One (sick?) stayed on at the Arizona-Sonora Desert Museum near Tucson until 22 Dec. in 1974 (Monson). A male seen and heard at the Desert Museum, 6 and 7 Mar. 1976 (S. Alden).

The smaller race nesting in saguaros is tentatively *P. s. hesperia* Brewster, while the birds nesting in the Transition Zone are thought to be *P. s. arboricola* Behle. The occurrence of both subspecies, especially the latter, on migration and at considerable distances from their breeding areas and in mixed roosting flocks, has been detailed in *The Birds of Arizona.*

FAMILY CORVIDAE: JAYS, MAGPIES, AND CROWS

279. *Perisoreus canadensis* (Linnaeus). Gray Jay. Common resident in fir and spruce of the White Mountains.

Arizona birds are of the subspecies *P. c. capitalis* Ridgway.

280. *Cyanocitta cristata* (Linnaeus). Blue Jay. Two records: one just northwest of Page, Coconino Co., 31 Oct. (*Nov. 1*) to 9 Nov. *1976* (ARIZ, photo, J. Middleton); and one seen near Teec Nos Pos, extreme northeastern Arizona, 30 May 1977 (K. Kaufman et al.)

281. *Cyanocitta stelleri* (Gmelin). Steller's Jay. Common resident of pine, fir, and spruce forests throughout state. Winter range extends into evergreen oaks of southern Arizona. Large flights occur in some years into lowlands, especially in southern and western Arizona, when the birds may be found over the entire desert, even to near Yuma. One remained at Organ Pipe Cactus National Monument to 14 June 1968 (R.L. Cunningham).

C. s. diademata (Bonaparte) is the breeding form in all Arizona with the possible exception of the Chuska Mountains, and makes up most of the birds occurring on the desert in flight years. *C. s. macrolopha* Baird is thought to breed in the Chuska Mountains. In some flight years it makes up the larger part of those birds found in the lowlands of southern Arizona.

282. *Aphelocoma coerulescens* (Bosc). Scrub Jay. Common (but local in southern Arizona), west and south to Hualapai and Baboquivari-Quinlan Mountains. In most winters a few descend to Lower Sonoran brush, orchards, and trees, chiefly along the streams of central Arizona, and to brush on Harquahala and Kofa Mountains; and in occasional years it is quite common in such lowland areas throughout the state to the lower Colorado Valley. Migrates across the Mogollon Plateau at Flagstaff in some autumns.

> *A. c. woodhouseii* (Baird) is a pale form that nests over most of Arizona, and seems to make up only a small part of the birds found in the lowland deserts in winter. *A. c. suttoni* Phillips probably nests in the northeast, and is thought to make up the bulk of the birds visiting the desert.

283. *Aphelocoma ultramarina* (Bonaparte). Arizona (Mexican) Jay. Common resident of evergreen oaks in southeastern and central Arizona, west to Baboquivari-Quinlan and Santa Catalina Mountains, and north sparingly to a number of points below the Mogollon Rim as far west as the Mazatzal Mountains of Gila and Maricopa Cos. There are very few records outside the Upper Sonoran Zone, mainly from the adjacent pine forests.

> The form found in Arizona is *A. u. arizonae* (Ridgway).

284. *Cissilopha sanblasiana* (Lafresnaye). San Blas Jay. Accidental. Two taken from flock of about eight near Tucson, *19 Dec. 1937;* one in same locality, *19 Dec. 1938,* and another there *15 Jan.*

1939. Statement in *Birding* IX(6):264(m) that these probably escaped from captivity is negated by the specimens themselves.

The race is *C. s. nelsoni* Bangs and Penard.

285. *Pica pica* (Linnaeus). Common (Black-billed) Magpie. Common resident in recent years (since about 1970) at Teec Nos Pos in the extreme northeast, and southward between Many Farms and Round Rock, all on the Navajo Indian Reservation. Prior to 1970 a scarce visitant in the same area, but before 1885 said to be common in parts of northeastern Arizona. The occupied habitat consists of cottonwoods along drainages, and orchards. Also two old specimens: near Winslow, *8 Dec. 1853,* and nestling from Rio Puerco at Navajo Springs, Apache Co., *27 June 1873.* Sparse in fall in northwestern Arizona north of the Grand Canyon, with records from Crystal Springs, Kaibab Plateau, 7 Nov. 1968 (H.G. Reynolds), and House Rock Valley east of the Kaibab Plateau, 13 Oct. 1973 (D.E. Brown), west to the Mt. Trumbull area, 30 Oct. 1968 (J.H. Riffey) and 21 Oct. to 28 Dec. 1968 (P. Bundy), and north to Utah line; also one at Las Vegas Bay, Lake Mead, Nevada, 27 Oct. 1972 (photo, C.S. Lawson).

286. *Corvus corax* Linnaeus. Common Raven. Fairly common resident almost throughout open parts of Arizona wherever nesting cliffs or trees are available. Sparse in Flagstaff area, lower Colorado Valley below Ehrenberg, and as a summer resident near Phoenix. Large congregations occur in northern and eastern Arizona at times.

C. c. sinuatus Wagler is the form breeding in Arizona.

287. *Corvus cryptoleucus* Couch. White-necked Raven. Common summer resident of yucca-mesquite-grassland association of southeastern Arizona (including the city of Nogales) north to Safford area, ranging fairly commonly into lower, less grassy brush, especially in upper Santa Cruz Valley. Limits of nesting range uncertain, but may extend to west edge of Papago Indian Reservation. Winters over most of breeding range, although large numbers appear to leave in conspicuous migrations in mid-Nov. Casual north to Pine, Gila Co., *June 1967* (REA, skeleton, R. Fuller). The two species of raven area easily confused; the so-called "white" neck is not a usable field criterion.

288. *Corvus brachyrhynchos* Brehm. Common Crow. Locally common resident of open parts of entire Mogollon Plateau, down Salt River to its confluence with the Verde, and down the San Francisco River to Clifton; also in the Chuska Mountains and the Defiance Plateau of the Navajo Indian Reservation, and perhaps elsewhere in the north, especially along the South Rim of the Grand Canyon. During winter may be seen in adjacent areas, as far from the breeding range as the Big Sandy and lower Colorado Valleys (up to 70 along Colorado River in Arizona above Needles, California, Jan.–Mar. 1973, and about 300 in the winter of 1978–79; astonishingly, more than 600 in the winter of 1976–77, and more than 1000 in Nov.–Dec. 1978 and in Nov. 1979 at Cibola National Wildlife Refuge along the Colorado River in Yuma Co.). Crows have also been found in summer in the Prescott and central Gila Co. areas, but nests haven't been found.

C. b. hesperis Ridgway has been taken across northern Arizona in the winter. Birds breeding north of the Mogollon Plateau possibly may be referable to this race, but additional specimens are needed, especially adults. *C. b. hargravei* Phillips, with larger wing and tail, breeds principally along the Mogollon Rim, winters there and in valleys below the Rim; probably also north of Mogollon Plateau, but specimens are needed. The wintering birds in the west have been undetermined.

289. *Gymnorhinus cyanocephalus* Wied. Pinyon Jay. Common resident of juniper-pinyon regions in northern and central Arizona (south possibly to Prescott area and Natanes Plateau north of San Carlos, and west to at least the Hualapai Indian Reservation and the Mount Trumbull area). Sometimes invades adjacent forests. Wanders erratically in large flocks in fall and spring (less common in winter), individuals or small groups sometimes reaching the southwestern part of Arizona and the lower Colorado River.

290. *Nucifraga columbiana* (Wilson). Clark's Nutcracker. Common resident in boreal zones to timberline in the San Francisco and White Mountains, also on the Kaibab Plateau and possibly in the Chuska Mountains and on Bill Williams Mountain; has bred casually on South Rim of Grand Canyon (1943). During fall and winter there are occasional large-scale invasions of other mountains (with intermediate invasions on a much reduced scale), when it ranges sparsely also into lower country, even to the Colorado River and the Mexican border in the southwest; following these the birds may linger well into the summer in mountains, and even at Boulder City, Nevada, as in 1951. (One seen at Bahia de Los Angeles, Baja California, 12 Nov. 1972, R. Chapin.)

FAMILY LANIIDAE: SHRIKES

291. *Lanius excubitor* Linnaeus. Northern Shrike. Apparently regular, but uncommon, in open parts of Upper Sonoran and Transition Zones in winter from the Mogollon Plateau northward and northwestward, especially from Fredonia and Flagstaff east to New Mexico. Reports from southern Arizona may be questionable, owing to confusion with the following species. One was seen repeatedly near Elgin in Santa Cruz Co., 15 Dec. 1974 to 22 Mar. 1975 (G.S. Mills et al.); one was carefully identified near Portal, 30

Dec. 1976 (J. and R. Witzeman); one was found near Poston, Yuma Co., *9 Jan. 1978* (ARIZ, M. Lange); and one was photographed at Arlington, Maricopa Co., *10 Nov. 1979* (ARIZ, K. Ingram).

Arizona birds are referable to *L. e. borealis* Vieillot unless *L. e. invictus* Grinnell is truly separable.

292. *Lanius ludovicianus* Linnaeus. Loggerhead Shrike. More or less common summer resident throughout open parts of state (except in brushless grassland) below Transition Zone, rather uncommon (at least in midsummer) along Mexican border west of Baboquivari Mountains. Fairly common transient in Transition Zone, at least in fall. Winters commonly in Lower Sonoran Zone, less commonly in open Upper Sonoran Zone even into evergreen oaks.

The breeding race is *L. l. excubitorides* Swainson, in which we include *L. l. sonoriensis* Miller and *L. l. nevadensis* Miller. *L. l. gambeli* Ridgway winters statewide, when it may outnumber *excubitorides* in the north but is perhaps less common in the south. Both races migrate across the Mogollon Plateau.

FAMILY PARIDAE: TITMICE, VERDINS, AND BUSHTITS

293. *Parus atricapillus* Linnaeus. Black-capped Chickadee. The only Arizona specimen is from Betatakin Ruin, Navajo National Monument, *23 Oct. 1936,* where up to ten at a time were seen throughout Oct. 1935. Other records are: Pipe Spring National Monument, Christmas Bird Counts in 1963, 1967, and 1978; one in cottonwoods at Teec Nos Pos, extreme northeastern Arizona, 26 Nov. 1976 (D. Stotz, J. and R. Witzeman) and *2 Feb. 1977* (ARIZ, photo, Monson). The species breeds along the San Juan River in extreme north-western New Mexico.

Arizona birds probably are *P. a. garrinus* Behle or *P. a. nevadensis* (Linsdale).

294. *Parus gambeli* Ridgway. Mountain Chickadee.
Common resident in pine and spruce-fir forests,
locally into pinyon-juniper in northeast, throughout
mountains except Hualapais and Mexican border
ranges. Two were noted in the Hualapais in July
1977 (K.V. Rosenberg, A. Higgins) and one 10 Aug.
1979 (B. Parfitt, M. Butterwick), as were a few at
high elevations in the Huachucas in 1971 and 1973–
74 in the breeding period (C. McMoran). In winter
ranges uncommonly into Upper and rarely Lower
Sonoran Zone areas adjacent to its breeding range in
northern Arizona, and at Tucson and Phoenix,
casually to the Colorado River (one seen 14 Nov.
1976 in Bill Williams Delta vicinity was monitored
through the winter and collected *19 Mar. 1977,*
ARIZ, K.V. Rosenberg; and two at Cibola National
Wildlife Refuge, Yuma Co., month of Dec. 1977, P.
Mack).

The nominate race occupies the central and southern
parts of the state. *P. g. inyoensis* (Grinnell) occupies
the Williams area westward, and in winter has reached
Bill Williams Delta and Mammoth, lower San Pedro
Valley. It has been taken in the Carrizo Mountains,
Navajo Indian Reservation, *18 Oct. 1978* (US, J.T.
Marshall). *P. g. wasatchensis* Behle is found on both
rims of the Grand Canyon, and is also the form found
eastward and northeastward from there. In winter it
descends to the Lower Sonoran Zone at Supai, Cataract
Canyon.

295. *Parus sclateri* Kleinschmidt.Mexican Chick-
adee. Common resident in pine and spruce-fir forests
of the Chiricahua Mountains. There is a winter sight
record for adjacent, lower Swisshelm Mountains
which are southwest of the Chiricahua Mountains
(20 Jan. 1924). A specimen labeled "Huachuca
Mts." was doubtless actually taken in Chihuahua.
One was taken in Clanton Canyon, Peloncillo Mountains, New Mexico side, *1 July 1963* (University of

Michigan, J.P. Hubbard). Sight records for the Santa Catalina Mountains have yet to be verified and are unlikely.

296. *Parus wollweberi* (Bonaparte). Bridled Titmouse. Common resident of Upper Sonoran woodlands of southeastern and central Arizona, north to Mogollon Rim (as at Oak Creek Canyon), and west to Juniper, Weaver, Pinal, and Baboquivari Mountains. Nests in Lower Sonoran Zone willow-cottonwood-mesquite locally, at least in Camp Verde region and along lower San Pedro River upstream to mouth of Aravaipa Creek; may have nested in 1950s in the Tucson vicinity. Regular winter visitant to willow-cottonwood association along larger streams and in city parks in southern and central Arizona, west to Phoenix and Sacaton. A sight record from above Supai, Cataract Canyon, 23 Sept. 1950 (Phillips); another sight record from near the bottom of the central Grand Canyon, 17 Mar. 1975 (S. Stockton); and a specimen from the Planet Ranch, lower Bill Williams River, *21 Mar. 1977* (ARIZ, A. Higgins; first noted 17 Feb. by J. Bays).

The race found in Arizona is *P. w. phillipsi* van Rossem.

297. *Parus inornatus* Gambel. Plain Titmouse. Fairly common to common resident in Upper Sonoran Zone of northeastern, northern, central, and locally southeastern Arizona; west to Mount Trumbull and the Cerbat, Hualapai, Bradshaw, Superstition, Galiuro, and Chiricahua Mountains. Has been noted in winter in Redington Pass between the Santa Catalina and Rincon Mountains (1972 and 1973, R. Chapin et al.; 1980, W. Hopf). Casual at foot of Santa Catalina Mountains, *28 Nov. 1928,* and in bottom of Grand Canyon, *18 Nov. 1912;* also at east foot of Rincon Mountains, 14 Feb. 1971 (J. Ambrose).

Arizona birds are the gray *P. i. ridgwayi* Richmond, of which *P. i. plumbescens* (Grinnell) is a synonym.

298. ***Psaltriparus minimus*** (Townsend). Bushtit.
Rather common resident of Upper Sonoran woodlands, and even chaparral and scrub oaks, throughout Arizona, including the Harquahala Mountains.
Wandering flocks are sometimes seen in other zones,
including mesquite thickets and fir forest, July to
Mar. One record from Mohave Mountains, southwestern Mohave Co., *27 Apr. 1938*. Nested once in
palo verde along Salt River east of Phoenix (near
Blue Point cottonwoods, Feb.–Apr. 1973, R.R.
Johnson and J. Simpson); in desert scrub at Roosevelt Lake, spring of 1980 (K.V. Rosenberg); and in
grape vine below Patagonia Lake, Santa Cruz Co.,
20 Mar. 1973 (Monson, T. Parker). In recent
winters has occurred, usually in small numbers, to
Colorado Valley (including one specimen in the Bill
Williams Delta, *2 Dec. 1975,* ARIZ, K.V. Rosenberg;
and two specimens on or about *26 Feb. 1977* from
flock of ten about 16 km [10 mi] north of Ehrenberg,
Yuma Co., ARIZ, A. Higgins, D. Wells).

   P. m. plumbeus (Baird) is the race found in northeastern Arizona. Birds of the remainder of the state are
   the shorter-tailed *P. m. lloydi* Sennett, from which *P.
   m. cecaumenorum* Thayer and Bangs and *P. m.
   providentialis* Arvey are apparently inseparable.

299. ***Auriparus flaviceps*** (Sundevall). Verdin.
Fairly common resident of the entire Lower Sonoran
Zone except bottom of Grand Canyon, and including the Virgin River Valley of the extreme northwest;
also among mesquites and even evergreen oaks along
lower edge of Upper Sonoran Zone. Casual near
Prescott in Upper Sonoran Zone, *10 Sept. 1940*
(CM, A.C. Twomey). Has evidently increased with
the spread of mesquite.

   A. f. acaciarum Grinnell is confined to the Colorado
   River and the southwest. Birds farther east become
   darker and are intermediates toward *A. f. ornatus*
   (Lawrence).

FAMILY SITTIDAE: NUTHATCHES

300. *Sitta carolinensis* Latham. White-breasted Nuthatch. Common resident throughout Transition and lower Canadian Zones, also locally among larger trees of the Upper Sonoran Zone (though no nesting record for Baboquivari Mountains); also locally in riparian Lower Sonoran Zone (Santa Cruz Valley). Fairly regular, Aug. to early Apr., in nearby Upper Sonoran Zone, in major flight years even to lower Colorado River (Bill Williams Delta, *10 Nov. 1950;* and near north end of Imperial National Wildlife Refuge, 28 Oct. 1955, Monson, and *26 Nov. 1961,* US, Monson).

> *S. c. nelsoni* Mearns is the resident Arizona race. *S. c. aculeata* Cassin of the western coast ranges was taken at the mouth of the Verde River, *30 Sept. 1950,* a major flight year. *S. c. tenuissima* Grinnell comes into the western half of Arizona during flight winters.

301. *Sitta canadensis* Linnaeus. Red-breasted Nuthatch. Resident in all, or nearly all, of boreal zones. During the fall sometimes found in Transition and Sonoran Zones, usually in large trees but casually in desert shrubs, ranging west to Colorado River in flight years; most regular as a fall transient in mountains and mesas of the north, west to Hualapai Mountains. One casual summer record from Tuba City, western Navajo Indian Reservation, *2 July 1936.*

302. *Sitta pygmaea* Vigors. Pygmy Nuthatch. Abundant resident in ponderosa pines throughout Arizona, and to some extent in adjacent heavy pinyon-juniper. Wanders to timberline, once to bottom of Grand Canyon, and a few times to lowlands (Phoenix; Superior; Tucson; Babocomari River, northwest of Sierra Vista, Cochise Co.; Patagonia; and even to Yuma, *20 Sept. 1902*—specimen lost).

Two were noted at Boulder City, Nevada, 8 Aug.
1950 (W.M. Pulich).

All extant Arizona specimens are *S. p. melanotis* van
Rossem.

FAMILY CERTHIIDAE: CREEPERS

303. *Certhia americana* Bonaparte. Brown Creeper.
Rather common summer resident of boreal zones
and, in the south, Transition Zone, throughout
Arizona, west to Kaibab Plateau and Bradshaw and
Santa Rita Mountains. Winters fairly commonly
through Transition Zone and Upper Sonoran Zone
woodlands. Sparse winter visitant in large trees
along rivers, particularly in Camp Verde and Tucson
areas (where not uncommon in some winters), and
west to lower Colorado River. One singing in Hualapai Mountains, 21 June 1978 (K.V. Rosenberg),
where at least two seen 27 July 1977 (Rosenberg, A.
Higgins).

The Arizona forms: 1. The eastern and nominate race
was collected several times near Tucson from *1936* to
1954, and is about equally as numerous in winter in the
southern and western lowlands as the following. 2. *C.
a. montana* Ridgway breeds in those mountains north
of the Chiricahua and Rincon Mountains, migrating to
lower areas after the breeding season, including the
Lower Sonoran Zone. The population at Prescott is
variably intermediate toward *C. a. leucosticta* van
Rossem (according to A.M. Rea). 3. *C. a. albescens*
Berlepsch is resident in the Huachuca and Santa Rita
Mountains. Intergrades with it and *montana* occur in
the Chiricahua and Rincon Mountains. 4. *C. a. zelotes*
Osgood is occasional (three specimens) in southern
Arizona, and also was taken near Prescott in *Oct. 1979*
(SD, Rea). A specimen from Cazador Spring, San

Carlos Indian Reservation, reported in *The Birds of Arizona* as *C. a. caurina* Aldrich, upon reexamination proves to be intermediate *zelotes* X *occidentalis* Ridgway.

FAMILY CINCLIDAE: DIPPERS

304. *Cinclus mexicanus* Swainson. Dipper. Fairly common resident along the few clear, swift, permanent mountain streams of Arizona, along the southern rim of the Mogollon Plateau from Oak Creek Canyon to Black River and Eagle Creek, in the general White Mountains region, and in the bottom of the Grand Canyon. It is also found sparingly in the rougher parts of the Chuska Mountains, Sierra Ancha, and Pinaleno and Santa Catalina Mountains, but not yet known to nest in the last two ranges. In recent years (1970–79) has been found more or less regularly in winter in Cave Creek Canyon of the Chiricahuas and Ramsey Canyon of the Huachucas—this perhaps due more to a large increase in observers in these areas than to any change in numbers; only one or two individuals are found each season, however. An unsuccessful nest with eggs in Cave Creek Canyon, May *1973* (photo, *3 May,* ARIZ, W. Spofford). Old records from the Huachuca Mountains in Aug. 1902 and *28 May 1903*. Rarely wanders at almost any time of the year to other mountain streams, as near Castle Hot Springs, Yavapai Co., Jan. 1965 (according to S. Demaree), and near Fort Rock, eastern Mohave Co., 7 Nov. 1950. Even more unusual records were those of individuals in a steep potholed canyon on the north side of Kitt Peak, Quinlan Mountains, *18 Jan. 1975* (ARIZ, photo, A. Hesselberg), and at Parker, 22 Oct. 1980 (L. Abbott, R. Martin et al.).

C. m. unicolor Bonaparte is the race generally found in Arizona, including a specimen from the Chiricahuas. The Huachuca specimen is of the darker nominate form.

FAMILY TROGLODYTIDAE: WRENS

305. ***Troglodytes troglodytes*** (Linnaeus). Winter Wren. Local and sparse to uncommon winter resident, generally in the densest brush of the more permanent streams, from the Transition Zone down to the Lower Sonoran Zone, in various parts of the state, including the lower Colorado Valley. It can be seen even at isolated places where a small amount of water and some lush vegetation is present, as at the Arizona-Sonora Desert Museum near Tucson, 23 Mar. 1975 (Monson).

Arizona birds, east to Alpine (*Nov. 1935*), are one of the dark northwestern mainland races, *T. t. pacificus* Baird or the very similar *T. t. salebrosus* Burleigh; but a photograph of a Portal bird, *21 Nov. 1976* (ARIZ, W. Spofford) seems to be paler, at least ventrally, and probably represents *T. t. hiemalis* Vieillot, which is to be expected in eastern Arizona. Additional specimens from eastern Arizona are badly needed.

306. ***Troglodytes domesticus*** (Wilson). Northern House Wren. Common summer resident in dense brush and fallen trees from Transition Zone to timberline in all mountains possessing forests. Winters commonly in better-vegetated areas of Lower Sonoran Zone of southwestern Arizona and the lower Colorado Valley east to the Phoenix region, Tucson, and Patagonia, sparsely farther east (even to upper Huachuca and Chiricahua Mountains) and north (one Pipe Spring National Monument, Dec. 1973, R. Wilt; and one at Springerville, 16 Dec. 1978, Christmas Bird Count). In migration common in southwestern Arizona, fairly common northeastward where chiefly restricted to permanent streams. Two seen on Verde River east of Phoenix, 29 May 1975 (S. Terrill), were very late.

T. d. parkmanii Audubon is the race found throughout the western United States. Some intermediates toward *T. d. cahooni* Brewster breed in the Huachuca and Santa Rita Mountains, occasionally in the Chiricahuas to the Pinalenos, and have been designated as *T. d. vorhiesi* Brandt; supposedly resident north to the Rincon Mountains. *Vorhiesi* is assigned by the A.O.U. Check-list to a separate species, *"T. brunneicollis* Sclater,"* the "Brown-throated Wren."

307. *Troglodytes bewickii* (Audubon). Bewick's Wren. Common to abundant resident in Upper Sonoran brush and woodland from the Mogollon Rim south and west, to mouth of Verde River and the southern tip of Nevada and the Topock area along the Colorado River; found nesting at Planet Ranch on the lower Bill Williams River in 1978 (K.V. Rosenberg). Summer resident locally and generally uncommon in pinyon-juniper zone over the rest of the state, and in mesquite–willow–cottonwood association along parts of Lower Sonoran Zone rivers. Winters commonly throughout that part of its breeding range that lies south and west of the Mogollon Plateau, along streams in extreme southwestern Utah, and among dense weeds and brush of the Lower Sonoran Zone west to the Colorado River, less commonly on the Hualapai Indian Reservation, at Pipe Spring National Monument, the west side of the Navajo Indian Reservation, and at Springerville. Sparse in extreme western Arizona in winter in the 1950s. Migrates sparsely across the Mogollon Plateau.

Arizona birds are nearly all of the palest, grayest United States race, *T. b. "eremophilus* Oberholser." A specimen from Bard, California, near Yuma, *18 Dec. 1923* (SD, L.M. Huey) is the dark, shorter-tailed southwestern California race *T. b. charienturus* Oberholser, while another from Bard, *13 Dec. 1916* (SD, Huey) is nearest *T. b. drymoecus* Oberholser, paler and more reddish than *charienturus.* A bird from Calabasas (a former location at the joining of Sonoita Creek and the Santa Cruz River), *22 Oct. 1889* (US, L. Stejneger) is *T. b. cryptus* Oberholser, which breeds in Kansas, Oklahoma, and much (?) of New Mexico, as are one from Patagonia, *18 Feb. 1952* (DEL, Phillips) and one from Virden, Hidalgo Co., New Mexico, *26 Dec. 1952* (LSU, K.W. Haller).

308. ***Campylorhynchus brunneicapillus*** (Lafresnaye). Cactus Wren. Common resident almost throughout the Lower Sonoran Zone, especially in cholla cactus, but also in open mesquite trees and shade trees in towns; lacking only along the Colorado River above upper Lake Mead. It is a common resident in extreme southwestern Utah (according to W.H. Behle and S.P. Hedges), and it also has been found in the Grand Wash Cliffs in extreme northwestern Arizona (J.H. and M.M. Riffey). Recently it has been found in the upper Verde Valley, east of and at Montezuma Well, Yavapai Co., 20 Jan. 1975 (A. S. Hyde) and 30 Mar. 1979 (C.S. Tomoff); along Spring Creek near Oak Creek, 1979–80 (S. Emslie, Tomoff); east of Camp Verde, 1979–80 (Tomoff); and one calling near Clarkdale, 11 Oct. 1977 (Tomoff).

Arizona birds are of the large pale northwestern race *C. b. anthonyi* (Mearns), with heavy black spotting concentrated on the lower throat and chest.

309. ***Cistothorus palustris*** (Wilson). Long-billed Marsh Wren. Local resident along the lower Colorado River and in marshes of the lower Gila and Salt

Rivers as far upstream as Granite Reef Dam, also possibly at Picacho Reservoir and near Arizona City, both Pinal Co. (R.L. Todd), although no nests found there yet. Common winter resident and migrant at reed-grown ponds and canals, including Tuba City, western Navajo Indian Reservation, in winter; less common in winter at frozen marshes on and near the Mogollon Plateau and in the Flagstaff region.

Resident birds are dark and are currently referred to *C. p. aestuarinus* Swarth, when that race is distinguished from *C. p. paludicola* (Baird); these disperse somewhat to an unknown extent after breeding, at least to Wikieup in the Big Sandy Valley. *C. p. plesius* (Oberholser) and the duller *C. p. pulverius* (Aldrich) are the common migrant and wintering birds. The brighter, redder *C. p. laingi* (Harper) is a sparse fall transient in the southeast (two specimens, US).

[*Cistothorus platensis* (Latham). Short-billed Marsh Wren. Hypothetical. Three or four reported from Arizona portion of San Simon Cienega, on the Arizona-New Mexico boundary, 10 Dec. 1979 (R.J. Morse).]

310. *Catherpes mexicanus* (Swainson). Canyon Wren. Rather common resident about cliffs, hills, and adjacent buildings and even high dirt banks in Sonoran zones throughout Arizona near available water, but quite uncommon and variable over the years in southwest, and along lower Colorado River not farther south than Parker Dam. Ranges exceptionally into low Transition Zone during late summer, but also may breed there locally, as south of Williams. A considerable movement into the region in and about Phoenix was noted in Oct.–Nov. 1979 (several observers; photo, ARIZ, K.V. Rosenberg).

The small, pale, somewhat reddish *C. m. conspersus* Ridgway is the only race known so far in Arizona, though many specimens from the southeast, south from Tucson, approach somewhat the darker *C. m. meliphonus* Oberholser of northwestern Mexico. No specimens of winter visitors are available.

311. *Salpinctes obsoletus* (Say). Rock Wren. Common summer resident in open rocky situations from timberline and above down to Upper Sonoran Zone, though locally scarce recently (e.g., Hualapai Mountains, San Francisco Peaks); less common in Lower Sonoran Zone, including dirt banks along streams (as at Santa Cruz River at Tucson, 23 May 1975, Monson), but present in scattered, small numbers to the low desert mountains ranges of Yuma Co. and in the Colorado Valley as far south as Parker Dam. Winters commonly in open, broken areas of the Sonoran zones of southern Arizona, but mostly absent then in northeastern Arizona east of Tuba City area and to the north of Holbrook (one seen at Ganado, 16 Dec. 1979, M.W. Loder).

The Rock Wren of Arizona is of the widespread pale nominate form.

FAMILY MIMIDAE: MOCKINGBIRDS AND THRASHERS

312. *Mimus polyglottos* (Linnaeus). Northern Mockingbird. Rather common summer resident in the less densely wooded parts of the Sonoran zones that afford thornbrush, including many towns and cities. Less common except in wettest years west of the Baboquivari Mountains, the mouth of the Salt River, and the Kingman region. Especially common resident of Maricopa Co. cities and Yuma. Winters commonly in most of southwestern Arizona west of Santa Cruz Valley and south from Roosevelt Lake, Wickenburg, and Davis Dam, and in upper Gila Valley; less commonly in and near Tucson and Safford, and, at least in some years, the lower canyons of the Santa Rita and Huachuca Mountains; exceptionally in southeastern Arizona aside from areas previously noted, and near Supai, Cataract Canyon. Three recorded at Springerville, 24 Dec. 1979 (Christmas Bird Count). Migrant and wanderer on Mogollon Plateau. Only a straggler in open pine–grass (Transition Zone) in Arizona, though common there locally in northern Sonora. There are peculiar seasonal fluctuations in the numbers of Mocking-birds in southern Arizona still not fully understood.

Arizona birds are the widespread northern nominate race, of which *M. p. leucopterus* (Vigors) is a synonym.

313. *Lucar carolinensis* (Linnaeus). Gray Catbird. Locally a fairly common resident in dense bush-willow association (Transition and high Upper Sonoran Zones) in the Springerville-Greer region (also one nest at Show Low in 1937); possibly also in recent past in Oak Creek Canyon and on the west side of the Chuska Mountains. Otherwise sparse, only about 15 records to the end of 1980, from Pipe Spring National Monument, 31 May 1979 (K. Kaufman), Lees Ferry, Coconino Co., and Four Corners, Colorado (*22 May 1913*, DEN, H.H. Sheldon) in the north to Phoenix and eastward in the south (with one exception, a record from the lower Bill Williams River, 26 Sept. 1978, B. Whitney). Only one southern or central Arizona specimen (*16 Oct. 1956*, SWRS, P. Marshall). One seen singing near confluence of Little Colorado River with its South Fork, west of Springerville, 25 Dec. 1980 (S. Parker).

Arizona specimens are *L. c. ruficrissa* (Aldrich), with paler crissum (sex for sex).

314. *Toxostoma rufum* (Linneaus). Brown Thrasher. Sparse fall and winter visitor to chiefly the Sonoran zones of southern Arizona, mostly in recent years. In the north, eight singles reported in all, including three in summer; and one in winter at Springerville, 16 Dec. 1978 (Christmas Bird Count).

Arizona specimens are *T. r. longicauda* (Baird), the large pale western race.

315. *Toxostoma bendirei* (Coues). Bendire's Thrasher. Rather common to local summer resident of the open parts of the Sonoran valleys almost statewide, except for Sulphur Springs Valley (where breeding is unproven although singing birds present in spring), and the plains north of Williams (including entire Grand Canyon region). Found especially where stretches of open ground meet tall dense bushes and/or cholla cacti. Winters, mostly sparingly, from the Phoenix, Casa Grande, and Coolidge areas southeast to Tucson; even more scarcely farther south and east to near Nogales, Portal, and even possibly to southwest of Duncan in Greenlee Co., but not farther west than northwestern Maricopa Co. and possibly the Ajo Mountains (one reportedly spent winter of 1978–79 at farmhouse near Yuma, V. Hink et al.). Migrants apparently return to Tucson and Sulphur Springs Valley in late Jan., and possibly to Duncan area (T.B. Johnson) in mid-Jan.

316. *Toxostoma curvirostre* (Swainson). Curve-billed Thrasher. Very common resident of cholla cactus association, rather common in other dense thorny brush and even in towns, of the Lower Sonoran Zone west to the Growler and Kofa Mountains, the Big Sandy River, and possibly west to the Hualapai Mountains; uncommon to sparse west of Growler Mountains to Cabeza Prieta Mountains. Local in extreme southeast (including Sulphur Springs Valley). Sparse fall, mostly winter, straggler to the Colorado River, Camp Verde, Fort Apache, and southeastern Nevada.

The nominate race is found in the extreme southeast. From there west for a short distance occur intergrades of atypical *curvirostre* at higher altitudes, and *T. c. palmeri* (Coues) in the valleys; *palmeri,* lacking white in the wings and tail, is the race of most of Arizona. A specimen (US) from Ash Creek, Pinaleno Mountains, is also close to *curvirostre* (of which *T. c. celsum* Moore is a synonym).

317. *Toxostoma lecontei* Lawrence. LeConte's Thrasher. Uncommon, usually very local, resident in open creosote bush, low scattered mesquite, and salt bush deserts of extreme western and southwestern Arizona, east in the Gila Valley even to near Queen Creek in Pinal Co. between Queen Creek (town) and Florence Jct., pair with nest, end of Mar. 1978 (K. Kaufman), and near the Coolidge-Florence airport south-southeast of Coolidge, singing male, at the same time (Kaufman), and farther southeast as far as the western side of the Avra Valley, Pima Co. (but on the main Papago Indian Reservation not found southeast of the Santa Rosa Valley). Formerly found in the Gila Valley east to the Florence region. Permanent residence remains to be proven in some areas north of the Gila Valley. Apparently lacking in the Wikieup-Kingman-Hoover Dam region, so a specimen from Union Pass between Kingman and Davis Dam in *Sept. 1865* may have been a vagrant or migrant. This thrasher has been found in extreme southwestern Utah (according to Behle et al.), but its status there and in adjacent Arizona is unclear.

The pale nominate race is the one found in Arizona.

318. *Toxostoma crissale* Henry. Crissal Thrasher. Common resident in dense, tall brush along rivers, larger washes, and brushy canyons of Lower Sonoran Zone; locally in dense broad-leafed chaparral, in open rocky situations with dense brush patches, and in deep brush in otherwise open situations, in Upper Sonoran Zone, south and west of the Mogollon Plateau; but absent in the deserts west of Growler Mountains and Papago Well in western Pima Co.

Has been observed in summer in the Toroweap Valley, Grand Canyon National Park (R.R. Johnson). It is a permanent resident in extreme southwestern Utah (according to W.H. Behle). Uncommon fall migrant in northern Arizona: from near South Rim of Grand Canyon east to lower Little Colorado Valley and even the Shumway-Concho area, where it could possibly be resident (seen in July 1876). One seen at or near Pipe Spring National Monument, 28 Dec. 1966 (Christmas Bird Count) and 24 Jan. 1973 (R. Wilt).

The nominate race occurs over most of Arizona. *T. c. coloradense* van Rossem is found along the Colorado and Big Sandy Rivers, with possible stragglers farther east; it is the palest race.

319. *Oreoscoptes montanus* (Townsend). Sage Thrasher. Fairly common summer resident of sage-brush areas of northeastern and possibly north-western Arizona, south possibly but sparsely to Springerville. Fairly common migrant on open plains, often abundant from Avra Valley, Pima Co., west and northwest in spring. Usually less common as a winter resident in sparse brush or scattered juniper of Sonoran Zone plains and low foothills of southern Arizona, decidedly uncommon along lower Colorado River; also found in winter in the Little Colorado Valley as far up as Springerville, and perhaps in the extreme northwest. Sparse migrant across higher plateaus. Casual (juvenile) near Gleeson, west of Elfrida, Cochise Co., *4 June 1940,* and seen at Flagstaff 11 Dec. 1938, and 7 Nov. 1975 (G. Foster).

FAMILY TURDIDAE: THRUSHES, BLUEBIRDS, AND SOLITAIRES

320. *Turdus migratorius* Linnaeus. American Robin. Common summer resident of openings in Transition and boreal zones, and now locally in moist Upper Sonoran woodland along the main canyons (as at Patagonia), throughout Arizona, including the Hualapai Mountains recently (two seen, one singing, June 1978, K.V. Rosenberg, M.L. Lange, and one seen 19 June 1979, S. Goldwasser et al.). Since 1965, one or more pairs have nested each summer in Tucson; in 1977, a pair nested at Blythe, California (Anita Higgins et al.); in 1977 and probably 1978 nesting took place in Willow Valley, on the Arizona side of the Colorado River and above Needles, California (according to Rosenberg); and in 1980 at Phoenix (S. Demaree, H. Longstreth). Also reported in summer in the Tucson Mountains, 5 *June 1964* (US, S.H. Levy); at Littlefield in the extreme northwest, 10 June 1964 (including juvenile, D.L. Carter); at Poston, Yuma Co., 4 July 1978 (according to Rosenberg); at Parker, 16 Aug. 1953; near Kingman, *12 June 1959*; and in the Cerbat Mountains of Mohave Co., about 1960. Winters commonly to abundantly in berry-bearing Upper Sonoran woodlands and in large towns of the Sonoran zones, somewhat irregularly in mistletoe-mesquite association, and uncommonly in Transition Zone.

Arizona birds are the pale *T. m. propinquus* Ridgway, with little or no white in the tail.

321. *Turdus rufo-palliatus* Lafresnaye. Rufous-backed Robin. A west Mexican species that has occurred since 1965 as a fall-winter visitor in southern Arizona every year but 1979, following its first occurrence in *1960* near Nogales. As many as ten individuals were reported in 1975–76, and generally one can expect about five to appear in any given year. The species has been found as far east as Guadalupe Canyon, as far west as the Phoenix region, and one was reported near Bridal Veil Falls, Cataract Canyon, 15 Nov. 1975 (T.L. Danielson). It is usually found in Arizona in deciduous tree situations, especially in fruiting canyon hackberries. Practically all Arizona records fall between 21 Oct. and 18 Apr.; one was found near Patagonia, 27 June 1975 (D. Stotz), and one was reported from Guadalupe Canyon, 3 to 4 June 1980 (C.R. Brown et al.).

322. *Geocichla naevia* (Gmelin). Varied Thrush. Although found in *1956, 1958,* 1965, and 1970, this species did not occur more than rarely in Arizona until 1972–73; since then it has been found in very small numbers as a winter visitor across southern Arizona (except in 1974 and 1976). Most of the records have come from the Tucson Valley and, in 1977–78, from the lower Colorado Valley–Bill Williams Delta area. However, it has occurred as far east as the east side of the Chiricahua Mountains; north to near Prescott, 20 Dec. 1977 (V. Miller); just below the Utah line at Moccasin, Mohave Co., 29 Sept. 1974 (R. Wilt) (exceptionally early!); and at Tuweep Ranger Station, North Rim of Grand Canyon, 30 Nov. to 2 Dec. 1977 (photo, L. Haight et al.). May occur as high as Transition Zone (Flagstaff region, several records). Generally found in heavy riparian or irrigated woodland, including that in mountain canyons.

The racially identifiable Arizona specimens (females) are the grayer *H. n. meruloides* (Swainson).

323. *Ridgwayia pinicola* (Sclater). Aztec Thrush. Two records, both in 1978: one in Madera Canyon, Santa Rita Mountains, 20 May (M. Bierly, A. Heilman), and one at 1700 m (5600 ft) in Huachuca Canyon, Huachuca Mountains, *30 May* to at least 15 June (ARIZ, photo, G. Beringer; first found by D. Danforth). The latter bird was observed by at least 50 people.

324. *Hylocichla mustelina* (Gmelin). Wood Thrush. Sparse fall migrant, recorded north to Sanders, Apache Co., *6 Oct. 1978* (ARIZ, photo, S. Terrill;

first seen by G. Rosenberg) and west to Phoenix, 16 Oct. 1971 (R. Bradley, S.M. Demaree). One winter record, Tucson, 23 Jan. to 26 Mar. 1972 (G. Gregg et al., banded), and one spring record, near Portal, 29 May 1976 (K. Zimmer et al.).

325. *Catharus guttatus* (Pallas). Hermit Thrush. Common summer resident of boreal zones and down locally into shady canyons in the Transition Zone. Rather common winter resident in Sonoran zones of southern and central Arizona, especially in dense Upper Sonoran woods and brush and in shady portions of major river valleys. During migration found even in the most arid desert mountain ranges, where also sparse and irregular in winter. Transient, but sparse, in most nonbreeding areas in northern Arizona, from early Sept. to early Nov. and again in late Apr.

A highly complex species. 1. The small dark nominate race is the commonest winter visitant, from mid-Nov. to early Mar., particularly in the mountains, but unknown between mid-May and Oct. It is at least an occasional transient in the north, though hardly any specimens as yet. 2. *C. g. verecundus* (Osgood), somewhat redder above, is a common winter visitant except north of the Gila Valley in the east, where it is an uncommon transient; present mainly from mid-Oct. to mid-Mar. This is the race to which *C. g. nanus* (Audubon) is misapplied in the A.O.U. Check-list. We tentatively include here the dark *C. g. vaccinius* (Cumming), occasional to the Colorado Valley. 3. A third small, rather dark race is *C. g. oromelus* (Oberholser); it winters in the same area as the preceding, darker races, except no typical specimens from the Colorado Valley.

Paler races: 4. *C. g. slevini* Grinnell, small and lightly spotted, winters rather commonly in the lowlands and at the foot of the mountains of extreme southern

Arizona, chiefly in the Patagonia area, occasionally west to the Colorado Valley, east to Graham Co. It is common in migration, when there is also one northern Arizona record (southern Navajo Co., *27 Oct. 1920*). We include here, as a brown phase, *G. c. jewetti* Phillips. 5. *C. g. sequoiensis* (Belding), intermediate, is a fairly common transient from southeastern Arizona to the Hualapai Mountains, in the higher mountains in fall but in the lower parts and foothills of the mountains in spring. Rare in winter, known only from the Chiricahua Mountains. Only two definite records from northern Arizona. 6. The large, boldly spotted *C. g. auduboni* (Baird) is the breeding race, also a rather common transient in the mountains (uncommon in valleys); probably only casual in winter, in the southeast. *C. g. polionotus* (Grinnell) is a synonym.

7. The rich brown eastern and northern *C. g. nanus* (Audubon) has been found twice, presumably accidental: at Parker, *29 Nov. 1953,* and at the mouth of the Salt River, *2 Nov. 1975* (REA, A.M. Rea). This is the *C. g. faxoni* Bangs and Penard of the A.O.U. Checklist.

326. ***Catharus ustulatus*** (Nuttall). Swainson's Thrush. Rare summer resident of the cork-bark fir forest of the San Francisco Peaks. One sang through June 1978 near the confluence of the Little Colorado River with its South Fork in the White Mountains region (B. Jones), and again 7 July 1979 (S. Terrill, G. Rosenberg) and in *July 1980* (Jones et al.; ARIZ, photo, K.V. Rosenberg) two to three were singing there. Also one singing west of Sheep Crossing in the White Mountains, 14 July 1979 (D. Stotz, S. Parker). Fairly common spring migrant through southern and western Arizona from Huachuca Mountains west, north to Kingman region, uncommon farther east and in central Arizona; only three May records in the north within Arizona, but four specimens from Four Corners on Colorado quadrant,

May 1913 (DEN, H.H. Sheldon). Generally un-
common in fall, when limited mostly to the Gila
River and south; five were reported from Kayenta,
Teec Nos Pos, and Canyon de Chelly, all on the
Navajo Indian Reservation, 9 to 11 Oct. 1980
(Stotz, Parker). One present in ranch yard north of
Tucson, 28 June to 1 July 1974 (S. Burk). Some
beginning observers confuse this species with the
Hermit Thrush, and vice versa.

> The dark reddish nominate race is the most common
> race in southern Arizona at all times except the start of
> spring migration. *C. u. oedicus* (Oberholser), grayer
> but with the tail also reddening a bit at its base, is sparse
> but widespread in the south in spring, with but one
> record from the north, *28 May 1887* near Mormon
> Lake; only two fall records, which come from the Castle
> Dome Mountains in Yuma Co., *5 Sept. 1956,* and the
> Gila River Indian Reservation, *1 Oct. 1968* (REA,
> A.M. Rea). *C. u. swainsoni* (Tschudi) is the breeding
> race, more olive and more heavily spotted; it has also
> been detected sparsely in migration from Camp Verde
> east- and southeastward, and occurs, probably more
> regularly, in the northeast (Four Corners, above). One
> specimen (Huachuca Mountains, *27 May 1901,* may
> be the very gray *C. u. incanus* (Godfrey).

327. *Catharus minimus* (Lafresnaye). Gray-
cheeked Thrush. One specimen, Cave Creek, Chiricahua Mountains, *11 Sept. 1932.* No creditable
sight records.

> The specimen is the large, grayish *C. m. aliciae*
> (Baird).

328. *Catharus fuscescens* (Stephens). Veery.
Breeds in willow-dogwood association along Little
Colorado River several miles west of Eagar, where
taken *3* and *4 July 1936,* and seen repeatedly since
1975, including one of a pair feeding a Brown-
headed Cowbird barely able to fly, 28 and 29 July
1977 (D. Stotz et al.). Not found in 1978, but nest

collected in 1979 (ARIZ, B. Jones), and present again in 1980 (Jones). No more than two pairs have been found at this only known breeding locality in Arizona. A few sight records from other localities not verifiable.

The Arizona specimens are in too poor plumage for racial identification.

[*Catharus aurantiirostris* (Hartlaub). Orange-billed Nightingale-Thrush. Hypothetical. One watched for more than one-half hour at a spring near top of Pinal Mountains in mid-Apr. 1974 (G. Nicholson, according to L. Yaeger).]

329. *Sialia sialis* (Linnaeus). Eastern Bluebird. Uncommon local resident in evergreen oaks and nearby pines from the Huachuca Mountains west to the Pajaritos Mountains. Has nested since about 1960 at Southwestern Research Station, Chiricahua Mountains; in cottonwoods at Patagonia beginning in 1971 (Monson); in Happy Valley east of Rincon Mountains in both Pima and Cochise Cos., July 1976 (Monson); and in Bear Canyon at 1830 m (6000 ft) in Santa Catalina Mountains since 1976 (D. Danforth et al.). Sparse (?) at Patagonia as long ago as *15 Apr. 1945* (CM, A.C. Twomey). One observed at Summerhaven, Santa Catalina Mountains, 20 May 1965 (S.M. Russell et al.). Seen rarely in winter about Tucson, sometimes in small flocks.

The nominate race has been taken casually in winter in the lowlands (Tucson, Patagonia). The paler Mexican race, *S. s. fulva* Brewster, the "Azure" Bluebird, is the resident one and is essentially nonmigratory; additional Tucson specimens are needed.

330. *Sialia mexicana* Swainson. Western Bluebird. Common summer resident in open Transition and lower Canadian Zones (and in northeastern Arizona, among the larger trees of Upper Sonoran woodlands) west to the Huachuca, Santa Catalina, Bradshaw, and Hualapai Mountains, and Mount Trumbull; now scarcer in the southern mountains. Four noted in open deciduous trees at Moccasin, Mohave Co., 1 Sept. 1974 (R. Wilt). Winters abundantly in berry-bearing Upper Sonoran woodland, uncommonly in open Transition Zone woods, and irregularly in farmlands and on the desert wherever mistletoe occurs.

> We refer Arizona birds to *S. m. occidentalis* Townsend, considering *S. m. bairdi* Ridgway not satisfactorily separable. One or two specimens resemble *S. m. anabelae* Anthony.

331. *Sialia currucoides* (Bechstein). Mountain Bluebird. Common summer resident of open parts of northern Arizona from pinyon-juniper woodland up to timberline, south to the entire Mogollon Plateau region and west to Ash Fork and beyond Mount Trumbull. Winters abundantly in more open berry-bearing parts of Upper Sonoran Zone, uncommonly in Transition Zone openings, and commonly in most years south of its breeding range in farmlands, grasslands, and open berry-bearing woods and brush. Seen in lowlands as late as 6 May 1978, near Poston, Yuma Co. (J. Drake), but seldom after early Apr.

332. *Myadestes townsendi* (Audubon). Townsend's Solitaire. Rather common summer resident in high Transition and boreal zones of northern Arizona, west to the Kaibab Plateau and San Francisco Mountains and south to White Mountains. Migrant and post-breeding wanderer in other parts of Transition Zone. Winters commonly in berry-producing woods of Upper Sonoran Zone, sparsely in Lower Sonoran Zone valleys and canyons, and even at times in the desert mountains of extreme southwestern Arizona, remaining rarely to early June.

Summer sight records for Chiricahua Mountains (11 July 1956) and in oak woodland near Ruby, Santa Cruz Co. (3 July 1971, R. Stallcup et al.).

All Arizona specimens to date are the paler nominate race, but there are no summer specimens from southern Arizona.

FAMILY SYLVIIDAE: OLD WORLD WARBLERS, GNATCATCHERS, AND KINGLETS

333. *Polioptila caerulea* (Linnaeus). Blue-gray Gnatcatcher. Rather common summer resident in open woodlands, chaparral, and even riparian brush, of the Upper Sonoran Zone, and locally in higher parts of adjacent mesquite associations (at least in the west), west to the Ajo, Castle Dome, Kofa, and Hualapai or even Mohave Mountains. Common winter resident of wooded river valleys of Lower Sonoran Zone from the Tucson area and the Salt and Big Sandy Rivers southward, and west to the Colorado River. Sparse fall transient in higher forests (a few records, mid-July through Aug.); common transient in western deserts north of Gila River. A nesting pair found along Sonoita Creek 8 km (5 mi) below Patagonia in 1976 (B. Harrison).

Arizona birds are *P. c. obscura* Ridgway, of which *P. c. amoenissima* Grinnell is considered a synonym.

334. *Polioptila nigriceps* Baird. Black-capped Gnatcatcher. Family, including three fledglings, collected *22 June 1971* on Sonoita Creek 19 km (12 mi) (*not* 8.5 km) northeast of Nogales (ARIZ, S. Speich), after the birds were first detected on 22 May by B. Harrison. A few unconfirmed sight reports from the same locality up to 1975; one of these, 26 June 1975 (G.S. Mills) is supported by a taped recording of calls.

The race is the larger *P. n. restricta* Brewster.

335. *Polioptila melanura* Lawrence. Black-tailed Gnatcatcher. Fairly common resident of open desert brush in the Lower Sonoran Zone, commoner westward and rather local east of the San Pedro Valley; not found in Verde Valley or the bottom of the Grand Canyon, nor of course anywhere in the northeast. It occurs along the Colorado River to the upper end of Lake Mead. One was taken 16 km (10 mi) west of Prescott, *14 Sept. 1940* (CM, A.C. Twomey), and a male was seen and heard south of Grand Canyon Village, 15 May 1978 (K. Kaufman). Although there are no specimens, this gnatcatcher probably ranges into extreme southwestern Utah (according to W.H. Behle). One was taken at Bunkerville, Nevada, *9 May 1891* (US, A.K. Fisher), and another at Overton, Nevada, *12 May 1966* (ZION, R. Wauer). It may therefore occur in the Virgin River Valley in extreme northwestern Arizona.

Arizona birds are the pale *P. m. lucida* van Rossem.

336. *Regulus satrapa* Lichtenstein. Golden-crowned Kinglet. Fairly common resident in boreal zones from Santa Catalina and Chiricahua Mountains north and northwestward to the Kaibab Plateau. Fairly common fall and winter resident in some of the higher forests of Arizona, especially White Mountains, reaching lower Transition Zone, including the Santa Rita Mountains (?). Sparse winter visitant in Lower Sonoran woodlands, with records mostly from Tucson and Phoenix vicinities; since 1976–77 regular but sparse in lower Colorado River Valley. Found once in Sierra Pinta, Yuma Co., *27 Dec. 1957*. One banded along Rio Magdalena near Imuris, Sonora, 5 Feb. 1964 (A. Collister).

The breeding race is *R. s. apache* Jenks, extending in winter west and south to the Hualapai and Santa Rita Mountains, rarely down into Upper Sonoran oaks, and once to Lower Sonoran Zone (Wickenburg, flock,

1959). *R. s. amoenus* van Rossem is a synonym of *apache*. The other lowland wintering birds, as specimens attest, are largely of the nominate race, but no specimens from recent flights, nor from Sonora.

337. *Regulus calendula* (Linnaeus). Ruby-crowned Kinglet. Common summer resident of the more extensive boreal zone forests of northern and locally southeastern Arizona, west and south to the Kaibab and entire Mogollon Plateaus and the Pinaleno, Santa Catalina, and Chiricahua Mountains. A record of at least five singing birds in the Hualapai Mountains, 21 June 1978 (K.V. and G. Rosenberg, T. Brush) is contrary to all previous observations in these mountains, which have produced no Ruby-crowns during the summer. Common transient throughout state. Winters commonly in the Lower Sonoran Zone, more sparingly in Upper Sonoran Zone and forests south and west of the Mogollon Plateau, and sparsely upon, or north of, that plateau.

According to Hubbard and Crossin (*Nemouria* 14:20-21), it is doubtful that any satisfactory separation from nominate *R. c. calendula* can be made east of the Pacific coast.

338. *Peucedramus taeniatus* (Du Bus). Olive Warbler. Fairly common summer resident, scarcer northward, in Transition and (locally) Canadian Zones of southeastern Arizona, north to the south edge of the Mogollon Plateau and west to the Santa Rita and Santa Catalina Mountains. Since 1974 has been found farther north and northwest in summer, viz. the Mazatzal Mountains in Maricopa Co. (S. Terrill et al.), the Sierra Prieta just west of Prescott (C.S. Tomoff), and Bill Williams Mountain (Tomoff). Uncommon winter resident in most, if not all, of its breeding range (chiefly adult males); also ranging at that season down to the Upper Sonoran Zone in its breeding mountains and to adjacent lower ranges lacking in much ponderosa pine, such as the Dragoon and Patagonia Mountains. Exceptionally reported on southeastern slope of the San Francisco Peaks, 19 Mar. 1972 (S.B. Vander Wall, K. Sullivan). In removing this species from the Parulidae, we follow George (AMNH *Novitates* 2103, 1962, 1-41).

The Arizona race is the pale *P. t. arizonae* Miller and Griscom.

FAMILY MOTACILLIDAE: WAGTAILS AND PIPITS

[*Motacilla alba* Linnaeus. White Wagtail. An adult in summer plumage was seen in Arroyo Cajón Bonito in extreme northeastern Sonora, less than 10 km (6 mi) from the Arizona boundary, 30 Apr. 1974 (Monson, C. McMoran, V. Roth).]

339. *Anthus spinoletta* (Linnaeus). Water Pipit. Breeds above timberline in the San Francisco and White Mountains. Recorded on the Kaibab Plateau in June 1971 (F. Gehlbach) and on 25 July 1973 (R. Wilt). Generally distributed about water, and even occurs on open plains in Sonoran and Transition Zones on migration. Common winter resident at streams, ponds, irrigated fields, etc., throughout the Lower Sonoran Zone; sparse to uncommon in winter in open Upper Sonoran Zone. Two near Poston, Yuma Co., 27 May 1980 (B. Woodbridge), one at water-hole east of Dragoon Mountains, 24 June 1972 (W. Anderson), and another at Willcox the same day (G. Gregg, F. Tainter). One was eating bird seed beneath a feeder in a heavy snowstorm at Portal, 7 Dec. 1978 (S. Spofford).

Breeding birds are *A. s. alticola* Todd. The abundant transient and winter resident is *A. s. geophilus* "Oberholser," if this is truly separable from *A. s. pacificus*

Todd, as characterized by Lea and Edwards. True *pacificus* occurs more regularly than *A. s. rubescens* (Tunstall). One heavily streaked specimen from Naco, Sonora, *6 June 1958,* (DEL, J.R. Werner), the only summer pipit *specimen* below timberline, was finally referred to *A. s. japonicus* Temminck and Schlegel.

340. *Anthus spragueii* (Audubon). Sprague's Pipit. Rather sparse and local winter resident across the southern part of the state, in grasslands as on the Sonoita Plains and east of the Chiricahua Mountains (Monson), and in irrigated fields as four specimens and others seen near Scottsdale in the Phoenix vicinity, *1963–64* and *1964–65* (US, T.D. Burleigh) and several records 1974 and later west of Phoenix (K. Kaufman et al., including photo, ARIZ, *6 Feb. 1979,* K.V. Rosenberg). Also once in open desert of the Tule Desert, Yuma Co., *30 Dec. 1958.* Reported along lower Colorado River in 1949 (Topock, 27 Sept.), in 1977 (near Parker, 23 Dec., Rosenberg), in *1978* (taken near Poston, *18 Dec.,* ARIZ, R. Dummer), in 1979 (Cibola National Wildlife Refuge, 16 Feb., B. Whitney); and in winter of 1979–80 in the Dome Valley east of Yuma (two to three, according to R. Martin). One seen at Wikieup, Big Sandy Valley, 18 Oct. 1953 (Phillips), and one at Tuzigoot National Monument, Yavapai Co., 19 Oct. 1980 (S. Terrill). One record from the north: one at Teec Nos Pos in the extreme northeast, 5 Oct. 1980 (Rosenberg et al.).

FAMILY BOMBYCILLIDAE: WAXWINGS

341. *Bombycilla garrulus* (Linnaeus). Bohemian Waxwing. A sparse, erratic winter visitor along Lakes Mohave and Mead, and at Grand Canyon South Rim. Also two, east side of Baboquivari Mountains, 10 Feb. to 10 Mar. 1932; one at Benson, 5 Dec. 1948; seen at Page, Coconino Co., winter of 1963–64 (R. Russell, H. Townsend); one at Seven

Springs, Maricopa Co., 1 May 1969 (E. Radke, D. Turner); one at Flagstaff, 9 Feb. 1979 (C. LaRue); and about 40 at Ganado, Navajo Indian Reservation, 18 Feb. 1979 (M.W. Loder). About 200 reported in Virgin Mountains on Nevada border, 2 Feb. 1966 (R. Russell). About 1700 at Las Vegas Bay, Lake Mead, Nevada, 25 Jan. 1969 (C.S. Lawson), and has occurred irregularly at Farmington, New Mexico (A.P. Nelson). Data on two specimens labeled "Phoenix" (G.S. Miller Collection, British Museum) are perhaps questionable.

342. *Bombycilla cedrorum* Vieillot. Cedar Waxwing. An erratic winter visitant in Sonoran zones south and west of Mogollon Plateau, often abundant in May in valleys and canyons, with occasional birds or flocks remaining even into June (even one 12 July 1953 at Parker). One noted at Martinez Lake above Imperial Dam, 29 Aug. 1976 (K. Kaufman, J. and R. Witzeman), also one at Parker, *31 Aug. 1980* (ARIZ, photo, K.V. Rosenberg). Migrant in the north, not known to remain all winter except sparsely (three at Moccasin, Mohave Co., 23 Dec. 1963, R. Wauer; one to ten at Flagstaff feeding station, winter 1970–71, G. Foster; and one at Ganado, Navajo Indian Reservation, 16 Dec. 1979, M.W. Loder).

343. *Phainopepla nitens* (Swainson). Phainopepla. Present in different areas in varying roles, seasonally; probably few, if any, individuals are sedentary or nonmigratory. It is also entirely possible for two or more populations, of different seasonal status, to be at the same place. The Phainopepla is a winter resident in the southwest (east to include Big Sandy Valley and Papago Indian Reservation), where it breeds in spring and then absents itself from May (although some birds may remain, even in numbers, to early July) until late Aug., or, more usually, early Oct. Possibly some, or most, of these western populations move to the coastal regions of California in summer (G.E. Walsberg, *Univ. Cal. Publ. Zool.* 108). The species is a summer resident in the central (north to Sedona, Coconino Co.) and southeastern parts of the state, locally abundant, in the Lower Sonoran (and locally Upper) Zone in brush and trees containing mistletoe; it bred in 1876 near Fort Apache in Upper Sonoran Zone. It is a common winter resident in the Lower Sonoran Zone of southern Arizona, except in the Verde Valley where it is uncommon, and in most of the southeast east of the Santa Cruz Valley where it is sparse. In the extreme northwest and adjacent Utah it has been found nesting, and, in Arizona, wintering as well (R. Wauer et al.).

There is a sprinkling of summer records from the Upper Sonoran parts of northern Arizona, especially where *Forestiera neomexicana* berries are available, but also in mistletoe-infested pinyon-juniper, and it is said to breed locally in the Snowflake area and perhaps near Mount Trumbull in the northwest. In some winters it remains north and east of usual winter range (as well as altitudinally above usual range), principally where juniper infested with mistletoe is present, as far as Guadalupe Canyon in the southeast (Monson) and Sedona in the north, and even to the extreme northwest corner (R. Wauer). Large concentrations in summer where Mexican elder and *Rhamnus californicus* berries or wild grapes are available. About 40 found in cottonwoods at Pahranagat National Wildlife Refuge, Lincoln Co., Nevada, about 100 km (62 mi) northwest of the northwest corner of Arizona, in June and July 1975 (C.S. Lawson).

Arizona specimens are mostly the northern race *P. n. lepida* Van Tyne. The nominate race was taken at Payson in *Feb. 1888* (AMNH, E.A. Mearns), and south of Tucson (two specimens), *24 Apr. 1940* (CM, A.C. Twomey).

[*Ptilogonys cinereus* Swainson. Gray Silky-Fly-catcher. Hypothetical. One observed briefly with Phainopeplas about 6 km (4 mi) southwest of Patagonia, 17 July 1980 (R. Stallcup).]

FAMILY STURNIDAE: STARLINGS

344. *Sturnus vulgaris* Linnaeus. Starling. Common resident in urban and agricultural areas of Sonoran zones statewide; also in high Upper Sonoran and in Transition Zones human population centers like Flagstaff, Show Low, and Springerville. First found in the state at Lupton in early 1946; first specimen from Parker, *16 Nov. 1946* (ARIZ, Monson); first nest near Glendale, Maricopa Co., in 1954. Apparently not common in the north until about 1965.

FAMILY VIREONIDAE: VIREOS

345. *Vireo atricapillus* Woodhouse. Black-capped Vireo. A male was captured in a mist net, measured, and weighed at the Tanque Verde Guest Ranch east of Tucson, *4 Apr. 1970* (C.E. Corchran).

[*Vireo griseus* (Boddaert). White-eyed Vireo. Hypothetical. Three satisfactory sight records: Pima Canyon, Santa Catalina Mountains, 13 Nov. 1966 (E.O. Willis); Montezuma Well, Yavapai Co., one singing, 1 and 8 Aug. 1976 (H. Snyder); and one at Round Rock, Navajo Indian Reservation, 11 Oct. 1980 (D. Stotz, S. Parker). Erroneously credited to Arizona by the A.O.U. Check-list.]

346. *Vireo huttoni* Cassin. Hutton's Vireo. Rather common summer resident in the denser evergreen oak brush and woods of southeastern and central Arizona, north sparingly to the Prescott region, the Mazatzal Mountains, and the Whiteriver-Fort Apache area, west to the Baboquivari-Quinlan (Monson) and Santa Catalina Mountains. Fairly common

winter resident in mountains west to the Baboquivari-
Quinlan and Santa Catalina Mountains, north rarely
to Salt River and perhaps the foot of Natanes Plateau
in Gila Co.; mostly in streamside trees and brush and
in lower oaks. Found uncommonly in fall in the
higher conifer forests adjacent to breeding areas.
Sparse to uncommon in Lower Sonoran mesquites in
valleys in winter west to Phoenix area. Sparse in fall
west to the Colorado River Valley from the Bill
Williams Delta south, chiefly in mesquites and
willows.

Arizona specimens to date belong to the pale, large
subspecies *V. h. stephensi* Brewster.

347. *Vireo bellii* Audubon. Bell's Vireo. Common
summer resident in dense low brush, especially
mesquite associations along streams, up to the top of
the Lower Sonoran Zone, including recently the
bottom of the Grand Canyon, and at least since 1940
extreme southwestern Utah (according to W.H.
Behle). Largely absent from along the Mexican
border beyond Ajo. Scarce along Colorado River in
the 1950s, but apparently once again common.
Cowbird parasitism is believed to be responsible for
such irregularity. One seen at Pipe Spring National
Monument, 15 May 1973 (R. Wilt), and noted at
Prescott in the spring of 1979 (C.S. Tomoff). Sparse
in winter: Topock, 7 Feb. to *7 Mar. 1951;* one in Bill
Williams Delta, 24 Nov. 1953; one singing on Organ
Pipe Cactus National Monument, 11 Feb. 1970 (R.
Cunningham); one near Parker Dam (Arizona side?),
28 Nov. 1964 (G. McCaskie); one near Parker, 18
Dec. 1978 (K. Kaufman, E. Cook); and one on
lower Bill Williams River, 25 Nov. 1979 (K.V.
Rosenberg). One noted at Magdalena, Sonora, 22
Dec. 1978 (K.V. and G. Rosenberg).

The race breeding in Arizona is *V. b. arizonae* Ridgway.
There is one specimen of the more yellowish *V. b.*

medius Oberholser from the Gila River at Cochran Buttes east of Florence, *8 May 1978* (SD, A.M. Rea).

348. *Vireo vicinior* Coues. Gray Vireo. Fairly common to common summer resident in junipers of the Upper Sonoran Zone, often quite local, in southeastern to northwestern Arizona, but absent from the Mexican border ranges west of the Chiricahua Mountains and from the area east of the Grand Canyon and north of the Little Colorado River and St. Johns. A sparse migrant in Lower Sonoran Zone of southern and western Arizona during Sept. and from late Mar. to early May. Winters in small numbers in the mountains of southern Yuma Co., and not rare in winter near Sonoyta in Sonora (*Nov. 1955*); also the following scattered winter records eastward: near Tucson, *31 Dec. 1949* and 31 Dec. 1974 (last by Monson); lower Cave Creek Canyon, Chiricahua Mountains, 13 Nov. 1964 (Monson); and west of Marana, Pima Co., 14 Jan. 1967 (S.M. Russell). Erroneously reported from Hoover Dam (specimens are *V. bellii*).

349. *Vireo flavifrons* Vieillot. Yellow-throated Vireo. Sparse migrant across southern Arizona; nine records, including three specimens: Chiricahua Mountains, *8 May 1948;* near Mammoth, *17 Aug. 1948;* and Bill Williams Delta, *10 Oct. 1953.* Sight records from other localities include Sierra Pinta, Yuma Co., 4 June 1956; Phoenix, 29 Aug. 1969 and 18 Aug. 1971 (S. Demaree) and 17 Sept. 1974 (B. Burch); and Arizona-Sonora Desert Museum, Pima Co., 30 May 1976 (Monson). One northern Arizona record, a bird seen near Kayenta, Navajo Indian Reservation, 30 May 1979 (K. Kaufman et al.).

350. *Vireo solitarius* (Wilson). Solitary Vireo. Common summer resident in Transition Zone throughout Arizona, and in the heavier vegetation of the

Upper Sonoran Zone (locally and irregularly ranging down after breeding into cottonwood association of both Sonoran zones). Common in migration statewide, principally in southwest in spring and mountains in fall. Winters in small numbers in willow-cottonwood association of Lower Sonoran Zone of southern and central Arizona, also in towns, dense mesquites, and casually in evergreen oaks, west to the Colorado River as far north as the Bill Williams Delta, and east to the Tucson and Patagonia regions (sparsely on upper San Pedro River).

> The breeding race is the gray-and-white *V. s. plumbeus* Coues; it also makes up a small percentage of wintering birds at Tucson and in the lower Colorado River Valley. The smaller yellow-and-green *V. s. cassinii* Xantus is the common transient and represents the bulk of the wintering birds. Neither of the similar (but larger and brighter) eastern races has been collected in the state.

351. *Vireo virescens* Vieillot. Red-eyed Vireo. Sparse transient (visitant) in deciduous trees throughout the state, more common in the north, records from mid-May through early Nov. (including summer months).

> The race found in Arizona is *V. v. caniviridis* Burleigh, slightly paler above than the nominate race. *V. v. flavoviridis* (Cassin), the "Yellow-green Vireo" of tropical North America north to northern Sonora, is casual in southern Arizona (one sound recording in July 1969, D.V. Borror; a number of records of one individual in June 1975, all in the Patagonia vicinity; and one observed near Theba, west of Gila Bend, *13* to 15 *July 1980,* G. Rosenberg et al., ARIZ, photo by R. Witzeman). *V. v. hypoleucus* van Rossem is considered a synonym of *flavoviridis.*

352. *Vireo philadelphicus* (Cassin). Philadelphia Vireo. Still only four specimens: two near Tucson,

10 Nov. 1939 and *7 Oct. 1953;* one in King Valley, south of Kofa Mountains, *27 Oct. 1954;* and one at Komatke, Gila River Indian Reservation, *12 Oct. 1963.* It is hard to know how many of a number of sight records since 1974 should be credited; those with more than one experienced observer involved are for the Salt River southwest of Phoenix, 6 to 7 Oct. 1977 (S. Terrill et al.), one near Kayenta, Navajo Indian Reservation, 1 Sept. 1978 (G. Rosenberg et al.), one at Richville, Apache Co., 5 Oct. 1978 (Rosenberg et al.), and one at Tucson, 27 to 28 Sept. 1980 (W.D. and R. Eastman et al.).

353. *Vireo gilvus* (Vieillot). Warbling Vireo. Rather common summer resident in the willows, maples, dense box-elders, and especially aspens from the Hudsonian Zone down, locally and irregularly, to the Upper Sonoran Zone; west to the Santa Catalina and Hualapai (July 1977 and June 1978, K.V. Rosenberg et al.) Mountains. (Not in such Lower Sonoran Zone places as St. Thomas, Nevada, and St. George, Utah, as stated by A.O.U. Check-list). Common in migration throughout the state. Unusually late spring migrant records are one west of Poston, Yuma Co., 28 June 1977 (P. Mack), and one singing at Cibola National Wildlife Refuge, Yuma Co., 17 June 1978 (K.V. Rosenberg). An unusually late fall record was of a bird seen near the confluence of the Little Colorado River and its South Fork, west of Springerville, on 22 Oct. 1978 (K. Kaufman, G. Rosenberg). Casual in late winter: 23 Feb. 1945, Baboquivari Mountains, and 17 Feb. (year?), near Phoenix. Also one on 19 Dec. 1978, Bill Williams Delta (K. Kaufman, W.C. Hunter).

V. g. brewsteri (Ridgway) is the breeding race, but is apparently scarce as a migrant, especially in fall. *V. g. swainsonii* Baird is the common migrant. The somewhat intermediate *V. g. leucopolius* (Oberholser) is less common.

FAMILY PARULIDAE: WOOD WARBLERS

354. *Mniotilta varia* (Linnaeus). Black-and-white Warbler. Sparse visitant, usually in deciduous trees, in southern and central Arizona, with most records from Sept. through May, but also including several summer records, among them singing birds. Six records for the north: Pipe Spring National Monument, 24 to 26 Sept. 1974 (R. Wilt); Nutrioso, Apache Co., 29 June and 6 July (B. Jones); Teec Nos Pos in extreme northeast, 23 May 1977 (B. Harrison) and 1 June 1979 (S. Parker, D. Stotz); and confluence of Little Colorado River with its South Fork, west of Springerville, 13 Sept. and 1 Nov. 1979 (B. Jones). Lacking in winter east of Santa Cruz Valley, except for individuals in Garden Canyon, Huachuca Mountains, 1 Dec. 1974 (R.T. Smith), and at Cooks Lake, lower San Pedro Valley, winter of 1978–79 (Monson).

355. *Protonotaria citrea* (Boddaert). Prothonotary Warbler. Sparse migrant. Three specimens: Tucson, *1 May 1884,* Chiricahua Mountains, *8 Sept. 1924,* and between Cortaro and Rillito, near Tucson, *21 Oct. 1967* (S.M. Russell). Five credible sight records: lower Sabino Canyon, Santa Catalina Mountains, 10 Sept. 1976 (B. Jones et al.); Bill Williams Delta, 10 May 1977 (K.V. Rosenberg); St. David, 6 June 1978 (D. Danforth); Bonita Creek northeast of Safford, *5 June 1979* (ARIZ, photo, T. Clark); and Ganado Lake, Navajo Indian Reservation, *17 Aug. 1980* (K. Kaufman et al., ARIZ, photo by S. Terrill).

Authors' note: Since completion of our manuscript, a singing Swainson's Warbler, *Limnothlypis swainsonii* (Audubon) was found on the South Fork of the Little Colorado River, several miles west of Springerville, 12 June 1981. Its song was tape-recorded the following day. Record by G. Rosenberg et al. This adds a hypothetical species to the list of Arizona birds.

356. *Helmitheros vermivorus* (Gmelin). Worm-eating Warbler. Very sparse migrant (one summer report) in southern Arizona. One at Boyce Thompson Southwestern Arboretum, Superior, 20 to 22 Oct. *1979* (ARIZ, photo, S. Terrill, *21 Oct.;* first seen by K.V. Rosenberg). Eight other southern Arizona sight records, from Chiricahua Mountains, Santa Rita Mountains, San Pedro River, Bill Williams Delta (singing 10 May 1977, Rosenberg), Prescott (5 and 6 July 1977, C.S. Tomoff), and Tucson. Except for Superior, Prescott, and Tucson (6 to 15 Nov. 1979) records, all reports range from 30 Mar. to 21 May. One northern Arizona report, Flagstaff, 24 Sept. 1966 (R.P. Balda).

357. *Helminthophila chrysoptera* (Linnaeus). Golden-winged Warbler. One specimen, 2 and *3 Nov. 1968* (ARIZ, E. Radke and R.L. Cunningham) at Quitobaquito, Organ Pipe Cactus National Monument. Also seen along Little Colorado River west of Eagar, 26 July 1972 (Monson) and 28 June 1973 (E. and S. Cardiff), and in Bill Williams Delta, 8 Oct. 1978 (B. Whitney).

358. *Helminthophila pinus* (Linnaeus). Blue-winged Warbler. Casual; one record, Bill Williams Delta, *5 Sept. 1952.*

359. *Helminthophila peregrina* (Wilson). Tennessee Warbler. Three specimens, Chiricahua Mountains, *7 Apr. 1925;* Komatke, Gila River Indian Reservation, *20 May 1972* (AMR, A.M. Rea); and Gila-Salt River confluence, *31 Dec. 1975* (AMR, Rea). Nearly 50 sight records, 1972 through 1980, all in migration periods, in central and southern Arizona; not yet found west of Organ Pipe Cactus National Monument and Gila Bend vicinity. At least seven sight records for the north, all in Springerville-South Fork of the Little Colorado River and eastern Navajo Indian Reservation regions.

360. *Helminthophila celata* (Say). Orange-crowned Warbler. Locally a summer resident in dense decid-uous cover, chiefly willow thickets, in the Canadian Zone of eastern Arizona (White, Chuska, Pinal, and Pinaleno Mountains, and one locality in the Santa Catalina Mountains), possibly sparingly farther west (Mormon Lake; Flagstaff, 1968, S.W. Carothers; San Francisco Mountains, 1980, D.R. Pinkston; and Bill Williams Mountain, 1975 and 1976, C.S. Tomoff). Common transient statewide. In southern and central Arizona, winters uncommonly from Patagonia and lower San Pedro River west in dense brush and deciduous trees; commonly along the lower Salt River and along the Colorado River north to at least Davis Dam. Probably winters along Virgin River in extreme northwest. Rare (?) in winter in Upper Sonoran Zone, west side of Santa Catalina Mountains, 22 Dec. 1977, when two seen (Monson). Two midsummer records from southwestern Arizona: Kofa Mountains, 25 and 26 June 1956, and Colorado River 37 km (23 mi) above Yuma, 1 July 1957. Wintering Orange-crowned Warblers are a possible confusing source of winter sight records for other wood warblers, including Nashville and MacGilliv-ray's Warblers.

H. c. orestera (Oberholser) is the common form in Arizona at most times and places. The nominate form occurs as a sparse (?) transient from Tucson eastward, and winters occasionally at Tucson and Patagonia, at least. *H. c. lutescens* (Ridgway) is a fairly common transient, in spring restricted to the southeast east to the Huachuca Mountains, but in fall found virtually state-wide; it is sparse in winter. A single adult from the Chuska Mountains, *3 Sept. 1978* (US, J.T. Marshall) is too dark, and contrastingly patterned below, for any of these, and is referred to *H. c. sordida* (Townsend), though short-billed.

361. *Helminthophila ruficapilla* (Wilson). Nashville Warbler. Common summer resident of low deciduous brush in the higher mountains throughout Arizona, chiefly in Transition and Canadian Zones; also breeds along low streams north of and below Mogollon Plateau (Keams Canyon, Monson; Holbrook; Carrizo Creek, Fort Apache Indian Reservation, S. Terrill) in Upper Sonoran Zone. Descends locally (Santa Catalina Mountains, Prescott region) to foothills in July. Fairly common, sometimes common, transient throughout Arizona, especially southwestward, in large brush and weeds and deciduous trees. Three winter sight records from Phoenix and vicinity in 1974 and 1975; one at Bisbee, 29 Dec. 1971 (L. Jones); and one at Flagstaff, 16 Dec. 1979 (Christmas Bird Count).

H. r. ridgwayi (van Rossem), the Nashville Warbler of the A.O.U. Check-list, is a fairly common to common transient throughout Arizona, and may be the wintering race, at least in part. *H. r. virginiae* (Baird), the Virginia's Warbler, is the breeding form, and is also an uncommon transient, more common in spring, in the Lower Sonoran Zone west to the Pajaritos Mountains and the Big Sandy Valley, sparsely to the Colorado River. One seen at Pipe Spring National Monument, 7 Oct. 1978 (S. Terrill et al.).

362. *Helminthophila luciae* (Cooper). Lucy's Warbler. Abundant summer resident in dense mesquite and cottonwood-mesquite associations of the Lower Sonoran Zone, fairly common in desert willow-ash-walnut-sycamore-evergreen oak association of Upper Sonoran Zone, in most of southern and central Arizona, including the Prescott region and below the Mogollon Rim, as well as along the entire Colorado River and in the Virgin River Valley of the extreme northwest. Absent from deserts west of

Growler Valley and the northeast side of the Kofa Mountains, and usually from most of Phoenix area. In the 1950s was scarce along the lower Colorado River, but has since recovered. Most birds undertake their fall migration by early Aug. Casual on and just north of Mogollon Plateau on migration, also one at Valentine, Mohave Co., *5 Oct. 1948*. Two winter records, for Salt River near Phoenix, 18 Dec. 1976 (K. Kaufman, B. Jones) and 3 Dec. 1977 (D. Stejskal, B. Foster); one crippled bird at Tucson to 2 Dec. 1979 (D. Stotz et al.).

363. *Parula americana* (Linnaeus). Northern Parula. Sparse transient, less common as a summer or winter visitant, across southern Arizona; mid-winter records are from Tucson and Phoenix areas west, and are relatively few. Two northern Arizona records: Lakeside, 12 Sept. 1977 (Monson) and Springerville, 30 May to 4 June 1978 (B. Jones). Apparently bred in northern Sonora, *1952*.

All Arizona and northern Sonora specimens, and probably all sight records, pertain to the nominate race. *P. a. pulchra* (Brewster) has been taken somewhat farther south in Sonora.

364. *Dendroica petechia* (Linnaeus). Yellow Warbler. Common summer resident in willows, cottonwoods, boxelders, and sometimes sycamores, of Sonoran zones and even low Transition Zone almost throughout the state, but peculiarly absent from some areas. Has bred once in willows of lower Canadian Zone on San Francisco Peaks (*1938*). Sparse to absent in recent years as a nesting bird along the lower Colorado River. Evidently locally reduced or exterminated by cowbird parasitism.

Common migrant in all parts of Arizona except unbroken woodlands. Very sparse in winter along the lower Colorado River from Parker south; also three sight records for Phoenix area and one photographed at Green Valley, south of Tucson, *14 Jan. 1974* (ARIZ, A. Brison).

D. p. rubiginosa (Pallas), the darkest race, is apparently a statewide fall migrant except perhaps in the northeast corner, and a sparse late spring migrant around Yuma. *D. p. "amnicola* Batchelder,"next darkest, is a migrant, widespread through the northeast in fall and also taken west to the Colorado River as far south as the latitude of the Big Sandy Valley; sparse in spring, when recorded only in the southwest, from Sonoyta, Sonora, to the lower Colorado Valley. *D. p. morcomi* Coale, medium dark, is a very common transient, and the only two winter specimens are of this race, as is also the breeding specimen from the San Francisco Peaks. True *morcomi* apparently breeds along the upper Colorado River south barely into Arizona. The remaining northern Arizona breeders from the Springerville area north are intermediate toward *D. p. sonorana* Brewster, the pale breeding bird of southeastern, central, and northwestern Arizona, north to the Mogollon Rim and (formerly) along the lower Colorado River.

365. *Dendroica magnolia* (Wilson). Magnolia Warbler. Sparse transient and casual winter visitant; about 15 records, including specimens from Topock, *11 Nov. 1951,* and Tucson, *6 Nov. 1955.* Sight records from Bill Williams Delta; Tempe; Chiricahua Mountains; North Rim of Grand Canyon; near confluence of Little Colorado River and its South Fork; Tes Nez Iah, Round Rock, and Kayenta, Navajo Indian Reservation; Bonita Creek near Safford; and Tucson. Most records are of fall migrants; the one winter record is from the lower Bill Williams River, 24 Dec. 1977 (G. Rosenberg) until 24 Jan. *1978 (19 Jan.,* ARIZ, photo, K.V. Rosenberg).

366. *Dendroica tigrina* (Gmelin). Cape May Warbler. One old specimen, probably from Tucson, in autumn of *1875.* Three other records on migration:

Laguna Dam, California side, *23 Sept. 1924;* along Sycamore Creek at Sunflower, Maricopa Co., 3 Oct. 1976 (S. Terrill, J. Witzeman); and at Boyce Thompson Southwestern Arboretum, Superior, 23 Apr. 1977 (S. Terrill et al.). Accidental in winter at Boyce Thompson Arboretum, 17 Nov. 1978 to at least 7 Apr. 1979 (S. Terrill et al., ARIZ, photo, K.V. Rosenberg), and at Tucson, 26 Jan. to late Mar. 1980 (F. and W. Hopf et al.).

367. *Dendroica caerulescens* (Gmelin). Black-throated Blue Warbler. Mostly a sparse fall migrant, with about 46 records in all from all parts of the state. Much less common in the spring, when only six records, all of them from the Chiricahua Mountains except for *30 Apr. 1955* when one was found freshly dead in the Ajo Mountains for the first state record and one for 30 May 1972 in Madera Canyon, Santa Rita Mountains (F.M. Murdoch et al.). One summer record, 17 June 1973, from near Barfoot Park in Chiricahua Mountains (T. Heindel). Three winter records: Indian Gardens, Grand Canyon, 11 Jan. 1978 (W.H. Buskirk), Yuma, 23 Dec. 1978 (G. Robinson), and lower Garden Canyon, Huachuca Mountains, 7 Dec. 1979 to 29 Feb. 1980 (R.T. Smith, C. McMoran et al.).

Arizona records are presumably the widespread nominate race.

368. *Dendroica coronata* (Linnaeus). Yellow-rumped Warbler. Common summer resident throughout boreal zones (less common in adjacent Transition Zone) except in the Hualapai Mountains and, apparently, central Arizona. Common migrant everywhere. Common to abundant winter resident of Lower Sonoran Zone and, locally, deciduous riparian Upper Sonoran Zone or even evergreen oaks of southern, central, and western Arizona, except in

driest desert portions; sparse in winter in other parts
of Upper Sonoran Zone in the south. May be more
common locally (increasing?) in winter in north than
records indicate (cf. at least eight in junipers near
Snowflake, 31 Jan. 1977, Monson, P.M. Walters;
six at Ganado, Navajo Indian Reservation, 16 Dec.
1979, M.W. Loder); and (number?) at Flagstaff,
1979–80 (according to J. Coons). Casual at Patagonia, 1 July 1980 (K. Garrett).

The nominate race is casual in Arizona, only one
specimen, lower Aravaipa Canyon, *14 Apr. 1940*. It
and the following form are known as the Myrtle
Warbler. *D. c. hooveri* McGregor is a sparse to
uncommon winter visitant to Lower Sonoran Zone
rivers and farms in western and southern Arizona, and a
sparse transient (chiefly in spring) in eastern, central,
and northern Arizona, including the mountains. Recorded
once at Springerville, 16 Dec. 1978 (Christmas Bird
Count).

D. c. auduboni (Townsend) is the common winter
resident. It and the following form are known as
Audubon's Warbler. *D. c. memorabilis* (Oberholser) is
the breeding form; it also occurs as an early fall and
spring migrant, and winters in some parts of the state.

369. *Dendroica nigrescens* (Townsend). Black-
throated Gray Warbler. Common summer resident
in pinyon-juniper woodland and other dense vegetation of high Upper Sonoran Zone, and apparently
also Gambel oak thickets, of eastern Arizona west to
the Baboquivari Mountains, Bradshaw Mountains,
and the Grand Canyon region; it has been found
recently (feeding young) in the Hualapai Mountains
(July 1977 and June 1978, K.V. Rosenberg et al.).
Fairly common statewide on migration. Winters
uncommonly in cottonwood-willow and sycamore-
mesquite associations from the lower San Pedro

Valley (1978–79, Monson) and Santa Cruz Valley west to the Colorado River, where sparse.

The nominate race is the more common migrant and winter resident. *D. n. halsei* (Giraud), slightly larger, is the breeding race; it appears to be sparse as a migrant and winter resident, but more study is needed to ascertain its true status.

370. *Dendroica virens* (Gmelin). Black-throated Green Warbler. Sparse transient, both spring and fall, throughout state, perhaps 25 creditable records in all. One summer record, a bird singing near Patagonia, 30 June 1971 (P. Norton). One winter record, Sycamore Canyon, Pajaritos Mountains, 2 Jan. 1978 (G. Rosenberg, K. Kaufman, D. Stotz). Hybrids of Townsend's and Hermit Warblers may closely resemble this species, and immatures are easily confused with immatures of Townsend's and Hermit Warblers. Many sight records are doubtless erroneous. No authenticated record (specimen) between late May and early Oct.

Arizona specimens belong to the large-billed nominate race.

371. *Dendroica townsendi* (Townsend). Townsend's Warbler. Transient throughout Arizona, very common at higher altitudes, only fairly common in lowlands. Sparse to uncommon along eastern edge and unrecorded in northeast in spring. A sparse winter resident, sometimes found even in mountains, of mostly deciduous trees, from Portal west to Phoenix region; in some winters (since 1972–73) has been occasional to uncommon in Phoenix vicinity.

372. *Dendroica occidentalis* (Townsend). Hermit Warbler. Abundant fall transient at high altitudes, scarcer at somewhat lower elevations, uncommon in Lower Sonoran Zone. Common spring migrant at all altitudes in southern Arizona west of the San Pedro River, north to Salome and the Mohave Mountains; sparse farther east and north to Verde Valley, unrecorded then in north. Singles reported from Bill Williams Delta area, 31 July 1977 and 14 Aug. 1978 (both K.V. Rosenberg), would seem extraordinarily early at that elevation. A winter record from Big Sandy Valley, *17 Feb. 1958;* also one in lower Sabino Canyon, Santa Catalina Mountains, winter of 1964–65 (D. Prentice), and possibly as many as four Dec.–Jan. records at Phoenix and vicinity in 1975 to 1977.

373. *Dendroica cerulea* (Wilson). Cerulean Warbler. A singing male found in lower Madera Canyon, Santa Rita Mountains, 18 May *1979* (C. Clark), and photographed *20 May* (ARIZ, Monson et al.) is the only documented record. Another singing male was seen about 1800 m (5900 ft) in Cave Creek Canyon, Chiricahua Mountains, 28 May 1970 (B. and M. Schaughency et al.).

374. *Dendroica fusca* (Müller). Blackburnian Warbler. Sparse in fall west to central Arizona. Singles photographed near confluence of Little Colorado River and its South Fork west of Springerville, *5 Oct. 1978* (ARIZ, S. Terrill, first seen by K. Kaufman) and at Boyce Thompson Southwestern Arboretum, Superior, *20 Oct. 1979* (ARIZ, K.V. Rosenberg); another at the Arboretum, *21 Oct. 1979* (ARIZ, photo, Terrill, first seen by G. Rosenberg). The first bird recorded in the state was at the Arizona-Sonora Desert Museum near Tucson, 8 Oct. 1973 (Monson). Since then, other than those photographed, 13 other creditable records, all in late Sept. or early to mid-Oct., from Tempe, Prescott, west of Springerville, and the eastern Navajo Reservation east to the New Mexico line.

375. *Dendroica dominica* (Linnaeus). Yellow-throated Warbler. A male photographed at Patagonia-Sonoita Creek Sanctuary, *2 June 1972* (ARIZ, B. McKnight). Unverified sight records for Guadalupe Canyon in the extreme southeast, 14 May 1972 (C. Littlefield) and 20 July 1975 (R. Dean), and for Verde River east of Phoenix, 14 Apr. 1979 (K.V. Rosenberg).

376. *Dendroica graciae* (Baird). Grace's Warbler. Common summer resident of Transition Zone throughout the state. Seven Sonoran zones records on migration: two at Phantom Ranch, bottom of Grand Canyon, 7 to 10 May 1929 (F.M. Bailey); St. David, 19 Apr. 1939; Gila River Indian Reservation, 29 Apr. 1967 and 26 Sept. 1968 (A.M. Rea); Pipe Spring National Monument, 26 Sept. 1974 (R. Wilt); Mule Mountains northwest of Bisbee, 19 or 20 Aug. 1978 (D. Danforth, W. Roe); and Arivaca, 24 Sept. 1978 (G. Gregg).

377. *Dendroica pensylvanica* (Linnaeus). Chestnut-sided Warbler. Sparse transient, in fall to late Dec.; about 30 records in all, from Prescott and Pipe Spring National Monument southeastward, but not farther west than Phoenix and Wikieup, Big Sandy Valley, in the south (except for near Poston, Yuma Co., 18 Dec. 1978, S. Terrill). Unrecorded from the northeast, save for individuals singing at Teec Nos Pos, Navajo Indian Reservation, 23 May 1977 (B. Harrison), and at Round Rock, also Navajo Indian Reservation, 1 June 1979 (D. Stotz). Five specimens, from near Tucson; near Nogales; Pinaleno Mountains; Phoenix; and Wikieup.

378. *Dendroica castanea* (Wilson). Bay-breasted Warbler. Sparse in spring and mid- to late fall. Three photographs (all ARIZ): Southwestern Research Station, Chiricahua Mountains, *6 May 1972* (T.

Parker et al., photo by C.E. Pinkard; bird also seen 5
and 7 May); Arizona-Sonora Desert Museum near
Tucson, *23 Nov. 1973* (W. Anderson, Monson); and
Ganado Lake, Navajo Indian Reservation, *6 Oct.
1978* (K. Kaufman et al., photo by S. Terrill). Also
sight records for Tucson, 7 Dec. 1975 (D. Stotz et
al.); San Pedro River north of Mammoth, 15 May
1978 (Terrill); Bill Williams Delta, 9 Oct. 1978 (B.
Whitney); near confluence of Little Colorado River
and its South Fork west of Springerville, 1 to 3 June
1980 (B. Jones), and at Theba, west of Gila Bend, 16
to 22 Nov. 1980 (G. Rosenberg, J. Witzeman et al.).

379. *Dendroica striata* (Forster). Blackpoll
Warbler. Sparse visitant in recent years from May to
late Oct. Three specimens: Jose Juan Tank, Cabeza
Prieta National Wildlife Refuge, Pima Co., *14 June
1968* (ARIZ, S.M. Russell), near Red Rock, Pinal
Co., but locality in Pima Co., *18 Sept. 1971* (ARIZ,
S. Speich), and Tuzigoot National Monument,
Yavapai Co., *19 Oct. 1980* (ARIZ, S. Terrill). One
male photographed in Phoenix, 18 to *20 July 1974*
(ARIZ, T. and D. Stejskal). Other sight records
(seven in fall of 1980!) from Quitobaquito, Organ
Pipe Cactus National Monument; Arivaca Jct.,
Pima Co.; Imperial National Wildlife Refuge,
Colorado River; Tanque Verde Ranch east of Tucson;
Tucson; near Blythe, California; Ganado, Navajo
Indian Reservation; Parker; near Phoenix; and
Tempe.

[***Dendroica discolor*** (Vieillot). Prairie Warbler.
Hypothetical. Three sight records, all in winter at or
near Tucson: 7 to 8 Dec. 1952; 14 Jan. 1965 (F.
Thornburg); and 31 Dec. 1974 to 5 Jan. 1975 (R.
Norton, P. Burr et al.).]

380. *Dendroica palmarum* (Gmelin). Palm
Warbler. One taken in open desert about 16 km (10

mi) northeast of Scottsdale in the Phoenix vicinity, *12 Oct. 1964* (US, T.D. Burleigh); another specimen from Tucson, *8 Nov. 1969* (ARIZ, F. Tainter). Also 16 southern Arizona sight records, including wintering birds at Nogales in 1963–64 and again in 1964–65 (B. Harrison), at Lake Pleasant, Maricopa Co., 2 Jan. to 26 Feb. 1966 (R. Norton et al.), and at Wikieup, Big Sandy Valley, 29 to 30 Jan. 1951, ranging from near Safford and Nogales on the east to Parker; three in spring, Walnut Grove, Yavapai Co., 29 Apr. 1956; Roper Lake, Safford, 25 Apr. 1977 (T. Parker et al.), and Nogales, 27 Apr. 1979 (C. Clark). Two northern Arizona reports, Tuweep Ranger Station, North Rim of Grand Canyon, 4 to 10 Dec. 1976 (M.M. Riffey), and Richville, Apache Co., 22 Sept. 1979 (S. Terrill et al.). Also one on California side of Colorado River above Imperial Dam, 22 Sept. 1942; and one on Nevada side at Davis Dam, 9 Oct. 1979 (S. Goldwasser).

The specimens are of the dull nominate race, the "Western" Palm Warbler.

381. *Seiurus aurocapillus* (Linnaeus). Ovenbird. About 35 records, all for May-June, Sept.-Oct., and Dec.-Jan., mostly from southern Arizona but also from the northeast, including *five* at Teec Nos Pos, 15 Oct. 1977 (S. Terrill et al.). Except for one at Parker, 23 Dec. 1977 (A. Gast, B. Edinger), all winter records are from the Phoenix vicinity. Four specimens, near Pioneer Pass, Pinal Mountains, *17 June 1968* (ARIZ, E.L. Smith); in Grand Canyon near confluence with Bright Angel Creek, *14 Sept. 1974* (MNA, R.R. Johnson); at Portal, *5 Oct. 1975* (ARIZ, D. Bogle); and Phoenix, *22 June 1977* (ARIZ, S. Demaree). The first Arizona record was from Walnut Grove, Yavapai Co., 4 May 1955.

The two June specimens are of the nominate race, and the other two we have identified as the slightly duller *S. a. cinereus* Miller.

382. *Seiurus noveboracensis* (Gmelin). Northern Waterthrush. Rather uncommon transient throughout state, along streams and in areas of damp ground. Waterthrushes reported as of this species recorded on Christmas Bird Counts at Phoenix and (once) near Parker, 20 Dec. 1976, but there is no specimen later than *4 Dec. 1964,* Sabino Lake, Santa Catalina Mountains (ARIZ, R.D. Ohmart). The earliest fall date is from Mormon Lake, near Flagstaff, *17 Aug. 1934.*

Geographic variation is slight. Apparently two subspecies may be recognized in fresh fall plumage (but doubtfully by spring): nominate (eastern) *noveboracensis* is more olive-tinged above, less gray or dark, than the widespread western *notabilis* Ridgway. Arizona specimens should mostly be *notabilis,* but a few seem inseparable from eastern birds; one of these, which flew into a window in Tucson *31 Oct. 1955* (ARP), is exceptionally late and could thus be a stray, but this is less likely with another Tucson bird (*26 Apr. 1934,* ARIZ, Phillips) and especially one from Blue Point, mouth of Verde River, *30 Aug. 1970* (MNA, R.R. Johnson and J.M. Simpson).

383. *Seiurus motacilla* (Vieillot). Louisiana Waterthrush. A very sparse transient and winter resident from the Huachuca Mountains west to the Pajaritos Mountains. A specimen from Pajaritos Mountains, *23 Jan. 1966* (ARIZ, B. Harrison), and one was banded and photographed at Tanque Verde Ranch east of Tucson, *31 July 1980* (ARIZ, P.M. Walters). In addition, there are the following sight records: Pajaritos Mountains (two localities), 22 Dec. 1966 to 15 Jan. 1967 (B. Harrison et al.) and 25 Dec. 1966 (E. Willis); Pajaritos Mountains, 17 Feb. 1968 (B. Harrison); Ramsey Canyon, Huachuca Mountains, about 20 Nov. 1971 to 11 Mar. 1972 (many observers); and Patagonia, 27 Apr. 1974 (B. Harrison et al.) and 25 Sept. 1976 (D. Stotz, M.

Hansen). Four specimens were taken in Sonora within 24 to 43 km (15 to 27 mi) of Nogales from *mid-Oct.* to *mid-Dec.* during the *1950s.* A water-thrush on the lower Bill Williams River on the unusually early dates of 31 July to 15 Aug. 1977 (K.V. Rosenberg, A. Higgins) was identified as this species, the identification being supported by the Tucson record above.

384. *Oporornis formosus* (Wilson). Kentucky Warbler. One specimen, Ramsey Canyon, Huachuca Mountains, *23 May 1959,* and one banded and photographed at Portal, *4 May 1974* (ARIZ, S. and W. Spofford). About 16 sight records, mostly in Chiricahua and Huachuca Mountains, but also at Tucson, 18 Sept. 1966 (F. Tainter); Winchester Mountains, 5 May 1974 (T. Parker); Patagonia, 19 May 1974 (D. Danforth); headquarters of Yuma Proving Grounds, Yuma Co., 20 June 1976 (K. and S. Spitler, a stunned bird examined in the hand); Phoenix, 3 to 5 Nov. 1977 (G. Rosenberg et al.); near confluence of Little Colorado River and its South Fork west of Springerville, 1 Sept. 1978 (S. Terrill et al.); Kino Springs near Nogales, 28 to 29 Oct. 1978 (C. Clark et al.); and at bottom of Grand Canyon, 18 June 1979 (R. Dummer, D. Laush). There are no July-Aug. records, and none between 5 Nov. and early May.

385. *Oporornis agilis* (Wilson). Connecticut Warbler. One record, Tucson, 15 and *16 Sept. 1979* (ARIZ, photo, J. Witzeman); bird first found by R. Bradley. Reported in A.O.U. Check-list as casual in Cochise Co.; basis of this statement unknown to us.

386. *Oporornis philadelphia* (Wilson). Mourning Warbler. One record, Pipe Spring National Monu-ment, *31 May 1974* (ARIZ, R. Wilt).

387. *Oporornis tolmiei* (Townsend). MacGillivray's Warbler. Fairly common summer resident in *Ribes*-willow thickets of the Canadian Zone and even the Transition Zone of the White Mountains and (very locally) the San Francisco Mountains and Bill Williams Mountain (the latter in 1975 and 1976, C.S. Tomoff); probably also in the area of Happy Jack, Coconino Co. (R.P. Balda, S. Fellers). Common migrant in brush throughout Arizona, except in unbroken forests. Three winter sight reports in Christmas Bird Count periods, one from Nogales in 1966 and two from Phoenix in 1976. Summer records for southeastern Arizona include one banded and photographed at Tanque Verde Ranch east of Tucson, *19 June 1980* (ARIZ, P.M. Walters), and Chiricahua Mountains, *18 July 1925.*

> The breeding race in Arizona is *O. t. monticola* Phillips; it is sparse as a migrant away from the breeding grounds. *O. t. austinsmithi* Phillips migrates rather commonly west to central Arizona, sparsely farther west; *O. t. tolmiei* (Townsend) migrates throughout; *O. t. intermedia* Phillips does not appear to be separable from *tolmiei.*

388. *Geothlypis trichas* (Linnaeus). Common Yellowthroat. Common summer resident at such reedy marshes as survive in the Sonoran Zones of Arizona, and sometimes in dense, tall grass or weedy fields in the southeast. Breeds up to lower edge of Transition Zone in White Mountains region. Common migrant at weedy, brushy, and swampy places throughout the more open parts of the state from the Transition Zone (where recorded in fall only) down, even occurring in the most arid desert sections sometimes in spring. Males winter rather commonly (females sparsely) along the lower Colorado River, and locally east as far as Safford, Tucson, and

Nogales (and the San Simon Cienega on the New Mexico line?).

G. t. *chryseola* van Rossem is the summer resident over most of Arizona; it also occurs as a migrant and winters at least at Picacho Reservoir, Pinal Co. G. t. *occidentalis* Brewster breeds along the Colorado River and in northern Arizona, is the common transient in southern Arizona (including the type specimen of G. t. *arizonicola* Oberholser), and winters from Tucson west. G. t. *campicola* Behle and Aldrich is a sparse migrant, and has been found in winter at Yuma. G. t. *arizela* Oberholser is chiefly a fall transient, with a few spring records in the southeast, and it has been found in winter at Picacho Reservoir. G. t. *yukonicola* Godfrey is hypothetical in Arizona: one at Bard, California, near Yuma, *3 Apr. 1930* (SD, S.G. Harter).

389. *Cardellina rubrifrons* (Giraud). Red-faced Warbler. Common summer resident of Transition and especially Canadian Zones, west and north to the Santa Rita, Santa Catalina, Hualapai (since 1977, T. Fears and K.V. Rosenberg), and San Francisco Mountains (since 1934); Bill Williams Mountain (1976, C.S. Tomoff); and, in the east, the White Mountains (since 1972, Monson). Recently found in summer on the North Rim of the Grand Canyon: 24 June 1975 (P.W. Post, S. Friedberg), 19 June 1976 (C.J. Ralph), 10 June 1977 (M.W. Larson), and 10 Aug. 1977 (R. Ringler). A male was found near the top of Baboquivari Peak, 7 June 1974 (Monson), and one was seen at Green Valley, south of Tucson, 2 June 1978 (A. Brison). Migrant in adjacent Upper Sonoran Zone during cold springs; three lowland records on migration, near Tucson, *26 Apr. 1940;* at Phoenix, 12 May 1971 (B. Burch et al.); and at Sun City, near Phoenix, 11 Oct. 1978 (R. Beveridge). Casual in foothills of Santa Catalina Mountains, 22 Feb. 1956.

390. *Wilsonia citrina* (Boddaert). Hooded Warbler. Sparse, somewhat irregular, vagrant in southern and central Arizona, mainly from Chiricahua Mountains west to Santa Rita Mountains, several of the records pertaining to singing birds heard repeatedly in the same locality, all between late Apr. and late Oct. except for one at Cooks Lake, lower San Pedro Valley, 27 Oct. to 20 Nov. 1978 (S. Terrill et al.). Extreme-range records include Bill Williams Delta, 29 June 1979 (T. Brush); near Prescott, 13 July to 22 Sept. 1979 (C.S. Tomoff et al.); and Littlefield in extreme northwestern Arizona, 18 May 1979 (M.M. Riffey). About 27 records in all. One specimen, Patagonia, *13 July 1947.*

391. *Wilsonia pusilla* (Wilson). Wilson's Warbler. Common to abundant transient in southern, central, and western Arizona, but apparently less numerous in the north. Records up to 16 June in the White Mountains area seem to be of late migrants rather than nesting birds. Sparse in winter in southern Arizona from St. David (13 to 14 Jan. 1973, D. Danforth et al.) and Patagonia west. One in tamarisks at Fredonia, 30 Nov. 1980 (L. and S. Terrill, G. and K.V. Rosenberg), was casually late. Feb. records are almost lacking, although "several" spent the winter of 1973–74 in the Phoenix area (according to J. Witzeman).

The nominate race is a rare but probably regular May transient in southeastern Arizona and casual farther northwest. *W. p. pileolata* (Pallas) is the abundant transient generally, except in early spring. *W. p. chryseola* Ridgway is a rather common spring transient in southwestern Arizona east to Tucson (occasionally farther northeast), more common and widespread in the fall when it has occurred east to the San Francisco and Chiricahua Mountains. The only winter specimen is *pileolata.*

392. *Wilsonia canadensis* (Linnaeus). Canada Warbler. Two specimens, Pipe Spring National Monument, *29 Sept. 1974* (ARIZ, R. Wilt), and Tucson, about *15 Aug. 1979* (ARIZ, M. McKitrick, skeleton only saved). Four sight records, lower Sabino Canyon, Santa Catalina Mountains, 6 to 7 Sept. 1975 (C. Kangas et al.); Tucson, 19 Oct. 1979 (K. Kaufman et al.); Boyce Thompson Southwestern Arboretum, Superior, 21 to *27 Oct. 1979* (ARIZ, photo, K.V. Rosenberg et al.); and Prescott, 3 Oct. 1980 (C.S. Tomoff).

393. *Setophaga ruticilla* (Linnaeus). American Redstart. A regular summer resident (not more than one or two pairs?) on Little Colorado River at confluence with its South Fork west of Springerville; nest and young found there, 14 July 1976, and nest collected (ARIZ) in 1979 after young fledged (B. Jones). Nested (unsuccessfully?) near Prescott in 1977 (C.S. Tomoff). Almost regular, but sparse, in midsummer, usually singing males, mostly in southeastern Arizona but sometimes in Phoenix region and along lower Colorado River. Occurs regularly, singly and in small numbers, as a sparse transient throughout Arizona, most frequent relatively in the northeast. Quite sparse in winter, with records from Tucson and Patagonia west to the Colorado River.

394. *Setophaga picta* Swainson. Painted Redstart. Common summer resident of the Upper Sonoran Zone (higher evergreen oaks, juniper, pinyon, etc., usually mixed with pines) of all southern and central Arizona, west to the Baboquivari Mountains and north to the Hualapai Mountains and the Mogollon Rim. Found post-breeding into the Transition and Canadian Zones of the same areas and sparsely down into lower limit of evergreen oak growth. Winters (not every year?) sparingly in some lower canyons of the Santa Catalina, Huachuca, Santa

Rita, Pajaritos, and Baboquivari Mountains; also, since about 1970, one or two at feeders at Portal and in Ramsey Canyon of the Huachuca Mountains in winter (a banded bird returned to Portal feeders for the eighth consecutive winter in 1980—S. Spofford). An occasional migrant in valleys and low foothills in southern and central Arizona, chiefly in the Tucson and Phoenix areas, casually to sparsely east to the San Bernardino Valley east of Douglas, early Apr. 1948 (H. Brandt), and west to the Ajo Mountains, 26 Mar. 1972 (according to R. Wilt), and the Colorado River from Davis Dam south (six records); one taken at Davis Dam (Nevada side), *27 Feb. 1976* (University of Nevada Museum of Biology, Las Vegas, C.S. Lawson). Sight records from Grand Canyon National Park are: Phantom Ranch, 2 Apr. 1956 (W.E. Dilley); North Rim, 3 June 1974 (H.C. Bryant); and just below South Rim, 21 Sept. 1958 (L. Hinchcliffe). At least two records from Zion National Park, Utah (according to W.H. Behle).

Arizona birds are of nominate *picta,* the widespread race with much white in the wing.

395. *Setophaga miniata* Swainson. Slate-throated Redstart. One found in Miller Canyon, Huachuca Mountains, 10 Apr. *1976* by R.K. Morse, was photographed *14 Apr.* (ARIZ, R. Norden), and was last seen 15 Apr. (B. Harrison).

396. *Euthlypis lachrymosa* (Bonaparte). Fan-tailed Warbler. One specimen, Baker Spring, north of Guadalupe Canyon, Cochise Co., *28 May 1961.*

The bird is the large, pale, olive-tinged *E. l. tephra* Ridgway.

397. *Basileuterus rufifrons* (Swainson). Rufous-capped Warbler. First found in *1977* in lower Cave Creek Canyon, Chiricahua Mountains, when a singing male was seen 9 May by M. Braun. Later, in July, a female was seen, and a nest with two eggs was located 19 July by H. Barker et al. On *17 July* one bird was photographed (ARIZ, M. Evans). The species was last seen 23 July (G. McCaskie, J. Dunn). The abandoned nest with four eggs was collected *1 Aug.* (AMNH, F. Ranson). Seen again in same locality, 8 Apr. 1978 (D. Stotz, K. Kaufman, E. Cook). The Rufous-capped Warbler was also recorded in Arroyo Cajón Bonito, extreme northeastern Sonora, 13 Sept. 1975 (a singing male, D. Danforth et al.) and again 16 May 1976 (at least three singing males, S.M. Russell, D. Lamm).

398. *Icteria virens* (Linnaeus). Yellow-breasted Chat. Very common summer resident of dense mesquite-willow-*Baccharis* and arrowweed associations along streams and at ponds in Lower Sonoran Zone; fairly common summer resident in deciduous brush along streams and in irrigated lands in Upper Sonoran Zone. May have bred at Museum of Northern Arizona in Transition Zone, Flagstaff (S. Carothers). Sparse transient elsewhere, including the Transition Zone and the arid deserts of southwestern Arizona, and more often garden shrubbery in cities. No winter records.

All Arizona specimens are *I. v. auricollis* (Deppe).

FAMILY THRAUPIDAE: TANAGERS

399. *Piranga ludoviciana* (Wilson). Western Tanager. Common summer resident in Transition and boreal zones throughout the state except from Prescott region northwest, where at least formerly not breeding (but several, mostly in pairs with males singing, in Hualapai Mountains, June 1978, K.V. Rosenberg et al.). Common, sometimes abundant, transient throughout Arizona, some fall birds arriving in low desert areas in early July, soon after the last spring migrants depart. Since about 1973, a diminution in numbers, both as resident and transient. A handful of winter records, mostly from Phoenix, but also from Tucson and once from Portal, *16 Dec. 1972* (ARIZ, photo, S. and W. Spofford).

400. *Piranga olivacea* (Gmelin). Scarlet Tanager. Very sparse, only nine records, all in the south (except two at Petrified Forest National Park, 3 and 4 June 1979, R. Thomas et al.) from Portal on the east to Wikieup and Quitobaquito on the west. First found in the state *18 May 1884*. All records fall between Mar. to June and Oct. to Nov. One banded and photographed at Blythe, California, 18 Oct. 1970 (H. Robert).

401. *Piranga flava* (Vieillot). Hepatic Tanager. Common summer resident in dense oaks, fairly common in pines and large pinyons, throughout southern and central Arizona. Local, mostly absent, in north (but at least six at Lakeside, Navajo Co., 12 Sept. 1977, Monson). No records from extreme northeast. Breeding range includes Hualapai and Baboquivari-Quinlan Mountains. Winters rather sparsely in Santa Cruz Co., from the Sonoita Valley west to the Santa Rita and Pajaritos Mountains; one was seen in Garden Canyon, Huachuca Mountains, 9 Feb. 1974 (J. Hoover). There are five winter records for the Phoenix region (some of which may have been immature Summer Tanagers?), and wintering birds were noted at La Morita, Sonora, southeast of Naco, Cochise Co., 18 and 25 Feb. 1973 (W. Ranney). Has been recorded on migration in lowlands about ten times, all in the south, from Tombstone (1 May 1974, D. Danforth) west to the Colorado River (about 29 km [18 mi] above Imperial Dam, *18 Nov. 1960*). A report from the extreme northwest (Virgin River) is unsubstantiated. One

record from California side of Imperial Dam, 19
Dec. 1973 (A. Collister) and another from the
California side near Parker Dam, 27 Mar. to 12 Apr.
1975 (R. Erickson, J. Dunn et al.).

Arizona birds belong to the dull northwestern race *P. f.
hepatica* Swainson.

402. *Piranga rubra* (Linnaeus). Summer Tanager.
Common summer resident in most of the willow-
cottonwood association of the Lower Sonoran Zone,
rather uncommon in other broad-leafed cover (sycamore, walnut) and even locally evergreen oaks of the
Sonoran zones, south and west of the Mogollon
Plateau; also (commonly?) to Beaver Dam Wash in
extreme northwest, and, recently, to bottom of
Grand Canyon. Sparse transient, Apr.-May and end
of July to Sept. in the Sonoran Zones away from its
breeding grounds; has strayed to 1980 m (6500 ft) in
the Pinaleno Mountains, *20 July 1940* (CM, A.C.
Twomey), to near the confluence of the Little
Colorado River and its South Fork west of Springer-
ville, 14 July 1976 (B. Jones et al.), and to Pipe
Spring National Monument, 24 to 26 Sept. 1974 (R.
Wilt). In winter has been found in the Phoenix and
Tucson regions, also south of Nogales in Sonora and
at Patagonia, and along the Colorado River near
Needles, California, 21 Jan. 1944 (Monson) and in
the Bill Williams Delta, 24 Dec. 1977 (D. Stejskal).
A molting male at Bard, California, near Yuma, 9
Apr. 1966 (G. McCaskie) perhaps represented a
wintering bird. The species apparently breeds in the
Virgin River Valley of southwestern Utah (R. Wauer
et al.), and in the spring of 1979 was recorded at
Durango, Colorado (E. Fox) and near Monticello in
southeastern Utah (F. Blackburn).

The nominate race is the only one known to winter in
Arizona, and apparently occurs sparsely in migration.
Otherwise, southern and eastern Arizona birds are *P. r.*

cooperi Ridgway; those of the Big Sandy Valley, and possibly the nearby upper part of the Colorado Valley, are *P. r. ochracea* Phillips, as are specimens from Tucson, *18* or *20 Apr. 1938* and *31 July 1953* (DEL, Phillips).

FAMILY EMBERIZIDAE: EMBERIZINE FINCHES

403. *Cardinalis cardinalis* (Linnaeus). Cardinal. Now a common resident (reports of altitudinal movements unconfirmed) of the taller and denser Lower Sonoran brush of southern and central Arizona, west to the Organ Pipe Cactus National Monument, the Gila Valley above Gila Bend, and Wickenburg; and north (mainly along rivers) to upper Verde Valley and the foot of the Mogollon Plateau in several places, west to upper Hassayampa Valley (Monson). In recent years (since about 1940?), also a small population along the Bill Williams and Big Sandy Rivers that extends to the Colorado Valley in the Parker area; this population is perhaps the source of vagrants to Poston and Yuma and to Needles, California. Resident in some numbers and locally of the Upper Sonoran Zone at Tonto Natural Bridge near Payson, Globe, Oracle, the Dragoon Mountains (D. Danforth et al.), and various localities in the Chiricahua Mountains (S. Spofford et al.). Uncommon to sparse at Prescott in winter; also a specimen from Horse Tank, Castle Dome Mountains, Yuma Co., *24 Feb. 1956*. Has considerably extended its range since 1870.

Arizona specimens belong to the race *C. c. superbus* (Ridgway).

404. *Cardinalis sinuatus* (Bonaparte). Pyrrhuloxia. Rather common summer resident in dense Lower Sonoran Zone brush of southeastern and south-central Arizona, from Guadalupe Canyon in the extreme southeast, the southern part of the San Simon Valley, and the upper San Pedro Valley, west over most of the Papago Indian Reservation to the Ajo region and the Gila River Indian Reservation, also locally in the southern half of the Sulphur Springs Valley (from Cochise area south). In *1958* and *1959* found westward to the Castle Dome and Mohawk Mountains of Yuma Co., as well as the Growler Valley in western Pima Co., where it persisted at least until 1962. It has occupied the Gila River Indian Reservation recently (A.M. Rea), and nested, at least in 1975, near Wickenburg (K. Kingsley). Winters over same range (except in parts of the San Pedro Valley) and also in the Patagonia area and other areas higher than the breeding range, even into evergreen oaks (i.e., Portal area, east sides of Santa Rita and Huachuca Mountains, Pajaritos and Baboquivari Mountains, Oracle vicinity). Wanders north in winter to Gila Bend, Phoenix (eight on Christmas Bird Count, 1976), near Superior, Globe (B. Jackson et al.), and San Carlos, as well as the lower San Pedro Valley. Coues' report from the Yuma district is to be disregarded. Nest found in June 1977 along Chemehuevi Wash about 40 km (25 mi) south of Needles, California (N. Green, P. Mack et al.).

Specimens from southeastern Cochise Co. belong to the nominate form. Other Arizona birds are of the race *C. s. fulvescens* van Rossem.

405. *Pheucticus chrysopeplus* (Vigors). Yellow Grosbeak. Six records, all in summer, since 1971: Patagonia, *8* to 30 *June 1971* (ARIZ, photo, J. and N. Strickling et al.); Southwestern Research Station, Chiricahua Mountains, 7 June 1974 (S.M. Russell); Patagonia, 21 June 1975 (E. and S. Cardiff et al.); Madera Canyon, Santa Rita Mountains, *4 June 1977* (ARIZ, photo, P. and J.A. Moroz); Ramsey

Canyon, Huachuca Mountains, 15–17 June 1977
(J. and C. Peabody, D. Danforth et al.); and near
Prescott, *26 July 1977* (C. and L. Ostrom, ARIZ,
photo by V. Miller). Some of these may be escapes,
but the seasonal pattern argues for natural occurrences.

406. *Pheucticus ludovicianus* (Linnaeus). Common
(Rose-breasted and Black-headed) Grosbeak. The
two races are treated separately:

The nominate race, or Rose-breasted Grosbeak,
has been found as a vagrant in Arizona every month
of the year, with the great preponderance of records
being in May-June and Oct.-Nov., and no winter
records in the north. Fewest birds are seen in Aug.-
Sept. and in Feb. and Mar. It is found throughout the
state, even in the Transition and boreal zones (i.e.,
Fish Creek north of Greer, Apache Co., a singing
male, 15 June 1976, Monson). There is no definite
evidence of breeding.

P. l. melanocephalus (Swainson), the breeding
form, and *P. l. maculatus* (Audubon) constitute the
Black-headed Grosbeak, a common summer resident
of the Transition Zone and, in southern Arizona, of
moist and high Upper Sonoran woodland, especially
about creeks and deciduous thickets. Common transient in most parts of the state below Canadian Zone,
rarely higher, with records of migrants spanning the
summer. A few winter reports from southern Arizona
since 1971 are mainly for Dec., with two or three for
early Jan. and none in Feb., from Portal west to the
Colorado River.

407. *Passerina caerulea* (Linnaeus). Blue Grosbeak. Fairly common summer resident of willow,
cottonwood, and moist mesquite-farmland and mes-
quite-grassland associations of the Sonoran zones,
including the northwest and Grand Canyon. Transient
even in high White Mountains, and probably bred
once, a male and two immature females at Big Lake,

8 Aug. 1940 (CM, A.C. Twomey); as well as transient casually in the arid southwest, at Papago Well, in extreme southwestern Pima Co., 26 Aug. 1959 (Monson) and along the Pinacate Lava Flow in extreme southeastern Yuma Co., *23 Apr. 1961* (US, R.D. Johnson). In some winters may be found in small numbers at St. David, Patagonia, and the Nogales region in weedy patches, sparsely at Phoenix and even scarcer along the Colorado River below Parker.

P. c. salicaria (Grinnell) is the race found along the Colorado River. Birds in the Big Sandy Valley and Organ Pipe Cactus National Monument are variable between it and the race occurring in the rest of Arizona, *P. c. interfusa* (Dwight and Griscom). Winter birds have not been determined, except for one from Parker, *18 Feb. 1951,* which is *salicaria.*

408. *Passerina cyanea* (Linnaeus). Common (Indigo and Lazuli) Bunting. The two races are treated separately:

The nominate race, or Indigo Bunting, formerly lacking in Arizona, in the 1970s was an uncommon but local summer resident in the lower Colorado River Valley, chiefly in the Bill Williams Delta and in the Topock-Needles area, according to K.V. Rosenberg et al., who accounted for over 40 singing males between the Topock area and the Imperial National Wildlife Refuge in 1977 and saw fledglings being fed at Needles, California; Topock; and Bill Williams Delta. It was found breeding at Indian Gardens, Grand Canyon, 31 July 1964 (three juveniles, D.L. Carter, D. Easterla); in the Oak Creek Canyon (south of Flagstaff) and Prescott areas by the 1940s; at Patagonia in 1967 (G. McCaskie); and possibly near Portal in 1978 (R.J. Morse) and definitely in 1980 (S. and W. Spofford). Small numbers, but sometimes as many as 12 in one area, usually males, are reported annually in most other areas of southern and central Arizona, usually in Sonoran zones but even to Transition Zone, where a pair was feeding one young in the Huachuca Mountains, 7 to 8 July 1979 (K.Kaufman). Records in the north are sparse (not more than ten), but this is probably because of a lack of observers. Mainly seen May to Sept.; one winter record, a male at a Portal feeder, 12 Jan. 1980 (M. Crutcher).

The Lazuli Bunting, *P. c. amoena* (Say), is a rather uncommon summer resident in willow associations of the Sonoran zones of central and northeastern Arizona, south and west to the bottom of the Grand Canyon, Prescott, Camp Verde, and possibly the Mazatzal Mountains (female on nest near Camp Creek [date?], S. Terrill) and Sierra Ancha. Common transient in brush and tall herbaceous vegetation throughout the less densely wooded parts of the state. Since about 1950, a large number of midsummer reports, generally of singing males, in southern Arizona indicate that many transient birds do not reach northern Arizona and beyond, but remain in the south all summer. However, there are no definite nesting records for the south. These midsummer reports include singing males and females in late July 1976, 1977, and 1979 at Topock and a singing male and a female in late June 1978 in a citrus orchard at Blythe, California (both according to K.V. Rosenberg). Winters locally (only since about 1939?) in weedy areas in small numbers (but up to 125 on the Nogales Christmas Bird Count, 21 Dec. 1966) in southern Arizona from the upper San Pedro Valley west to the Santa Cruz Valley, sparsely west to Phoenix and east as far as Douglas and Portal but not as far north as Safford.

> The extent of crosses between the two races in Arizona is unknown, but it does not seem to be significant. On the other hand, very few *c. cyanea* have been found breeding, and females are easily confused.

409. *Passerina versicolor* (Bonaparte). Varied Bunting. Locally a common to uncommon summer resident, breeding July-Sept., in low thorny thickets of the higher Lower Sonoran and low Upper Sonoran Zones in foothill canyons and washes of southern Arizona (west perhaps to the Ajo area), north to the Santa Catalina Mountains (in 1976–79, singing males seen in upper Aravaipa Canyon, Graham Co., J. Schnell and G.S. Mills) with the Pajaritos and Baboquivari Mountains the center of abundance; no records for Huachuca Mountains. Extralimital records are from: near confluence of San Francisco and Gila Rivers in Greenlee Co., 10 June 1975 (R. Bradley); the east side of the Mohave Mountains near the Colorado River, *27 Oct. 1949;* the Bill Williams Delta, 20 Sept. 1952; Wikieup, 1 to 6 Oct. 1952; and near Portal, summers of 1979 and 1980 (R.J. Morse). No satisfactory winter records, although 15 or more seen at Blythe, California, side of the Colorado River in *Feb. 1914,* including two specimens, *8* and *9 Feb.* One reported from Glenwood, Catron Co., New Mexico, 12 June 1977 (D. Mc-Knight).

With the exception of the Mohave Mountains specimen, which is the duller nominate race, Arizona birds are of the race *P. v. pulchra* Ridgway; *P. v. dickeyae* van Rossem appears to be a synonym.

410. *Passerina ciris* (Linnaeus). Painted Bunting. Sparse late summer and early fall visitant to southeastern Arizona, west to Nogales and Tucson areas; also casually to Aguajita Spring, Organ Pipe Cactus National Monument, 22 Sept. 1967 (R. Cunningham) and near Ehrenberg, Yuma Co., *8 Nov. 1976* (ARIZ, B. Anderson). Casual at Ganado, Navajo Indian Reservation, 17 Aug. 1980 (K.V. Rosenberg et al.). A winter record for Canoa Ranch near Green Valley, *27 Jan. 1965* (ARIZ, S.M. Russell). Until 1884 at least, a fairly common fall transient (not "casual," as stated by A.O.U. Check-list) in extreme southeastern Arizona, north to the Gila River and west to the Pinaleno Mountains and the Nogales area. Common to abundant in northern Sonora at times.

P. c. pallidior Mearns is the only race found in Arizona, as far as known.

411. *Pipilo chlorurus* (Audubon). Green-tailed Towhee. Rather common summer resident in low deciduous brush of the Transition and boreal zones of the White and San Francisco Mountains, Bill Williams Mountain (1976, C.S. Tomoff), and the Kaibab Plateau. Common transient in dense brush throughout Arizona. Winters fairly commonly in low, weedy brush of the Lower Sonoran Zone and adjacent areas of the Upper Sonoran Zone of central and central-southern Arizona; in most winters scarce in extreme west, southwest, and southeast. Following spring migration an occasional individual lingers in the south into mid- and late June, from near Patagonia and Tucson east.

412. *Pipilo maculatus* Swainson. Western or Patterned Towhee ("Rufous-sided," part; Spotted Towhee). Common summer resident in dense broad-leafed brush of the Upper Sonoran Zone, ranging locally into the Transition Zone and even up to the lower edge of the boreal zones. Winters commonly in the Upper Sonoran foothills of northwestern, central, and southern Arizona, and fairly commonly in brushy canyons and river valleys of Lower Sonoran Zone of southeastern Arizona; less commonly westward to the Colorado River, where it is a rather sparse transient and usually scarce in winter in most years. May be sparse in winter in Transition Zone. Reported commonly in area of Phantom Ranch, bottom of Grand Canyon, in Jan. 1937 (V. Veatch). Apparently sparse to uncommon in winter in the northeast.

Earliest names for any Patterned Towhee are *P. maculatus* Swainson and *P. macronyx* Swainson, 1827; since these were published simultaneously, as first revisers we select *maculatus* as the specific name. The Eastern, "Red-eyed," or "Rufous-sided" (part) *P. erythrophthalmus* (Linnaeus) is considered specifically distinct.

Arizona birds are chiefly of the race *P. m. montanus* (Swarth). *P. m. maculatus* Swainson is casual in winter, one specimen from Camp Verde in *1888*. *P. m. curtatus* Grinnell is equally common as *montanus* as a winter resident. *P. m. megalonyx* Baird occurs sparsely or casually in winter, all specimens being from south-western Arizona. A number of intermediate specimens (*montanus* x *curtatus, montanus* x *megalonyx*) have been taken.

413. *Pipilo fuscus* Swainson. Brown Towhee. Common resident in scattered low but dense brush in Lower Sonoran Zone and low Upper Sonoran Zone of most of southern, central, and northwestern Arizona, including the area about the head of Lake Mead (Mar. 1974 and Apr. 1975, A.M. Rea). Restricted to rocky hills and desert mining camps westwardly. Found west to the Mohave and Black Mountains of western Mohave Co., the Kofa Mountains, and the Ajo region west sparingly to Papago Well in extreme southwestern Pima Co. Island populations are found on the north side of the White Mountains region from west of Springerville to Sanders and Lupton. Three sight records along rims of Grand Canyon, from Village westward.

P. f. mesoleucus Baird is the race found in Arizona; *P. f. relictus* van Rossem is not considered separable.

414. *Pipilo aberti* Baird. Abert's Towhee. Common resident in southern, western, and central Arizona and extreme northwestern Arizona and southwestern Utah in dense undergrowth of the willow-cottonwood and large mesquite associations of the main streams of the Lower Sonoran Zone and some of their tributaries (i.e., Aravaipa Creek, lower Sabino Canyon of Santa Catalina Mountains, Happy Valley on the east side of the Rincon Mountains, Trout Creek in the Big Sandy drainage in Mohave Co.) and at isolated waters with dense brush (i.e., Cluff Ranch near Pima, Graham Co.; Rabbit Farm northeast of Bowie, Cochise Co.). It is also found in large mesquite associations in the Avra Valley, Pima Co. Strays outside of breeding season increasingly to such places as Boyce Thompson Southwestern Arboretum, Superior; Pima Canyon, Santa Catalina Mountains; Fort Huachuca sewage treatment plant; San Simon Cienega, Cochise Co.; and (since about 1970) the Nogales region. The Upper Sonoran Zone report ("Fort Whipple") is in error

> The nominate race (which includes *P. a. dumeticolus* van Rossem) ranges from the Colorado River east to the Phoenix area, except in the Big Sandy Valley, where the population is variable. *P. a. vorhiesi* Phillips occupies the Santa Cruz Valley eastward, probably including all upper Gila Valley birds. The lower Gila Valley birds (from confluence with San Pedro River downstream) are variable.

415. *Calamospiza melanocorys* Stejneger. Lark Bunting. Common to abundant winter resident (from late July to early May) in brushless, weedy, or barren-looking parts of the Lower Sonoran Zone and low Upper Sonoran Zone of southeastern Arizona north to San Carlos Indian Reservation; scarcer and irregular westward but common some years, even to southern Nevada, usually reaching the Colorado River only in fall. Apparently a fairly common transient in eastern Arizona in open Upper Sonoran Zone from Holbrook south to Fort Apache; rather sparse and irregular in spring farther west or north (but large flock south of Pipe Spring National Monument, 22 May 1973, R. Wilt). One seen at Pipe Spring, 24 Dec. 1967 (J. Schaack). Nested in *1973* at Chino Valley, Yavapai Co., when a juvenile, accompanied by five adult pairs, was taken after it had struck a fence, *24 July* (REA, L. Muehlbach). Extreme dates otherwise range from *9 July 1940* near Tucson to 3 June 1978 north of San Simon, Cochise Co. (S. and W. Spofford).

416. *Ammodramus sandwichensis* (Gmelin). Savannah Sparrow. Fairly common summer resident locally at lakes and moist fields on and just north of the Mogollon Plateau in the White Mountains (including Springerville area), also possibly Mormon Lake (and formerly Kayenta?). Heard singing at Willcox in two out of three years (1977–79, G.S. Mills) and seen there as late as 4 June 1977 (pair, K. Kaufman). Common transient at lakes, ponds, marshes, and in fields and level grassy spots throughout the state. Common to abundant in winter in irrigated valleys, grassy swales and plains (where rather irregular), and along bodies of water in Sonoran zones throughout southern and western Arizona. Also found locally in winter in weedy fields and grassy edges of lakes and ponds in northern Arizona, casually into Transition Zone (near Lakeside, *18 Dec. 1936,* and at Flagstaff, 18 Dec. 1971, Christmas Bird Count). Late summer straggler from south to lakes near Yuma; one authentic record, *15 Aug. 1902.* One seen south of Parker, 27 June 1978 (K.V. Rosenberg).

The Yuma summer record is that of the "Large-billed Sparrow," *A. s. rostratus* (Cassin). The breeding race is *A. s. rufofuscus* (Camras); it is almost unknown as a transient and winter resident. *A. s. brooksi* (Bishop) is a sparse winter visitant (?) in Arizona. *A. s. nevadensis* (Grinnell) is easily the commonest transient race, and is very common in winter. *A. s. anthinus* (Bonaparte) is also very common in winter.

417. *Ammodramus savannarum* (Gmelin). Grasshopper Sparrow. Common to fairly common summer resident in dense grassland and alfalfa fields of San Rafael and Babocomari Valleys, near Nogales, on the Sonoita Plains, (sparsely?) south of Sierra Vista, and southwest of Apache, Cochise Co. Bred commonly near Arivaca at least in 1979 (B. Harrison, Monson); in the same summer one was singing at Kansas Settlement, Cochise Co., on 12 July (Monson); a singing bird was on the Santa Rita Range Reserve in the summer of 1976 (S.M. Russell) and in May-June 1979 (K. Kaufman); and a male was found at Chino Valley, Yavapai Co., *12 July 1973* (REA, A.M. Rea, L. Muehlbach, L.L. Hargrave). Has bred (possibly irregularly) at Fort Grant, Graham Co., and perhaps once (1916) at Camp Verde. Sparse migrant along lower Colorado Valley. Fairly common winter resident in dense grass (usually mixed with low brush) of southeastern Arizona, west to the Papago Indian Reservation; lacking in central Arizona; uncommon and irregular (including Growler Valley, western Pima Co.) farther west, even to the Colorado River, where there are about six records, including two specimens (in harvested cotton fields near Poston, Yuma Co., *11 Jan. 1979,* ARIZ, J. Drake, and one on Cibola National Wildlife Refuge, Yuma Co., *18 Dec. 1979,* ARIZ, R. Dummer). Also a winter record years ago at mouth of Bill Williams River (not on Big Sandy River, as stated in the A.O.U. Check-list).

A. s. perpallidus (Coues) is the common race, except locally in the extreme south. *A. s. ammolegus* Oberholser is the breeding race, and although most move into Sonora for the winter, a few winter on or near the breeding grounds. A specimen from lower Gardner Canyon, Santa Rita Mountains, *28 Sept. 1958,* seems to be *A. s. pratensis* (Vieillot) (ARIZ, J.T. Bialac).

418. *Ammodramus bairdii* (Audubon). Baird's Sparrow. Until about 1878 an abundant transient and doubtless winter resident in the grasslands of southeastern Arizona, north to northern Graham Co. and west along the border to the Altar Valley; until about 1920 decidedly uncommon but still a winter resident about the bases of the Chiricahua and Huachuca Mountains. Now seemingly much sparser, especially in mid-winter, recent (1940 and later) records coming from only beneath these and the Santa Rita and Patagonia Mountains, the Sonoita Plains, the San Rafael Valley, and the upper Altar Valley. Has been found south of Bowie, Cochise Co. (*Apr.*); near Eagar, Apache Co., *14 Oct. 1934;* and once at Tucson, *28 Oct. 1977* (ARIZ, R. Henry).

[*Ammodramus caudacutus* (Gmelin). Sharp-tailed Sparrow. Hypothetical near California side of Imperial Dam, 29 Mar. 1975 (F. Heath, according to G. McCaskie).]

419. *Pooecetes gramineus* (Gmelin). Vesper Sparrow. Fairly common summer resident in dry grasslands from high Upper Sonoran Zone to boreal zones along and north from the Mogollon Plateau. Common migrant in open country generally. Winters commonly in weedy fields and grassy areas in Sonoran zones of southern and (locally) central Arizona, northwest to the Verde and Big Sandy Valleys and Davis Dam.

P. g. confinis Baird is the common transient and winter visitant. *P. g. altus* Marshall is the breeding subspecies, and occurs to an unknown extent as a transient and probably winter resident.

420. *Chondestes grammacus* (Say). Lark Sparrow. Locally a fairly common summer resident in brushy grasslands from high Lower Sonoran Zone to Transition Zone in eastern Arizona west to upper Altar Valley, Prescott region, and perhaps Grand Canyon region (also possibly in Mt. Trumbull area); but distribution between these points not continuous. Also nests found in 1939 at Quitobaquito, Organ Pipe Cactus National Monument; in 1977 in orchards around Blythe, California (D. Wells et al.); and in 1978–79 at orchards and farmhouses at Blythe and at Parker, Yuma, and Tacna in Yuma Co. (K.V. Rosenberg et al.). Common migrant in eastern Arizona, uncommon migrant west of the Baboquivari and Aquarius Mountains and the Phoenix region. Winters commonly in weedy farmlands and fairly commonly in grass-brush associations of the Lower Sonoran Zone of southern Arizona and the lower Colorado Valley, east and north to the San Pedro and Verde Valleys.

All Arizona specimens are *C. g. strigatus* Swainson.

421. *Spizella arborea* (Wilson). Tree Sparrow. Very sparse winter resident in brushy and weedy parts of the Transition Zone, and of Upper Sonoran Zone rivers and farmlands, on and northeast of the Mogollon Plateau. Ranges west and south to House Rock Valley, Coconino Co., 15 to 17 Nov. 1974 (R.L. Todd); Flagstaff; and the upper Black River in the White Mountains. Casual to the San Carlos area, Gila Valley, *11* and *22 Jan. 1937,* and to southern Nevada; near Indian Gardens, Grand Canyon, 12 Feb. 1939 (E. McKee); and south of Parker, 11 Feb. 1977 (two seen [!], K.V. Rosenberg). An old report near Tucson is unsubstantiated.

Arizona specimens are *S. a. ochracea* Brewster.

422. *Spizella passerina* (Bechstein). Chipping Sparrow. Abundant summer resident in open parts of Transition and boreal zones, and rather common in open wooded parts of Upper Sonoran Zone, west and south to the Hualapai Mountains, the Prescott region, Payson, Whiteriver, and the Big Lue Mountains in Greenlee Co. Also breeds locally in Upper Sonoran woods and Transition Zone of the Huachuca and Chiricahua Mountains, and possibly recently in the Santa Catalina and Pinaleno Mountains. One observed in Phoenix, 6 June 1974 (D. and P. Stejskal). Migrates throughout the state. Generally winters abundantly in oak-grassland (Upper Sonoran Zone) of central-southern Arizona, and commonly in farmlands and moister parts (grassy or wooded) of Lower Sonoran Zone throughout southern Arizona, north less commonly to Davis Dam, the Big Sandy Valley, the Camp Verde region, and the upper Gila Valley. Twelve reported at Springerville, 25 Dec. 1980 (Christmas Bird Count).

The common Arizona race is *S. p. arizonae* Coues. The darker nominate race occurs, chiefly in the east, but is probably only casual. *S. p. stridula* Grinnell and *S. p. boreophila* Oberholser are considered synonyms of *arizonae*.

423. *Spizella pallida* (Swainson). Clay-colored Sparrow. Sparse transient (formerly more common?), and possibly an even sparser winter resident, from Sonoita Valley east. Occurs sporadically west to Nogales and Tucson, and once to Altar Valley (29 Jan. 1956). Reports from as far west and north as the Ajo Mountains, Phoenix, and Sedona, and from the Springerville region, are unsubstantiated. Some published records are erroneous.

424. *Spizella breweri* Cassin. Brewer's Sparrow. Common summer resident in sage and other tall, fairly dense brush of Upper Sonoran Zone in the northern part of the Navajo Indian Reservation, and to an unknown extent farther west (nesting in Toroweap Valley, north of Grand Canyon in Mohave

Co., 1975, M.M. Riffey). A colony also in Lower Sonoran Zone, Camp Verde to Fossil Creek, in 1880s. There are single summer records for Flagstaff and near Tucson, but none for "Fort Whipple" (Prescott), where erroneously stated to breed by the A.O.U. Check-list. Common to abundant migrant in open areas statewide except in boreal zones, where uncommon. Abundant winter resident in Lower Sonoran Zone (except in drier open areas, with purer creosote bush stands, of the extreme southwest, where much less common; and except in uncultivated portions of the Colorado Valley); sparser in northern edge of Lower Sonoran Zone but winters to near Kingman, to southern Nevada, and to Pipe Spring National Monument (Dec. 1963–Jan. 1964, R. Wauer et al.).

> Arizona specimens are all of the nominate race, except for one specimen from Honeymoon on Eagle Creek, Greenlee Co., *23 May 1935,* and another from Komatke, Gila River Indian Reservation, *16 May 1965* (REA, A.M. Rea), which are tentatively referred to *S. b. taverneri* Swarth and Brooks.

425. *Spizella pusilla* (Wilson). Field Sparrow. One documented record: a bird at a feeder in Ganado, Navajo Indian Reservation, 10 to *17 Jan. 1980* (ARIZ, photo, M.W. Loder). One reported on or about 29 Nov. 1974 near Topock (J. O'Connell).

426. *Spizella atrogularis* (Cabanis). Black-chinned Sparrow. Fairly common summer resident in Upper Sonoran chaparral across Arizona from east to northwest below the Mogollon Rim, west to the Hualapai Mountains and Grand Wash Cliffs (D.H. Ellis, 1979); south locally to the Chiricahua and Mule Mountains and possibly the south end of the Huachuca Mountains (but not in Sonora, as stated in A.O.U. Check-list). Fairly common winter resident locally in scattered brush of high Lower Sonoran and

low Upper Sonoran hillsides of central-southern
Arizona, from the foot of the Natanes Plateau,
Graham Co., and the Santa Catalina Mountains
west to the Ajo Mountains. Also winters in most
years to the higher mountains of Yuma Co., where
seldom common, however. East of the San Pedro
Valley known as a wintering bird only in the Chiricahua Mountains, where locally resident. Very sparse
transient west to the Colorado River and lower
mountains and valleys of Yuma Co.; unrecorded in
open valleys of the southeast, and in the northeast.
Also known to breed in Toroweap Valley, Grand
Canyon National Park (R.R. Johnson), and in the
Beaver Dam Mountains and near Leeds in extreme
southwestern Utah.

> The race normally found in Arizona is *S. a. evura*
> Coues; *S. a. cana* Coues is a synonym. Some specimens
> from southwestern Arizona are tentatively referred to
> the darker *S. a. caurina* Miller.

427. *Aimophila carpalis* (Coues). Rufous-winged
Sparrow. Common resident locally in mixed bunch-
grasses and thornbrush of the Lower Sonoran Zone
in central-southern Arizona, from near Oracle, the
Tucson region (including east side of Rincon Moun-
tains, July 1976, Monson), and the north foothills of
the Santa Rita Mountains west across the Papago
Indian Reservation as far as Ventana Ranch and
Menagers Dam and probably to the vicinity of
Sonoyta, Sonora (D. Stotz et al.). In 1973 nested in
Upper Sonoran Zone south of Elgin (H.R. Pulliam).
Formerly more common and less local. In at least
some years following ample summer rains it spreads
out in winter to such localities as the Tumacacori
Mountains (1972–73, Monson); Tombstone and St.
David (1973–74, D. Danforth); Gardner Canyon in
the Santa Rita Mountains (1956–57, J.T. Marshall;
1973–74, Monson; Mar. 1977, S.M. Russell);

Nogales area (Apr. 1966, 1977–78 and 1978–79, B. Harrison et al.); north to near Coolidge (at least five, 12 to 24 Mar. 1978, K. Kaufman); and west to Quitobaquito (1974 and previously, R. Wilt).

Arizona birds are nominate *A. c. carpalis* (Coues).

428. *Aimophila ruficeps* (Cassin). Rufous-crowned Sparrow. Common resident of open, grassy, and rocky Upper Sonoran hillsides of southern Arizona, north sparingly to parts of the Mogollon Rim region (summer only?) and west to Kofa Mountains, the Sierra Estrella (A.M. Rea), and the Ajo Mountains. It is also found sparingly along most of the Grand Canyon, including Toroweap Valley (R.R. Johnson), where its range and status are poorly known; it breeds sparingly in southwestern Utah (according to W.H. Behle). The Rufous-crowned Sparrow is found sometimes in lowlands, as at the edge of the Gila River, at Bapchule on the Gila River Indian Reservation, *24 Oct. 1965* (REA, A.M. Rea); in agricultural field southwest of Phoenix, 5 Jan. 1976 (K. Kaufman, J. Witzeman); and in a backyard in Tucson not far from the University of Arizona campus, 15 Sept. 1978 (Kaufman, E. Cook).

Arizona birds are *A. r. scottii* (Sennett). *A. r. rupicola* van Rossem is a synonym, according to J.P. Hubbard. The Bapchule specimen (above) is *A. r. eremoeca* (Brown.).

429. *Aimophila botterii* (Sclater). Botteri's Sparrow. Rather uncommon summer resident (but frequency of breeding birds not known) from the southeastern corner of Arizona west to Nogales; Arivaca, Pima Co.; and the north foothills of the Santa Rita Mountains, usually in giant sacaton grass-mesquite association; also found in Oracle region in *1940*. First evidence of breeding in Arizona is found in a juvenile taken *22 Aug. 1893* at Fairbank, San Pedro

River (US, W.W. Price, R.L. Wilbur); subsequently, breeding was not established until a nest was found in *July 1967* in the east foothills of the Santa Rita Mountains (ARIZ, R.D. Ohmart). Formerly much more common, especially before 1895, when it ranged west to the Altar Valley and north to Fort Grant. The birds first appear in late May (but as early as 6 May 1967 east of Nogales, B. Harrison), singing in some years until mid-Sept. No winter records.

The Arizona subspecies is *A. b. arizonae* (Ridgway).

430. *Aimophila cassinii* (Woodhouse). Cassin's Sparrow. Common summer visitant or resident, much less common in winter, of the more extensive savannah areas and weedy (cf. *Amaranthus*) growths of the Lower and (less commonly) Upper Sonoran Zones in southeastern Arizona. Apparently largely absent in most years during Apr. and May, and sometimes in most of June. Ranges west to the Baboquivari Mountains, and north to the San Carlos Indian Reservation and beyond Globe (B. Jackson).

Elsewhere quite irregular, largely dependent on unusual rainy periods. Has been found exceptionally to west of Growler Mountains in *fall of 1959*; Monument 180 on Mexican border in southeastern Yuma Co., *25 Aug. 1961*; south side of Painted Rock Reservoir, Maricopa Co., July to Oct. 1974 (R. Norton et al.); about 45 km (28 mi.) north of Caborca, Sonora, Mexico, 18 July 1975 (several, S.M. Russell et al.); and at Sells, Papago Indian Reservation, 24 Mar. 1978 (Monson). Taken at Camp Verde, *21 July 1916*. A fledgling and an adult male collected in Chino Valley, Yavapai Co., *21 Aug. 1973* (REA, A.M. Rea), and birds singing there 11 July 1976 (C.S. Tomoff) and at Cordes Jct., Yavapai Co., in 1975 and 1976 (Tomoff). In the north, one record: numerous on 30 June and 1 July

1976 along Arizona Highway 61 between Witch
Well and the New Mexico state line in eastern
Apache Co. about 50 km (31 mi) north of St. Johns
(T.B. Johnson). Lacking in Phoenix region.

Not found nesting successfully in the state until
1965, near Tucson (not confirmed by specimen or
photo, R.D. Ohmart); since then, nests have been
found along the north side of the Santa Rita Mountains, about 20 km (12 mi) northwest of Benson
(S.M. Russell), and south of Elgin (D. Stotz); and
one nest was discovered west of the San Simon
Cienega near the New Mexico line (W. Principe, B.
Locke). Nest dates range from late July to early Sept.
The birds are more conspicuous in years of better
rainfall; in some such years (as in 1973, 1975, and
1978) birds begin singing in early Mar. and continue
through mid-Apr. when singing drops off to be
resumed with the advent of summer rains, at which
time they more usually commence singing, to continue into early Sept.

431. *Aimophila quinquestriata* (Sclater and Sal-
vin). Five-striped Sparrow. Summer resident of
thick brush of rocky canyon slopes in Lower Sonoran
Zone along Mexican border from Patagonia west to
the Baboquivari Mountains, and north to the west
side of the Santa Rita Mountains, where very local.
Apparently winters in same areas but in small
numbers. A presumed recent immigrant from Mexico, the first Arizona report was of a single bird at the
west base of the Santa Rita Mountains, *18 June
1957*. In 1969 breeding birds were found along
Sonoita Creek southwest of Patagonia (B. Harrison
et al.). In 1977 birds were discovered in the Pajaritos
Mountains in several canyons along the Mexican
border (G.S. Mills, Harrison et al.) and in Chino
Canyon on the west side of the Santa Rita Mountains (S.M. Russell et al.). In 1978 at least four birds

were found on the west side of the Baboquivari
Mountains (Mills et al.). One was seen 26 June 1979
in Pima Canyon of the Santa Catalina Mountains
(Monson).

The Arizona specimen is *A. q. septentrionalis* van
Rossem.

432. *Aimophila belli* (Cassin). Sage Sparrow.
Common to abundant summer resident of open
sagebrush (Upper Sonoran Zone) on the Navajo
Indian Reservation north of the Rio Puerco Valley,
west to Echo Cliffs and the Hopi Buttes (and
possibly in sage areas farther west?). Summer reports
elsewhere probably due to confusion with juvenile *A.
bilineata*. Winters commonly in most parts of
northern Arizona in Upper Sonoran grasslands and
low brush, and in southern Arizona in salt bush
associations with mesquite in the San Simon Valley
and from the Avra Valley westward and northwestward, less commonly in creosote bush areas. Also
occurs in winter in dense salt bush stands of lower
Colorado Valley. Casual fall transient on the high
prairies of the White Mountains (10 Oct. 1936).

The commoner Arizona race is *A. b. nevadensis*
(Ridgway). *A. b. canescens* (Grinnell), smaller, ranges
into western Arizona in winter as far east as the Gila
River Indian Reservation.

433. *Aimophila bilineata* (Cassin). Black-throated
Sparrow. Common summer resident of scattered low
brush or cactus in arid Sonoran zones throughout the
state, scarcer west of the Gila Bend and Organ Pipe
Cactus National Monument areas in the south.
Winters rather commonly in scattered Lower
Sonoran thorn-brush north to the Gila, upper Verde,
and lower Salt River Valleys (rarely north of Prescott,
13 Dec. 1960, and at Tuweep, North Rim of Grand
Canyon, 3 Jan. 1974, M.M. Riffey; and reported
from Pipe Spring National Monument in winter of
1963-64, R. Wauer), thence to the Hoover Dam

region and probably the Virgin River Valley of the extreme northwest. Uncommon west of the Castle Dome Mountains, Yuma Co., seldom reaching the extreme lower Colorado River, and absent from brushless grassland in the southeast. Sparse transient (and wanderer?) on the Mogollon Plateau and in the San Francisco Mountains region. An astonishing 294 listed on Kanab, Utah, Christmas Bird Count, 20 Dec. 1978, must be erroneous.

Arizona birds are *A. b. deserticola* (Ridgway).

434. *Junco hyemalis* (Linnaeus). Dark-eyed Junco. Includes "Gray-headed Junco." Very common summer resident in boreal zones forests of the Mogollon and Kaibab Plateaus. Fairly common summer resident in the adjoining Transition Zone, on the Coconino Plateau, and in the northeast. Reported sparingly south to Coronado Mountain north of Clifton, the Natanes Plateau, the Sierra Ancha, and the Mazatzal and Bradshaw Mountains; but no nest yet found in any of these ranges. Abundant transient throughout, more scarce in Lower Sonoran Zone and especially in the southwest. Abundant winter resident of open forests and woods of the Upper Sonoran Zone and above; rather common in the moister, more brushy areas of the Lower Sonoran Zone; also common in wet years in southwestern desert mountain ranges, north of the Gila River, sparse farther south.

Subspecies are found in Arizona as follows: 1. The nominate race (Slate-colored Junco) is quite uncommon but regular as a winter visitor in eastern Arizona, sparser in the west, but ranging all the way to the Colorado River, usually as single individuals in flocks of other races. 2. *J. h. henshawi* Phillips (*J. h. cismontanus* Dwight of the A.O.U. Check-list) is a fairly common winter resident (never in large numbers) in northeastern and central Arizona, less common farther south and west but reaching as far as Yuma. 3. *J.*

h. simillimus Phillips (Oregon Junco), *J. h. shufeldti* Coale of the A.O.U. Check-list, cannot be positively identified in the field, hence its status is not clear; apparently it is fairly common in southern and western Arizona, and may occur sparsely in northern Arizona. 4. *J. h. thurberi* Anthony (Thurber's or Sierra Junco) is apparently relatively common in southwestern Arizona; uncommon to fairly common east to Prescott, the Salt River Valley, and even the Chiricahua Mountains and sparsely to the San Francisco Mountains region. 5. *J. h. shufeldti* Coale (Shufeldt's Junco and Montana Junco), *J. h. montanus* Ridgway of the A.O.U. Check-list, is the abundant winter bird of the Oregon type in Arizona, especially in the northern woods. *J. h. oreganus* (Townsend) has been erroneously (?) reported from Arizona and southwestern New Mexico (A.H. Miller).

6. *J. h. mearnsi* Ridgway (Pink-sided Junco) is common in winter in the east, especially the White Mountains, but much scarcer westward, and apparently rather irregular west of the Prescott and Ajo Mountains regions. 7. *J. h. aikeni* Ridgway (White-winged Junco) occurred from Flagstaff east in the winter of 1936–37 and one was taken in Flagstaff, *23 Feb. 1971* (MNA, R.P. Balda). One was reported from Roll, lower Gila River, Yuma Co., 13 to 14 Nov. 1971 (A.M. Rea). 8. *J. h. caniceps* (Woodhouse) (Gray-headed Junco) is common in winter in eastern and central Arizona, but sparse to uncommon west of Flagstaff, Prescott, and Ajo Mountains regions. In wet years, it is common in winter in the Kofa Mountains. Two seen in the Hualapai Mountains, 26 or 27 July 1977 (K.V. Rosenberg, A. Higgins), and one in lower Cave Creek Canyon, Chiricahua Mountains, 27 June 1980 (K. Garrett) are of doubtful subspecific status (*caniceps* x *dorsalis*?). Atypical birds breed in the northeast north of the Little Colorado River. 9. *J. h. dorsalis* Henry (Red-backed Junco) is the breeding race except in the northeast, and is a sparse migrant and wintering bird in southeastern and central Arizona, except in valleys just below (south

of) its breeding range where it is generally common in winter. Intermediate juncos are frequent, representing birds whose breeding ranges are adjunct. Those breeding birds of both rims of the Grand Canyon are *caniceps* x *dorsalis.*

435. *Junco phaeonotus* Wagler. Yellow-eyed Junco. Abundant resident in Transition and boreal zones of southern Arizona, north and west to the Santa Rita, Santa Catalina, Pinal, and Pinaleno Mountains; nests as low as 1615 m (5300 ft) in some canyons with Arizona cypress. Winters also in adjacent Upper Sonoran Zone, but rarely reaching its lower edge. Lowland and straggling winter records include Seven Springs, Maricopa Co., 13 Jan. 1971 (S. Demaree); Patagonia, 2 Jan. 1965 (B. Harrison); Dragoon Mountains, 26 Jan. 1974 (D. Danforth); Tucson, 25 Oct. 1978 to 11 Jan. 1979 (G. Gregg); east side of Baboquivari Mountains, 1 Jan. 1979 (I. Nesbit); and Bisbee in the winter of 1978–79 (Danforth). Unusual in migration (?) in the Whetstone Mountains, *1907*; in the Superstition Mountains, 27 to 28 Oct. 1974 (R. Norton et al.); in the Dragoon Mountains in the fall of 1975 (Danforth); and in the Patagonia Mountains in early Oct. 1978 (Harrison).

The Arizona race is *J. p. palliatus* Ridgway.

436. *Zonotrichia leucophrys* (Forster). White-crowned Sparrow. Likely breeds near timberline in the White Mountains, where seen *11 July 1936*, and again 7 July 1976 (B. Harrison), as well as on North Rim of Grand Canyon, 1957 (D.J. McLean), where fledglings observed. In recent years has colonized the San Francisco Mountains (R.P. Balda et al., beginning in 1969). Very common transient in all brushy places. Abundant winter resident in weeds about tall brush, principally in farmlands and large washes, throughout the Sonoran zones, though less numerous north of the Mogollon Plateau and east of Tuba City. Leaves Mogollon Plateau and rims of the

Grand Canyon by early Dec. Has been seen sparsely (even at Tucson, 5 July 1966, F. Thornburg, J. Gates; in upper Aravaipa Canyon, Graham Co., 8 July 1979, G.S. Mills; and near Parker, 8 July 1978, K.V. Rosenberg) in summer in Lower Sonoran Zone, where it often lingers to early June. Recorded at Pipe Spring National Monument, 4 July 1974 (R. Wilt). One in the lower Colorado Valley, 27 Aug. 1980 (J.K. Meentz) was unusually early.

The nominate race (orange-billed, pale- or white-lored "Gambel's Sparrow") is the abundant winter resident and transient, present mainly from the end of Sept. to mid-Apr.; the three Lower Sonoran July birds (above) were of this race. *Z. l. oriantha* Oberholser (pinkish-billed, dark-lored) is principally a migrant in Sept.-Oct. and Apr.-May, but is sometimes frequent in winter in the south; it is the subspecies found in July in the White and San Francisco Mountains. The July 1974 bird at Pipe Spring was dark-lored, as was one at Tucson, 1 July 1978 (K. Kaufman). *Z. l. nigrilora* Todd (also dark-lored) has been taken four times in Arizona, at Nogales, Mesa, Eagar, and Topock.

437. *Zonotrichia albicollis* (Gmelin). White-throated Sparrow. Uncommon winter visitant, usually as single birds throughout state, but almost lacking (only five records from Colorado River Valley) west from Ajo Mountains, Phoenix, and Prescott, chiefly in Lower Sonoran Zone riparian brush, including foothill canyons; in some years actually fairly common in the Patagonia area. Most frequent in late fall and early winter. Records from east of Patagonia are chiefly from feeders at Portal. Has been recorded as high as above 1830 m (6000 ft) in the Santa Catalina Mountains (22 Dec. 1976, R. Kellman et al.). First recorded in Arizona in *1939*, it has decidedly increased in numbers since then, becoming regular in the 1950s and 1960s. A hybrid with *Junco hyemalis* was found at Boyce Thompson Southwestern Arboretum, Nov. 1978 to *Jan. 1979* (ARIZ, photo, K.V. Rosenberg).

438. *Zonotrichia atricapilla* (Gmelin). Golden-crowned Sparrow. Sparse to uncommon winter visitant in southern Arizona, considerably more common in Colorado River Valley (i.e., eight on Bill Williams Delta Christmas Bird Count, 19 Dec. 1978; three at Puerto Peñasco, Sonora, 3 Jan. 1965, S.M. Russell), mainly in riparian brush and at feeders in Lower Sonoran Zone, nearly all records being of single birds. Three winter records in the north, Fredonia, Coconino Co., 25 to 30 Dec. 1976 (B. Lewis), near Phantom Ranch, Grand Canyon, 23 Dec. 1976 (S.W. Carothers), and three (!) at Flagstaff, 16 Dec. 1979 (Christmas Bird Count). A handful of transient records in the north, mostly in Oct. and Nov. and only one in spring (Springerville, 25 Apr. 1953). Once found in Upper Sonoran Zone (not at feeder) in south: Molino Basin, Santa Catalina Mountains, 11 Dec. 1977 (E. Cook).

439. *Zonotrichia querula* (Nuttall). Harris's Sparrow. Sparse to uncommon winter visitant, mostly in riparian brush or hedgerows in Sonoran zones, but also occurring in Transition Zone, throughout state, but less frequent south of central Arizona; in some winters may be locally more common (cf., ten or more at Pipe Spring National Monument, 1972–73, R. Wilt; seven at Scottsdale, Maricopa Co., 1972–73, B. Carnes; three at Teec Nos Pos, extreme northeastern Arizona, 5 Feb. 1977, K. Kaufman et al.), in others may be sparse everywhere. One remained at a feeder at Martinez Lake north of Yuma until 22 Apr. 1980 (K. Irwin et al.). Apparently more common since the late 1960s.

440. *Melospiza lincolnii* (Audubon). Lincoln's Sparrow. Summer resident, perhaps not uncommon, of willows at higher elevations of the White Mountains; possibly also at Mormon Lake. Since 1969 has bred in Inner Basin, San Francisco Mountains (R.P. Balda et al.). Common migrant in dense low cover bordered by grass or weeds throughout state. Winters commonly in dense brush, reeds, and farm hedgerows of the main Lower Sonoran Zone valleys of southern Arizona, north to Phoenix, the Gila Valley, the Davis Dam area, and sparsely to Boulder City, Nevada. Also in more moist situations in Upper Sonoran Zone canyons in southeastern and central Arizona, as well as (at least locally) in the Prescott region. Exceptional at Flagstaff, 16 Dec. 1979, when seven seen on a Christmas Bird Count. Early Feb. records from the western part of the Navajo Indian Reservation represent early returning migrants. It does not usually winter at Flagstaff nor San Francisco Mountains, as stated in A.O.U. Checklist.

> Virtually all Arizona records are of the nominate race. *M. l. gracilis* (Kittlitz) is represented by only three Arizona specimens, from the Colorado River Valley (two) and east of Flagstaff.

441. *Melospiza georgiana* (Latham). Swamp Sparrow. Locally sparse, sometimes uncommon, and somewhat irregular, winter visitant to southern and central Arizona, usually in wet and weedy spots in the Lower Sonoran Zone; casually (?) as high as Prescott, 20 Dec. 1977 (Christmas Bird Count) and taken in Chino Valley, Yavapai Co., *9 Nov. 1975* (REA, L. Muehlbach). Has been found in northern Arizona in winter at Tuba City, 19 Dec. 1936, and in the Springerville region in late Nov. and Dec. 1978 (B. Jones, K. Kaufman). Transient in the White Mountains, where found at Lee Valley Reservoir, 10

Oct. 1973 (Monson). Virtually all records are of single birds, though the first specimen was from a flock of four, in *1915*.

All Arizona specimens but one are *M. g. ericrypta* Oberholser; the exception is from the Bill Williams Delta, *28 Nov. 1952*, and belongs to the nominate race.

442. *Melospiza melodia* (Wilson). Song Sparrow. Locally common resident in reed-sedge-brush types along major permanent rivers and at irrigation ponds and canals in southern and western Arizona, east in the Gila River drainage up the San Francisco River into New Mexico (June 1976, S. Terrill) and to San Bernardino Ranch in the extreme southeast; also resident along the Upper Colorado River (Grand Canyon region) and on permanent brush-lined streams of Upper Sonoran and Transition Zones on and adjacent to the Mogollon Plateau (chiefly in the White Mountains region). Rather common winter resident locally at reedy ponds, brushy streams, and farmlands with brush and weedy edges in the Sonoran zones valleys and even in the Transition Zone where it does not breed. Sparse transient elsewhere (cf. DeMotte Park, Kaibab Plateau, 2 Oct. 1974, Monson). Greatly reduced as a resident bird in the southeast in the present century because of habitat destruction.

Subspecies are found in Arizona as follows: 1. *M. m. montana* Henshaw is the breeding race of northern Arizona, and is by far the most common transient and winter resident statewide. 2. *M. m. fallax* (Baird) is the resident race of central and southeastern Arizona and in northern Sonora below Nogales; some birds migrate to become a sparse winter resident in southern Arizona non-breeding localities, east once to New Mexico line at San Simon Cienega. 3. *M. m. saltonis* Grinnell is resident along the lower Colorado and lower Gila Rivers, in some years at least migrating as far east as

Tucson to become a winter resident. 4. *M. m. juddi*
Bishop has been taken twice in Arizona in winter, near
Tucson and in the Ute (=Black) Mountains of Mohave
Co. 5. *M. m. fisherella* Oberholser has occurred
several times in southern Arizona as a wintering bird. 6.
M. m. merrilli Brewster has been found three times in
Arizona in fall, at Quitobaquito on Organ Pipe Cactus
National Monument, at Wikieup in the Big Sandy
Valley, and at Mammoth in the lower San Pedro
Valley. 7. *M. m. rufina* (Bonaparte) is casual in
Arizona, represented by a specimen from Continental,
Pima Co., *10 Jan. 1963.*

443. *Passerella iliaca* (Merrem). Fox Sparrow.
Local winter resident, usually in very small numbers
except in the Hualapai Mountains (and in some
years, the Kofa and adjacent mountains), in dense
Sonoran zones thickets and chaparral in western,
central, and southern Arizona (also once at bottom
of Grand Canyon, 30 Jan. 1975, S.W. Carothers)
south barely into Sonora (but one as far south as
Ures, 14 Jan. 1980, G. Rosenberg and S. Terrill).
Sparse transient in the San Francisco and White
Mountains regions; also recorded at Pipe Spring
National Monument, 13 Oct. 1974 (R. Wilt); at
Canyon de Chelly, 16 to 18 Oct. 1974 (R. Norton);
at Keams Canyon, Hopi Indian Reservation, 8 Sept.
1979 (C. LaRue) (extremely early!); and at Ganado,
Navajo Indian Reservation, 11 Jan. 1980 (M.W.
Loder). Accidental in western Arizona as late as *15
May* (*1956,* Kofa Mountains) and as early as 29
Aug. (1938, below Hoover Dam); also two at Hart
Prairie, San Francisco Mountains, on 26 May 1980
(D.R. Pinkston).

   P. i. zaboria Oberholser occurs occasionally in southern
Arizona, as does *P. i. altivagans* Riley. *P. i. schistacea*
Baird is the race that occurs regularly in Arizona. *P. i.
megarhyncha* Baird has been found twice: Ajo

Mountains, *24 Oct. 1947*, and Sierra Pinta, Yuma Co., *12 Dec. 1955. P. i. townsendi* (Audubon) has been found only once, Chiricahua Mountains, *28 Nov. 1914* (now at US).

444. *Calcarius mccownii* (Lawrence). McCown's Longspur. Mostly uncommon to sparse and irregular (formerly abundant) winter resident in grassy plains and valleys of eastern Arizona west to Willcox and the San Rafael Valley in Santa Cruz Co.; recorded formerly west to the Altar Valley, the Gila Valley south of Phoenix, the Agua Fria River east of Prescott, Camp Verde, and the northeast slope of the San Francisco Mountains; recorded recently near Phoenix, *6 Feb. 1979* (ARIZ, photo, K.V. Rosenberg, first found by S. Terrill) and (identified by notes only) two in the Bill Williams Delta, 24 Dec. 1977 (D. Stotz). About 250 found east of Cananea, Sonora, 23 Jan. 1977 (K. Kaufman, T. Parker, Stotz, J. and R. Witzeman).

445. *Calcarius lapponicus* (Linnaeus). Lapland Longspur. Sparse winter visitant, mostly as single birds and extending from Nov. to Mar. with records from Meteor Crater, Coconino Co.; western part of Navajo Indian Reservation (where it may be regular?); one east of Holbrook, 23 Dec. 1979 (G. Rosenberg et al.); one at Round Rock, Navajo Indian Reservation, 10 Oct. 1980 (D. Stotz, S. Parket); southwest of Phoenix (Dec. 1976, K. Kaufman et al.); south of Parker (three times in *1977*, including *25 Dec.*, ARIZ, K.V. Rosenberg et al., collected by M.L. Lange); near Poston, Yuma Co. (*1 Dec. 1979*, ARIZ, R. Dummer); and Martinez Lake, Colorado River, Yuma Co. (two Nov. records). Specimens found in other places (Phoenix, Petrified Forest National Park) were probably brought there by automobiles coming from undetermined regions, perhaps out-of-state, and the latter record should be deleted from the A.O.U. Check-list.

Arizona specimens are of the race *C.l. alascensis* Ridgway.

446. *Calcarius ornatus* (Townsend). Chestnut-collared Longspur. Abundant winter resident in the grasslands of southeastern Arizona north to Ash Flat on the San Carlos Indian Reservation, sparse to uncommon winter resident in agricultural fields about Phoenix and along Colorado River from Parker to Yuma, and fairly common migrant and winter resident in grasslands farther north, even up to the Canadian Zone (snow-cover permitting; cf. 150 northeast of Flagstaff, 20 to 26 Jan. 1980, J. Coons et al.). In fall migration occurs in small numbers (singly or in flocks of five or less, seldom in larger numbers) more or less regularly, usually on open land next to water, nearly statewide west to the Colorado River (where found north to Havasu Landing on California side of Lake Havasu, 25 Sept. 1952). Ten birds were reported incredibly from east side of the Sulphur Springs Valley in the area of the mouth of Pinery Canyon in the Chiricahua Mountains, 12 July 1976 (D.L. Pearson).

447. *Calcarius pictus* (Swainson). Smith's Longspur. One specimen: White Mountains, *24 Apr. 1953.* No other substantiated record, but possibly not as rare in Arizona and northern Sonora as this single specimen would imply.

FAMILY CARDUELIDAE: CARDUELINE FINCHES

448. *Coccothraustes vespertinus* (Cooper). Evening Grosbeak. Rather uncommon and erratic summer resident about deciduous trees in the Transition Zone of eastern and northern Arizona, west to the Grand Canyon (both rims), Bill Williams Mountain (June 1976, C.S. Tomoff), the Bradshaw Mountains, the Sierra Ancha, and the Santa Catalina and Santa Rita Mountains; apparently scarcer in recent years. Breeding at Flagstaff from 1964 to at least 1972 was induced by a year round feeding station (G. Foster et al.). Sparse and irregular transient and winter visitant in the wooded parts of the Sonoran zones throughout the state, in flight years even reaching the Colorado River (five records, including California side; between 1250 and 1500 at Boulder City, Nevada, 27 Oct. 1972, C.S. Lawson). Also generally sparse in winter in and near its breeding territory, but common locally in flight years. A strange desert appearance was of one at Covered Wells, Papago Indian Reservation, 23 Jan. to *10 Apr. 1976* (REA, A.M. Rea), apparently eating ironwood and palo verde seeds; individuals were seen at the headquarters area of Organ Pipe Cactus National Monument, 29 Apr. 1962 and 2 May 1964 (according to R. Wilt).

> The nominate race has been taken twice, in the Chiricahua Mountains and in Oak Creek Canyon, Coconino Co. *C. v. mexicanus* (Chapman) is the race breeding from the Santa Catalina and Chiricahua Mountains (and Sierra Ancha?) into Mexico. Otherwise, Arizona birds are *C. v. montanus* (Ridgway).

449. *Loxia curvirostra* Linnaeus. Red Crossbill. Irregularly common resident of the more extensive Transition and boreal zones forests. May occur in pinyons in winter. Sparse and irregular in the lowlands, mainly in winter, but staying into June in some years (even to 31 July 1974 and 7 Aug. 1975 at Phoenix, D. Stejskal, and to 18 July 1977 and 28 July 1979 at Tucson, D. Stotz; there were two, one, one, and two, respectively). Also present in Tucson after 2 Aug. 1966 (F. Thornburg, S.M. Russell). In occasional winters (about ten-year intervals?) much more common and widespread. Has apparently nested twice in city parks/cemeteries: an adult feeding a young bird on the ground at Tucson, 15

Apr. 1973 (R. Steffens), and a pair feeding a recently
fledged young at Phoenix, 26 Mar. 1976 (J.
Witzeman, K. Kaufman). Only five records for
Colorado Valley: one at Willow Beach below Hoover
Dam, *14 Nov. 1938* (Lake Mead Recreation Area
Museum, R.K. Grater, specimen now lost); five at
Parker, *23 Aug. 1953*; one in Bill Williams Delta, 17
Nov. 1976 (A. Higgins); two at Parker, 20 Dec.
1976 (K. Kaufman); and one in the Dome Valley
east of Yuma, 27 Nov. 1979 (S. Goldwasser, E.
Ferry).

> *See* Appendix, "The Races of Red Crossbill, *Loxia
> curvirostra,* in Arizona" for a discussion of the complex
> taxonomy of this species.

450. *Carpodacus purpureus* (Gmelin). Purple Finch.
Irregular fall and winter visitant, usually in quite
small numbers, in Sonoran zones in central and
southern Arizona east to Camp Verde, Globe,
Oracle, and Portal; also at 2195 m (7200 ft) in the
Santa Catalina Mountains, *20 Feb. 1975* (ARIZ,
Monson). Two taken on South Rim of Grand Canyon,
22 Dec. 1934, and one seen at Supai, 23 Sept. 1950,
are the only northern Arizona records. One at Portal,
19 June 1978 (K. Garrett), lingered unusually late.

> Taxonomy of the Purple Finch is uncertain. The
> nominate or eastern race has been taken once (*6 Jan.
> 1956*, Tucson). Other specimens all seem to be *C. p.
> californicus* Baird, unless *C. p. rubidus* Duvall is a
> valid race, as advocated by A.M. Rea.

451. *Carpodacus cassinii* Baird. Cassin's Finch.
Common summer resident in boreal forest openings
of the Kaibab Plateau; decidedly uncommon and
apparently irregular in Transition and Canadian
Zones elsewhere in northern Arizona, including the
Northern Arizona University campus at Flagstaff in
1976 (R.P. Balda). Irregularly abundant winter
visitant in high Upper Sonoran and, in southern

Arizona, open Transition Zone generally, and very
irregularly in small numbers into Lower Sonoran
Zone as at Tucson, Phoenix, Camp Verde,
Wickenburg, Salome, the Big Sandy Valley, the
Kofa Mountains, and even near Tule Well, Yuma
Co. (*8 Nov. 1960*). On the Mogollon Plateau it is
chiefly a transient, though sometimes wintering.

Summer resident birds are the nominate form. Some
winter birds are *C. c. vinifer* Duvall, but how commonly
it occurs is unknown.

452. *Carpodacus mexicanus* (Müller). House Finch.
Abundant summer resident in the less dense vegetation of the Sonoran zones, especially about towns
and ranches; in recent years has spread to towns and
ranches in the Transition Zone. Irregularly reaches
even Canadian Zone (Kaibab Plateau). In winter it
withdraws into lower valleys, and spreads out
commonly to the deserts of western and southwestern
Arizona.

All Arizona birds are referred to the widespread *C. m.
frontalis* (Say).

453. *Pinicola enucleator* (Linnaeus). Pine
Grosbeak. Uncommon to sparse resident in the
boreal forests of the White Mountains. Was present
on the Kaibab Plateau June and July 1929, but not
seen there since. Three were taken from a flock of ten
to 15 on the south slope of the San Francisco
Mountains, *2 Mar. 1967* (NAU, MNA; S.M.
Carothers, J.R. Haldeman, J. Hildebrand), and up to
25 were found there at least in the winters of 1968–
69 and 1979–80 (several observers). Specimens
were taken on South Rim, Grand Canyon, *15 Dec.
1950* and *6 Jan. 1957*. Of a few sight records out of
the breeding zone, the most credible are of two in the
Sierra Ancha, 9 May, and six there 10 May 1953
(A.S. Margolin et al.), two birds in the upper Santa
Catalina Mountains, 6 Nov. 1972 (S.M. Russell), a

pair at Prescott, 17 Aug. 1978 (S. Demaree et al.),
and one at Rustler Park, Chiricahua Mountains, 5
Nov. 1978 (L. Kiff et al.).

Arizona birds are of the race *P. e. montana* Ridgway.

454. *Leucosticte tephrocotis* (Swainson). Rosy
Finch. A few sight records from the Fredonia and
Sunset Crater National Monument areas (R. Wilt
and D. Magee, respectively). Specimens come from
the South Rim of the Grand Canyon, *27 Nov.* and *26
Dec. 1956,* and from the San Francisco Mountains,
Feb. 1967 (S.W. Carothers, J.P. Haldeman).

> The "black" subspecies, *L. t. atrata* Ridgway, accounts
> for most of all Arizona records except for the Sunset
> Crater and San Francisco Mountains birds which are
> mostly of the "gray-crowned" nominate race, but
> include *atrata* and a few *L. t. littoralis* Baird. There is
> an exception of a flock of *atrata* at Sunset Crater on 14
> Mar. 1971 (Magee).

[*Carduelis flammea* (Linnaeus). Common
Redpoll. Hypothetical. A report of six at Petrified
Forest National Park, 1 Dec. 1962, is completely
unsubstantiated.]

455. *Carduelis pinus* (Wilson). Pine Siskin.
Common summer resident (although few nests
reported) from the Transition Zone to timberline on
the Kaibab and Mogollon Plateaus, including the
San Francisco and White Mountains; rather
uncommon to sparse as a presumably breeding bird
southwest and south to Prescott (nest, 11 June 1973,
C.S. Tomoff) and the Mazatzal, Santa Rita, and
Chiricahua Mountains, and probably to Mt. Trumbull
in the northwest. Winters more or less commonly,
but to some extent irregularly, in weedy fields and
river valleys almost throughout the state, but rather
sparingly in the southwest and along the Colorado

River, sometimes appearing in flocks in the Sonoran zones by *10 Aug.* and remaining to early June.

Arizona specimens are of the nominate race. *C. p. macropterus* (Bonaparte) breeds in Mexico only. It is darker on the crown, though many northern birds are just as large.

456. *Carduelis tristis* (Linnaeus). American Goldfinch. A fairly common winter resident, irregular in numbers, in deciduous trees and weedy fields of the Sonoran and (locally) Transition zones, sometimes remaining to early June. A pair was watched building a nest at Teec Nos Pos in the extreme northeast, 31 May 1978 (A. Gast, S. Terrill). Has been seen on the Mogollon Plateau in summer, as well as in the Hualapai Mountains, but no summer specimens. Older summer records inside the Grand Canyon and on Navajo Mountain (Utah) require substantiation.

The nominate race occurs rarely in eastern and central Arizona. *C. t. pallida* (Mearns) is the usual race. *C. t. salicamans* (Grinnell) is represented by a single bird near Parker, *17 May 1948.*

457. *Carduelis psaltria* (Say). Lesser Goldfinch. Fairly common summer resident in deciduous trees and brush (especially willows and cottonwoods) in the Sonoran and (locally) Transition zones throughout Arizona; also found locally in evergreen oaks. The female of a pair was carrying nest material (small stick) in desert at Heart Tank, Sierra Pinta, Yuma Co., 25 Mar. 1978 (Monson). Irregularly common post-breeding visitor and winter resident in the Sonoran zones, less common in extreme northeast. Locally common post-breeding visitor in Transition Zone of Huachuca Mountains; in late summer visits Canadian Zone (Kaibab Plateau), and may winter irregularly in Transition Zone. Breeding season remarkably prolonged or irregular, from Jan. to Nov. The nominate race, usually green-backed, is the one occurring in Arizona.

458. *Carduelis lawrencei* (Cassin). Lawrence's Goldfinch. Irregularly common transient and winter visitant, sometimes in large numbers, in weedy areas and at watering places of the Sonoran zones across southern Arizona, north to the Globe and Prescott regions. In *1952* nested at Parker (nest, CAS), and recently has been found nesting along Verde River east of Phoenix (1977, S. Terrill; 1978, K. Kaufman, G. Rosenberg; 1980, A.E. Higgins) and in the Bill Williams Delta (1979, J. Bean, A. Laurenzi). Nonbreeding (?) birds are seen occasionally in May to early July, from the Phoenix region westward; juveniles were seen near Wickenburg, 10 July 1980 (C.S. Tomoff). A female was seen at Arivaca Jct. south of Tucson, 1 July 1972 (G. McCaskie), and a male was at Seven Springs, Maricopa Co., 10 July 1974 (D. and P. Stejskal).

FAMILY PLOCEIDAE: WEAVER FINCHES

459. *Passer domesticus* (Linnaeus). House Sparrow. Abundant resident of cities and towns, and rather common resident of large ranch headquarters, irrigated fields, etc., statewide. Became established in Arizona in the early 1900s, widespread by 1915.

Arizona birds are the nominate race.

FAMILY ICTERIDAE: MEADOWLARKS, BLACKBIRDS, AND ORIOLES

460. *Spiza americana* (Gmelin). Dickcissel. Sparse to uncommon transient with records mainly in Sept. in Sonoran zones valleys and farms (but also in Transition Zone at Flagstaff, 15 Aug. 1952, Mrs. O. Maddox, and at Lakeside, Navajo Co., 12 Sept. 1977, Monson). Three late winter records: Tucson, 20 to 24 Feb. 1972 (D. Lynn et al.); Nogales, 18

Mar. to 11 Apr. 1974 (J. Bache-Wiig et al.); and Tucson, 15 Feb. 1977 (J. Ambrose)—all at feeders. One near Springerville, 23 Nov. 1978 (D. Danforth, J. Bealer) would seem to be very late.

461. *Dolichonyx oryzivorus* (Linnaeus). Bobolink. A small breeding colony recorded near Show Low in 1937. A pair seen near Snowflake, 15–16 June 1968 (R. Norton). At least six observed in field west of Eagar, Apache Co., adjacent to the Little Colorado River, 16 June 1979 (D. Stotz, S. Parker), and a nest with eggs located in the same place and collected after being accidentally destroyed, *7 July 1979* (ARIZ, S. Terrill, G. Rosenberg, R. McKernon, W. Howe); a pair was in the same locality, 7 July 1980 (R. Dummer, Rosenberg). Otherwise a sparse migrant, chiefly in fall; among the localities of record are Teec Nos Pos in the extreme northeast; near Tombstone, Tucson, and the upper San Pedro Valley in the southeast; Phoenix; Lake Mohave in the northwest; and near Poston, Yuma Co., in the southwest (this last a singing male on 8 June 1977, A. Laurenzi). Five specimens near Wikieup, *2* to *10 Oct. 1952*, indicate a status other than "casual" (A.O.U. Check-list).

462. *Sturnella magna* (Linnaeus). Eastern Meadowlark. Fairly common summer resident of grassy plains and fields in southeastern, central-southern, and northern Arizona, but not north of the Little Colorado Valley and the Grand Canyon nor west beyond Coconino Co. as far as now known. Its centers of abundance are the Altar, Sonoita, San Rafael, upper San Simon, and Sulphur Springs Valleys, the Arivaca vicinity, the high prairies of the White Mountains, and the valleys near the Juniper Mountains in Yavapai Co. During winter, it is found in varying abundance in southern Arizona west to at least Arlington in the Phoenix region and to the Organ Pipe Cactus National Monument, but is rare

in the north except at Springerville. One collected
south of Poston, Yuma Co., *17 Mar. 1979* (ARIZ,
R. Dummer).

The race found in Arizona is *S. m. lilianae* Oberholser.

463. *Sturnella neglecta* Audubon. Western
Meadowlark. Common summer resident in the grassy
parts of northern and central Arizona (except most
places where *magna* occurs) and north of the Quinlan
Mountains, Pima Co.; locally in irrigated valleys
almost throughout Arizona except in the southeast
beyond Tucson. Nested at least once in Sulphur
Springs Valley in an exceptionally wet year (1941).
In wet years it remains and nests in well-vegetated
areas of southwestern Arizona. In the northwest it
apparently breeds in eastern Mohave Co. and along
the Utah border, but not as far west as the Kingman
region; we cannot believe it is a "common permanent
resident in the...desert areas" of adjacent Nevada.
Common in grassy and semi-grassy areas in migration.
In winter common in grassy parts of the Sonoran
zones and farmlands of southern and western Arizona,
rather uncommon in grassy or cultivated ponderosa
pine openings and in northeastern Arizona farmlands
and grasslands.

Arizona birds belong to the nominate race. *S. n.
confluenta* Rathbun is apparently casual in the state.

464. *Xanthocephalus xanthocephalus* (Bonaparte).
Yellow-headed Blackbird. Breeds in small colonies
at reedy lakes on and north of the Mogollon Plateau
and in the Chino Valley north of Prescott (1976,
C.S. Tomoff), and locally along the lower Colorado
and Gila Rivers. It probably breeds at Picacho
Reservoir in Pinal Co. Common in migration at
marshes and cattle pens, and in smaller numbers at
lakes, fields, and stock tanks throughout the state.
Winters abundantly, arriving in numbers by mid-
July, nearly all males, in marshes and farmlands
across southern and western Arizona (600,000

estimated roosting at Picacho Reservoir, Pinal Co., Nov. 1973, Monson); recorded at Washington, extreme southwestern Utah, 28 Dec. 1965 (R. Wauer). In southeastern Arizona at least, some often linger into May, and (in recent years only?) small numbers of nonbreeding birds sometimes remain throughout the summer. Yellow-headed Blackbirds were still roosting in large numbers at Hermosillo, Sonora, 26 Apr. 1977 (Monson).

465. *Agelaius phoeniceus* (Linnaeus). Red-winged Blackbird. Common to abundant resident in marshes and irrigated farmlands of Sonoran zones throughout the state, feeding in farmlands and roosting in marshes during the winter, when numbers augmented by birds from the north. Common summer resident at marshy lakes in the Transition Zone and higher in northern Arizona; uncommon and irregular in winter in the Transition Zone (but 195 at Flagstaff, 16 Dec. 1978, Christmas Bird Count). Occasionally found in migration at stock tanks and wells on the desert.

The following races are found in Arizona: 1. *A. p. nevadensis* Grinnell winters in the south, uncommonly but widespread; there is one northern specimen from Grand Canyon Village (*Nov. 1956*). 2. A specimen of *A. p. neutralis* Ridgway of southwestern California was taken at Supai, Grand Canyon (*Nov. 1912*). 3. *A. p. fortis* Ridgway breeds over the northeast half of the state and winters commonly south and west; it mixes with the following in northern central Arizona. 4. *A. p. sonoriensis* Ridgway is the common resident bird from Safford and the extreme southeast west in suitable areas to the lower Colorado River; the birds breeding south and southeastward from the Tucson region are intermediate with *A. p. fortis* and *A. p. nayaritensis* Dickey and van Rossem. 5. *A. p. arctolegus* Oberholser of the far north is represented by six females taken on the Gila River Indian Reservation (REA, A.M. Rea) and one at Globe (CU, R.W. Dickerman).

6. *A. p. caurinus* Ridgway is apparently a casual vagrant from the north Pacific Coast, with only two specimen records (one of these is from Sonoyta, Sonora, just across the border).

466. *Icterus spurius* (Linnaeus). Orchard Oriole. A very sparse migrant to southern Arizona, from the extreme southeast west to the Phoenix region. About 25 records in all, mostly in May and June, but one, an adult male, in winter near Phoenix, 11 Jan. 1974 (S. Terrill et al.). A singing male was seen on the California side of the Colorado River between Imperial and Laguna Dams, 15 June 1969 (G. McCaskie, A. Craig); an adult male was found northeast of Yuma, 20 May 1979 (Terrill); one was observed at the California side of Laguna Dam, 1 Oct. 1979 (K.V. Rosenberg); and one was reported at Theba, west of Gila Bend, 14 June 1980 (G. Rosenberg et al.). Only three specimens, two from the Chiricahua Mountains, *2* and *8 Sept. 1956,* and one from Komatke, Gila River Indian Reservation, *22 Oct. 1968* (REA, A.M. Rea).

467. *Icterus cucullatus* Swainson. Hooded Oriole. Common summer resident of large mesquite, palm, walnut, and sycamore, and, less numerously, in willow-cottonwood associations of the Sonoran zones across southern Arizona, north in recent years (since about 1940) to the Virgin River Valley and Beaver Dam Wash in the extreme northwest (including adjacent Utah) and the bottom of the Grand Canyon, and west to the Kingman region. In northern Arizona, a pair carrying nesting material was seen in cottonwoods near Chinle, Navajo Indian Reservation, 3 June 1971 (J.R. Haldeman, G.A. Ruffner). In migration occurs on deserts of extreme southwestern Arizona. Formerly casual in winter; the widespread use of hummingbird feeders has resulted in small numbers wintering since about 1965 from Nogales to Tucson (one record from Tombstone, 10 Dec. 1974,

N. Danforth) west to Phoenix and Yuma, although one found at the foot of the Sierra Pinta, Yuma Co., 27 Dec. 1957, was not being detained by a feeder!

Arizona breeding birds are of the race *I. c. nelsoni* Ridgway. No winter specimens are available to date.

468. *Icterus parisorum* Bonaparte. Scott's Oriole. Common summer resident of the evergreen oak and yucca associations in the mountains and foothills of southeastern and central Arizona, and in Joshua trees from Wickenburg region northwest; also (vegetative type?) along Beaver Dam Wash in the extreme northwest. Smaller numbers breed in the pinyons of most of northern Arizona (where extreme records are Teec Nos Pos in the northeast, 30 May 1977, D. Stotz et al., and Pipe Spring National Monument in the northwest, 27 to 28 May 1974, R. Wilt—this excludes the Beaver Dam Wash area), also in beargrass (*Nolina*) and *Yucca* in mountains of southwestern Arizona, almost to the Colorado River. Occurs as an uncommon migrant in the valleys of southeastern Arizona, casually at Flagstaff (juveniles, *1* and *5 Aug. 1947*), and sparsely in spring and summer in the immediate lower Colorado Valley. Winters sparsely and irregularly in recent years (beginning in 1965) from the Huachuca Mountains west to Organ Pipe Cactus National Monument, and more or less regularly at feeders in Tucson and Nogales (also once at Portal, 10 to 15 Feb. 1975, S. Spofford).

[*Icterus wagleri* Sclater. Black-vented Oriole. Hypothetical. One reported at a feeder in Cave Creek Canyon, Chiricahua Mountains, 17 July 1971 and for more than a week thereafter (J. Witzeman, I. Hicks). Probably bred originally in Patagonia Mountains, but there is no documentation (H. Brown).]

469. *Icterus galbula* (Linnaeus). Northern Oriole.
Breeds commonly in cottonwood-willow association
of the Sonoran zones except along parts of the
Mexican boundary; also sometimes in large mesquite
bosques and even open juniper-oak woodland. On
migration found largely in broad-leaved trees in open
country, also in mesquites and palo verdes in the low
desert; it ranges throughout the state, especially in
Lower Sonoran Zone. Hardly more than ten winter
records in all, from the San Pedro Valley west to the
Colorado River, but chiefly in the Tucson and
Phoenix vicinities and mostly since 1965.

The nominate race, known as the Baltimore Oriole, has
occurred only a dozen times; males have been photographed at Tucson, *23 Apr. 1978* (ARIZ, W.A. Davis,
R. and P. Keyworth), at Portal, *3* to *9 May 1978*
(ARIZ, S. Spofford), and at Lees Ferry, *4 Sept. 1978*
(ARIZ, S. Terrill, G. Rosenberg); also a specimen
from south of Nogales in Sonora, *12 Oct. 1954.* A male
mated with an *I. g. bullockii* and a nest was built and
young fledged in 1977 near the Colorado River about
16 km (10 mi) north of Blythe, California; the male was
present from about 16 May to 7 Sept. and photographed
(S. Clark, many other observers); the same mating took
place on the Verde River near Phoenix in 1980 (A.E.
Higgins et al.; photo, ARIZ, K.V. Rosenberg). *I. g.
bullockii* (Swainson), known as the Bullock's Oriole, is
the common breeding and migrant race. *I. g. parvus* van
Rossem is thought to be the breeding bird along the
lower Colorado Valley, and occurs in the Gila Valley
east to about Arlington, Maricopa Co. (according to
A.M. Rea) and even farther eastward; migrant specimens have been taken as far east as Mammoth, Pinal
Co., and Patagonia, and north to the Grand Canyon. A
winter specimen from Parker, *1 Feb. 1947,* is *parvus,*
but other winter specimens are *bullockii.*

470. *Icterus pustulatus* (Wagler). Scarlet-headed Oriole. Sparse to casual fall and winter vagrant to Tucson and vicinity. Pre-1978 records there are *19 Dec. 1886,* 30 Oct. to *26 Dec. 1948* (CAN), *19 Mar. 1952* (CAN), *31 July 1952* (CAN), and 17 Dec. 1975 to 12 Jan. 1976 (C. and E. Wolfe et al.), all single birds. From 1978 to 1980, Scarlet-headed Orioles appeared from year to year at northside Tucson hummingbird feeders. In one locality (Oro Valley), a pair appeared from 7 to 22 Oct. 1978, three (one male, two females) intermittently from 27 Sept. to 22 Oct. 1979, and a pair for an unknown period, Sept. to Oct. 1980 (all Monson et al.). At another location about 3.6 km (2.25 mi) distant, one male from 24 Oct. 1978 to 22 Mar. 1979, a pair from 11 Oct. to *15 Nov. 1979* (ARIZ, photo, W.A. Davis), and a male from 8 Oct. 1980 to 9 Feb. 1981 and a female from 2 Dec. 1980 to 13 Feb. 1981 (Davis), were observed. All males were immature. Casual at confluence of Gila and Salt Rivers (adult male), 4 Apr. 1976 (S. Terrill, S. Burge).

Arizona specimens are *I. p. microstictus* Griscom.

471. *Euphagus carolinus* (Müller). Rusty Blackbird. Sparse fall and winter visitant to at least southern Arizona (no definite records in the north; two reported as this species at Grand Canyon Village, 25 Apr. 1968, W.H. Hill). Records include eight specimens and less than a dozen sight occurrences. Their dates range from *24 Oct. (1887,* Camp Verde) to 10 Mar. (1977, 3 males, 2 females, Bill Williams Delta, K.V. Rosenberg, R. Bonney—this hardly seems credible).

472. *Euphagus cyanocephalus* (Wagler). Brewer's Blackbird. Common summer resident in the vicinity of willows and in well-watered farmlands on and just below the Mogollon Plateau and in the Springerville region; scarcer in the Chuska Mountains region, on the South Rim of the Grand Canyon (irregularly?), and on the Kaibab Plateau. Unknown in summer farther west. Transient throughout state, generally uncommon except in farmlands and feedlots. Abundant winter resident, principally in and near farmlands, south and west of the Mogollon Plateau; also winters sparingly at lakes and farms of Mogollon Plateau and northward. Two summer records in Lower Sonoran Zone: California side of Lake Havasu, *12 June 1947,* and Phoenix, *26 July 1953.* Also three birds in low Upper Sonoran Zone near Tuba City, Navajo Indian Reservation, *6 July 1936.*

Arizona specimens are currently assigned to the nominate race.

473. *Quiscalus mexicanus* (Gmelin). Great-tailed Grackle. Until the 1960s, a local resident in southeastern Arizona as far west as Phoenix, first appearing in Arizona at Safford in 1935 and later spreading to Douglas, Benson, Nogales, and Tucson. It had appeared along the lower Colorado River by *1964* (SD) and was nesting there in 1970 (G. McCaskie). New appearances were made in Puerto Peñasco, Sonora, in 1965 (D. Lamm), Lukeville, Organ Pipe Cactus National Monument, in 1967 (D. Greenburg), Prescott in 1971 (A.M. Rea), Globe in 1973 (nesting in 1977) (B. Jackson), Joseph City, Navajo Co., in 1973 (Monson), at the bottom of the Grand Canyon in 1974 (S.W. Carothers), Pipe Spring National Monument in 1974 (R. Wilt), nesting in Las Vegas in Nevada in 1976 (C.S. Lawson), at Seneca Lake, Gila Co., in 1977 (Monson), Eagar-Springerville in 1977 (Monson), and near Flagstaff in 1977 (R.L. Todd). No winter records for northern Arizona, unless five seen at Marble Canyon, Coconino Co., 30 Nov. 1980 (S. Terrill et al.) would constitute such a record.

Two races came into Arizona: *Q. m. monsoni* (Phillips) from the southeast and *Q. m. nelsoni* (Ridgway) from coastal Sonora. The former is thought to occupy the area from the San Pedro Valley east, while the latter is found in the remainder of the state; however, more material is needed to settle the question. A.M. Rea has found a mixed population in central Arizona, with *monsoni* influence predominant.

[*Quiscalus quiscula* (Linnaeus). Common Grackle. Nested at Farmington, New Mexico, less than 80 km (50 mi) from Arizona, in 1979–80 (A.P. Nelson); the species has been observed there in at least some summers after being first observed in Nov. 1968. Also, at least four at Blackrock, Zuni Indian Reservation, New Mexico, 28 Apr. to 30 May 1980 (A. Schmierer); the locality is only 24 km (14 mi) from Arizona.]

474. *Molothrus ater* (Boddaert). Brown-headed Cowbird. Common summer resident of the less densely wooded parts of the Sonoran zones, especially in southern and central Arizona; uncommon in pinyon-juniper areas and in adjacent ponderosa pine, casually even higher. Common transient south and west of Mogollon Plateau. Winters commonly in southern Arizona lowlands where there are livestock concentrations, notably at Parker, Yuma, Willcox, and in the Phoenix and Tucson areas. Two seen at Springerville, 16 Dec. 1978 (K. Kaufman, E. Cook).

M. a. "obscurus (Gmelin)" breeds over Arizona generally except in the northeast, where it is still local (?); it is the predominant race in winter. In the northeast in summer it is overlapped by the larger *M. a. artemisiae* Grinnell, which also occurs as a transient (arriving in July?) and as a winter visitor in the south. The nominate race occurs, probably regularly, in winter in the southeast west to Tucson.

475. *Molothrus aeneus* (Wagler). Bronzed Cowbird. Common summer resident (starting early in twentieth century) of irrigated areas, ranch yards, and sycamore canyons in southern and central Arizona, west to Organ Pipe Cactus National Monument and Wickenburg, north to the Phoenix, Globe, and Clifton regions, and east to the San Pedro Valley and extreme southwestern New Mexico; since 1950 sparsely along the lower Colorado River, and since about 1970 rarely to uncommonly northeast as far as between the Salt River and the Mogollon Plateau and northwest to Prescott. Has been found as high as 1950 m (6400 ft) in the Huachuca Mountains in 1975 and 1977 (Monson). A bird identified as this species was noted near Slide Canyon in the Mount Trumbull region in early June 1975 (N.J. Sharber, P. Shoemaker). Winters, usually in small numbers, at Tucson and in lesser numbers at Phoenix and in the Santa Cruz Valley above Tucson.

The Arizona race is *M. a. loyei* Parkes and Blake.

Appendix
The Races of Red Crossbill,
Loxia curvirostra, in Arizona

This species requires special discussion with its
independent little semi-species wandering around
the state. All four North American size classes
occur, and intermediates are relatively infrequent.
The four are distinguishable even in the skeleton,
particularly the skull, but are essentially alike in
calls, behavior, nesting (as far as known), and
plumage sequences. American ornithologists therefore do not call them *Loxia minor, L. pusilla, L.
bendirei,* and *L. stricklandi,* respectively, though
European ornithologists (faced with a quite similar
situation) have recently begun calling theirs *Loxia
curvirostra, L. scotica,* and *L. pytyopsittacus.*

Such a classification flows naturally from an over-
rigid species concept which defines species by
"reproductive isolation" alone without considering
their biology as a whole. Crossbills taken from the
same flock often show very similar characteristics,
and the grouping of these minor variations into
broader subspecies is sometimes a bit perplexing; a

particular series may resemble itself more than anything else. Unless crossbills speak a number of different "languages" undecipherable to our ears, we must deduce that they commonly maintain tight, exclusive little social systems, probably somewhat inbred (also in some areas, not Arizona, different races probably nest at different seasons); else such variations could hardly persist. These conclusions were reached after an arduous restudy by Phillips of most of the available North American Red Crossbills, from 1970 to 1976 (*see* the partial acknowledgements in *Bird-Banding* 48:110–111). Specimens were segregated and marked as follows:

Size Class I: smallest; *"sitkensis"* of A.O.U. Check-list. Most specimens are correctly *minor* (Brehm), as stated by Griscom, 1937; but in 1975–76 other color variants were noticed. True *sitkensis* of the west coast tends to be paler but cannot be consistently separated from true *minor,* which includes birds marked, in 1975–76, B, D, and M (for bright, dull, and typical *minor*), OY, and *sitkensis.* Other symbols used in class I were cf Az, Ct, K, Me, W, and WVa; these differed in color. Usual weight 21.5–29.9 gm.; extreme length in flesh usually 152–161; extent (extreme wingspan) 247–263; wing chord usually 80–85 mm, occasionally 78 to (male) 87; width of mandible at base (next to flesh and feathers) 8–8.8, rarely 7.8–9.0 mm.

Class II: small; includes *"minor"* and most of *"bendirei"* of A.O.U. (but not Brehm's and Ridgway's types). The only useful character found to tell eastern *"minor"* from western *"bendirei"* (*sensu* A.O.U.) was its blunt-tipped maxilla; but even this required that many sharp-billed eastern birds (including Griscom's type specimen of *neogaea*) be considered strays from the west (or south). The futile attempt at an east-west segregation was abandoned late in 1975; before then, birds were marked *neogaea* or *"bendirei"* (in quotes) according to whether or not the maxilla was more attenuate than in the old Maine population in general and particularly, in 1973–74, than the two sharpest-billed specimens of an August series of 21 from northern Maine (ANSP).

Thereafter, class II was divided on color, using the symbols A, C (for the more colorless, dull ones), NE, Ph, SE (for the darker Appalachian region birds, presumably *pusilla* "Gloger" Stresemann), and T. Usual weight 28 (females)–34.6 gm. Average extreme length ca. 166–167, extent ca. 277; wing usually 84–92 (female to 82.5, rarely 81.7); width of mandible 8.8–9.8 mm. (rarely 8.6–10.2 or more).

Class III: rather large; *"benti,"* and most of *"grinnelli,"* of Griscom and A.O.U.; but Ridgway's types of *bendirei* are really nearest this race, the common one in eastern Oregon, just as always considered before Griscom's erroneous reidentification as a smaller one. Color variation was minor; birds were marked *"benti,"* CypH, and *percna.* (Griscom's color variations are simply molt and wear.) Usual weight (male) 30.8–39.6 gm; length male 163.5–181 (female usually 165–173); extent male usually 285–300 (female 276–282); wing male 89.4–97 (female 85.5–92.5, rarely 94.5); width of mandible usually 9.8–10.4 mm.

Class IV: largest; all U.S.A. birds are *stricklandi,* and so marked. Usual weight 34.5–45 gm; length male usually 175–183; extent male usually 296–309 (female 294–304); wing male adult 96.6–104.5, once 95.5 and once 106.5 (female usually 97–98.5, less often 94–100.2); immatures, wing male 93.2–101.8 (female usually 93–96.6, occasionally 90.25–97.3). Width of mandible male 10.6–11.6, occasionally 10.2 (immature)–12.0 (female 10.6–11, occasionally 10.3–11.4).

In Arizona, *stricklandi* has long been well known as a frequent resident of the southeastern mountains, and it is not infrequent in those of northern Arizona when attention is paid to crossbills. Small young have been taken in *1881* and grown young in *1919* and *1949,* all in the Chiricahua Mountains.

Curiously, *stricklandi* usually molts 2 to 3 months before our other crossbills.

Class III, in Arizona, is represented by true *bendirei,* as explained above. In northern Arizona it has been taken almost every year that an ornithologist has searched for it; and it is nearly or quite as frequent in the southeastern mountains as *stricklandi,* being sometimes abundant. In recent years there are also verifiable lowland records: *Dec.* to *Feb.* at Phoenix and Tucson in *1962* (*Feb.,* Tucson), *1966–67,* and *1972–73* (ARIZ, MNA, DEL). An earlier specimen from Willow Beach, Colorado River below Hoover Dam, is apparently lost; it was identified as *"grinnelli,"* which should mean *bendirei* (or perhaps *stricklandi*) unless the identification was made on "geographic probability," as happens too often.

Classes II and I are much less frequent and perhaps never occur in Arizona in large flocks: maximum numbers less than 25 and seldom over five or six. Probably they do not breed here. Yet prior to 1962 they evidently reached our low valleys more often than did larger crossbills. In both classes a northern and a Rocky Mountain race reach us.

The dull northern class II birds are *neogaea* Griscom (*"bendirei"* of A.O.U., as explained above). Besides these names, they were marked A, C, NE, and T. They reach the Flagstaff region of northern Arizona fairly regularly, but are not known south of the Sierra Ancha in central Arizona (*26 Apr. 1957,* MNA).

The Rocky Mountain class II race was labeled "Ph". It may be known as

Loxia curvirostra vividior subsp. nov.

Diagnosis: moderately small as in *neogaea,* but bill often thinner. Crown, rump, breast, etc., more richly colored, being pervaded by an ochraceous tint, and thus in stronger contrast to the back, at least in most specimens (see below). Wing chord of male 86–91.5 (immature to 84.5), of female 82.5 and 83–88. Width of mandible at base 8.8–9.3 (immature male to 8.6).

Type: United States National Museum no. 128479, immature female; taken from nest, with set of 3 eggs, in "El Paso County," Colorado [= about 8–15 km from Monument], *13 Mar. 1893,* by George F. Breninger. Wing chord 82.5 mm.

Distribution: usually the high mountains of the western United States, presumably in spruce-fir associations, from Montana to Colorado and west probably to Deschutes Co., Oregon (and possibly Mt. Adams, Washington?). Wanders irregularly east to Kansas and the Great Lakes region as far as Michigan and northern Wisconsin (Phelps, Vilas Co.); west to Puget Sound; north to British Columbia (several years); and south to western Texas, southeastern Arizona, and northern California (Fort Crook, casually to Pasadena). Casual in Maine (Scarborough, *16 May 1877,* Princeton M.Z.), Massachusetts (chiefly Wayland, *30 Nov. 1882,* MCZ), Connecticut (Guilford, *4 Nov. 1903,* F), and New York (Lyons Falls, *5 May 1877,* and Locust Grove, *12 Apr. 1884,* British Museum of Natural History).

Remarks: A few specimens examined, notably 2 males from Netarts, Oregon, *11 Feb. 1915,* SD, are exceptionally bright over the *entire* upperparts; whether these represent *vividior* or a bright phase ("morph") of *neogaea* is unclear. *Vividior* sometimes has a very slender bill, compared to *neogaea,* but the wing is too long for Class I. Females are best for color comparisons in *L. curvirostra,* but red males are useful (off-color or patchy males are difficult).

Arizona specimens of *vividior* with specific locali-
ties are from Tucson, *30 Dec. 1960* (ARIZ, P.J.
Gould); near Tucson, *25 Jan. 1956* (ARP); Chirica-
hua Mountains, *13 May 1948* (two from flock,
ARP); and Inner Basin, San Francisco Mountains, *3
July 1969* (NAU, R.P. Balda).

Of Class I, *minor* (Brehm), marked *"sitkensis,"*
etc., as above, is the deep, bright northern and west-
coast race. It is represented by 2 Arizona specimens:
13 km. southeast of Springerville in piñons, *9 Sept.
1908* (US, C. Birdseye), and Parker, Colorado
River, *23 Aug. 1953* (ARIZ, Monson); each was
taken from a flock of five.

The remaining Arizona Class I, i.e., the nine *1950*
specimens (ARP), are of the duller Rocky Mountain
race (labeled W or cf Az). It may be known as

Loxia curvirostra reai, subsp. nov.

Diagnosis: very small, as in *minor* (Brehm),
though bill often heavier; wing chord usually 82–
84.7 mm (females 80.5–82.2), and width of mandible
8.2–8.8 mm. Duller below and on crown and back
than *minor,* the back less reddish (male) and thus
more strongly contrasted (at least to rump); female
also very dark- and dull-backed, in strong contrast to
the rich-yellow rump, and more deep-ochraceous
below. (Juvenal plumage apparently relatively
heavily streaked.)

Types: (in CAN) females, ARP original nos.
10347 and 10353; Dismal Lake, southeastern Sho-
shone Co., Idaho, *4 Sept. 1971;* collected by Amadeo
M. Rea and A.R. Phillips, respectively, and prepared
by Santos Farfán B. (dissected by A.R. Phillips).
Ovary of 10347 adult-looking with one ovum 1.8
mm in diameter (though still juvenal-plumaged on
median belly and partly so on breast, chest, upper
tail-coverts, and especially flanks); little fat. 10353
had ovary adult, ova up to 1 mm, belly bare but not

very thick, oviduct rather large (evidently used), plumage as in 10347, rather fat. Neither showed any molt. *Paratypes:* seven males in A.M. Rea collection, of same data.

Measurements of types: weight 23.8, 28.5 gm; extreme length 154, 161 mm; extent (extreme wing-span) 248, 250; wing chord 81.6, 83.8; tail 48.0, 49.5; width of mandible at base 7.4, 7.8; exposed culmen 13.5, 14.7; depth of bill at base 8.0, 8.5.

Distribution: Poorly known; chiefly from the type series (AMR, ARP) from the mountains of northern Idaho, a *1918* series from southern British Columbia (Okanagan), four skins from Sheridan, Wyoming, *July–Aug. 1908,* and flights to Lawrence, eastern Kansas, *Nov. 1887* (University of Kansas) and Arizona (San Francisco Peaks, Flagstaff, and Tucson), *30 Aug.–6 Nov. 1950* (ARP); but several Class I from the mountains of central Colorado are probably this race, though most are worn (*June*) or else off-color males.

Casual east to Minnesota (*1897,* Milwaukee Public Mus.; *1922,* University of Minnesota) and Michigan (*1885, 1941;* University of Michigan); and west and northwest to western Oregon, Vancouver Island, British Columbia (*30 May 1939,* F), and St. Lazaria Islands, Alaska (*11 Aug. 1912,* US).

Certain females from the Queen Charlotte Islands, British Columbia, are remarkably similar to *reai* (strays from the southeast?); their identity remains in doubt.

To the northeast, a good series of females from near Jasper National Park, Alberta (CM) are peculiarly colored, perhaps intermediate toward *minor;* they were marked K.

Etymology: Dedicated to Amadeo M. Rea, a careful ornithologist who played the key role in its discovery.

Remarks: Specimens of *reai* were marked W or cf Az.

The discovery of this, and other new and unsuspected races, in supposedly well-collected areas should serve as a reminder of the importance of continued collecting. Griscom, in his 1937 monograph, had already stressed the need to sample every flight of Red Crossbills; and our studies serve to underline his warning. As noted above, females are especially needed (and less often collected than males); but red-bodied males are also useful. Patchy or off-color males are very difficult to identify.

Obviously we have much more to learn about Red Crossbills, in and out of Arizona!

Index

231

Printed in the United States
1043200006B